Yankee Weathervanes

Illustrated with Drawings by Corinne Pascoe

Myrna Kaye

YANKEE WEATHERVANES

New York   E. P. DUTTON & COMPANY, INC.   1975

Library of Congress Cataloging in Publication Data

Kaye, Myrna.
Yankee weathervanes.

Bibliography: p.
1. Vanes—New England. I. Title.
NK9585.K39   739'.4774   74-19245

Lines from *Western Star*, by Stephen Vincent Benét (New York, 1943) reprinted by permission of Brandt & Brandt.

First Edition

10 9 8 7 6 5 4 3 2 1

Published simultaneously in Canada by Clarke, Irwin & Company Limited,
Toronto and Vancouver
ISBN: 0-525-23859-X
Designed by The Etheredges

Contents

v ·

Illustrations

weath-er-vane (we*th*'-ər-vān), noun.

1. a device, freely movable in the wind, which turns
to indicate the changing direction of the wind.

2. an indicator of changing ways and fashions.

This is the story of our weathervanes, in both meanings.

Preface

Folk art is history as it reflects the social attitudes, the skills, and the tastes of a given period.

C. MALCOLM WATKINS, CURATOR
DIVISION OF CULTURAL HISTORY
SMITHSONIAN INSTITUTION

Among the arts and artifacts which reflect the culture of our country, weathervanes have an exciting and unique place. This all-too-neglected art form is one art which is representative of all the people. Fine arts apprise us of the culturally and financially elite; folk arts tell of common people. Weathervanes are different; they tell the story of a whole culture.

For while the wealthy posed for Copley and the average man sat for limners, weathervanes stood atop elegant mansions and humble barns. While fashions changed and time passed, weathervanes decorated colonial clapboard and Victorian gingerbread. No other folk art affords as wide a view of America as the ubiquitous vane—the product of amateur and artisan, the craft of city and countryside, the adornment for church and stable.

In this book, I record the weathervane's story in pictures and words. On spires, weathervanes indicate the climate's varied winds; on these pages, they indicate the culture's various and variable ways. Drawings have been used instead of photographs to afford the reader the clearest and most accurate documentation possible.

The book concentrates primarily on the weathervanes of New England so that I can tell a comprehensive story. To focus mainly on New England seemed logical. America's vanes, like American society, began in settlements along the East Coast. In the nineteenth century, when vanes were popular across the continent, the home of the weathervane industry was the manufacturing Northeast. And although weathervanes have dominated the skyline wherever Americans lived, they have remained on their original perches longest in New England. (Not that vanes are secure on Yankee rooftops; increasingly, they are being doomed by fires, hurricanes, urban renewal, and most often by thieves. Many now decorate home interiors and enhance folk-art collections.) Finally, but perhaps of primary importance, history-loving New Englanders have preserved in town and state historical societies, in parish records and local libraries, the detailed information which made a weathervane study possible.

Some of the weathervanes which decorated New England buildings were manufactured outside of New England. Therefore, this history includes references to the work of Samuel Bent & Sons, J. W. Fiske, J. L. Mott Iron Works, E. G. Washburne & Co., and A. B. & W. T. Westervelt & Co., all of New York City. Because some New Englanders bought vanes manufactured elsewhere and because New England-made vanes were sold everywhere, the appendices (a list of American weathervane vendors and an illustrated list of weathervane manufacturers' cardinal designs) are national in scope.

With few exceptions, the vanes included in this book have New England histories. The arm and hammer vane (Fig. 74), made in Pennsylvania and now in the Shelburne Museum in Vermont, is included because it is a type of vane known to have been used in New England, but no New England example was available. Some weathervanes in museum collections and many in private collections have little or no documentation as to their origins. Many were collected before such data seemed important. The vanes which have been included here are examples of styles or types which have been found in New England. Vanes of styles typical of other sections of the country have been omitted from this study.

Notes containing sources of quoted material, documentation of historical information, and some supplementary information start on page 217. The notes are arranged by chapter and page.

This history could not have been written without the kind help and cooperation of many people. I am indebted to the following institutions and their staffs: Bostonian Society, Old State House, Boston, Mass.; Cary Memorial Library, Lexington, Mass.; Community Church, West Topsham, Vt.; Concord Antiquarian Society, Concord, Mass.; Concord Free Public Library, Concord, Mass.; Essex Institute, Salem, Mass.; Faneuil Hall, Boston, Mass.; First Baptist Church, Providence, R.I.; First Church in Cambridge, Congregational, Cambridge, Mass.; First Church of Christ in Marblehead, Marblehead, Mass.; First Congregational Church, Hamilton, Mass.; First Congregational Church, Ipswich, Mass.; First Congregational Church of Waltham, Waltham, Mass.; First Parish Church, Sandwich, Mass.; First Parish in Dorchester, Dorchester, Mass.; Greenfield Village and Henry Ford Museum, Dearborn, Mich.; Hall of Fame of the Trotter, Goshen, N.Y.; Hancock Shaker Village, Hancock, Mass.; Hirschl and Adler Galleries, New York; Index of American Design, Washington, D.C.; M. and M. Karolik Collection, Museum of Fine Arts, Boston, Mass.; Massachusetts Historical Society, Boston, Mass.; Merrimack Valley Textile Museum, North Andover, Mass.; Museum of Early American Folk Arts, New York; Nantucket Historical Association, Nantucket, Mass.; New York State Historical Association, Cooperstown, N.Y.; Old Dartmouth Historical Society, New Bedford, Mass.; Orthodox Congregational Church, Manchester, Mass.; People's Methodist Church, Newburyport, Mass.; Plymouth Fire Department, Plymouth, Mass.; Paul Revere House, Boston, Mass.; Abby Aldrich Rockefeller Folk Art Collection, Williamsburg, Va.; Shelburne Museum, Shelburne, Vt.; Union Congregational Church, Maynard, Mass.; Eleanor and Mabel Van Alstyne Folk Art Collection, Smithsonian Institution, Washington, D.C.; Waltham Historical Society, Waltham, Mass.; Wenham Historical Association and Museum, Wenham, Mass.; West Parish Congregational Church, West Barnstable, Mass.

Among those who graciously shared their talent, scholarship, information, or photographs were Mrs. Effie T. Arthur, Stephen Crocker, Robert C. Eldred, Joseph W. Fiske of J. W. Fiske Architectural Metals, Robert C. Hilton, the late Frank Lovering, Bette Lustig, Helene Margolskee, Barbara Nerenberg, Ralph Raynard of E. G. Washburne & Co., Sonia Reizes, Edward Thomas, Henry White, and especially Marjorie Childs Hunt, whose inspiration and scholarship were of incalculable value.

For encouragement and advice I am grateful to Joan Lautman, Chris Malagodi, Barbara Mende, Sabra Morton, Shirley Moskow, Doris Pullen, Jeri Quinzio, Catherine Rothery, and Molly Turner. A special thank-you to my family for sharing my interest, to Murray who proved a top-flight weathervane photographer and to the world's best weathervane spotters—Sharon, David, and Stephen.

M.K.

Lexington, Mass.
September 1974

Yankee Weathervanes

1.

Heritage From the Old World

STEPHEN VINCENT BENÉT
Western Star

By 1673 America's weathervane tradition was well established. When the Englishmen of Concord, Massachusetts Bay, North America, crowned their newly completed meetinghouse with the gilded vane shown in Figure 1, they were following a proud English tradition. One hundred and two years later, the men of the same village followed another old English tradition and fired the shot which made them Englishmen no longer.

To take up arms against their king to secure their rights had revered precedent. Armed nobles had forced King John to grant them the Magna Carta. Medieval England was the source of much that became American. And in that world of courageous knights and kingly grants, we begin the story of America's weathervanes.

Medieval England was fond of flags. Noble families had banners, emblazoned with their coats of arms, flying from their castle rooftops. Each helmeted and armored knight rode to war carrying a pennant marked with his heraldic device—a sign of identification, a medieval license plate.

The knight who first succeeded in implanting his pennant on the wall of a

1. *Flag. Iron, gilded.* $14\frac{1}{8}''$ *x* $14\frac{1}{8}''$. *Made in 1673 for the Concord, Mass., meetinghouse, by an unknown smith. Concord Free Public Library.*

besieged castle or town was rewarded with royal permission to affix to the highest part of his own castle a flag which, like the suit he wore to battle, was armored.

This grand privilege to fly a fane (the ancient word meant both flag and weathervane) was restricted to nobility, and even they required royal permission. The honorable fane, resembling its cloth predecessor, displayed the family crest.

Because a broadside breeze would have brought down a fixed metal banner, the knight's badge of honor was made with a swivel and swayed freely in the wind. Weathervanes were heraldic fanes first and only secondarily wind indicators.

Pointing wind direction was useful, however. In that era, the English longbow supplanted the lance in medieval weaponry. Archers, adjusting their aim to the way of the wind, must have glanced at the gilded vanes gleaming in the sun.

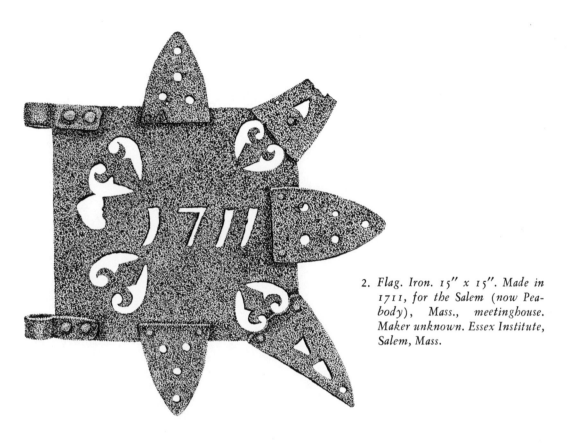

2. *Flag. Iron. 15" x 15". Made in 1711, for the Salem (now Peabody), Mass., meetinghouse. Maker unknown. Essex Institute, Salem, Mass.*

During Europe's Middle Ages and Renaissance, architects put finials on their buildings. Gilded spheres were most common. The crosses placed on top of churches often stood on spheres. A popular variety of the ball finial was the sunburst or star, a sphere with points radiating in all directions. Standing figures, statues, also adorned rooftops. On an English building, the finial which became most popular was the weathervane, usually affixed above a ball.

The crowning touch to a new edifice was often a vane marked with the building's date of completion. The numerals, usually pierced in the metal, were prominent in the pattern. By the seventeenth century, with the king's permission no longer required, vanes crowned most important buildings in Britain. The English emigrants took to their New England this familiar feature of the old.

3. *Flag. Brass. W. 15″. Made in 1688, for the Wenham, Mass., meetinghouse. Maker unknown. Wenham Historical Museum.*

The middle precinct of Salem, Massachusetts, petitioned for a separate parish in 1710. The 51- x 38-foot meetinghouse built the next year was given the traditional finishing touch—a proud fane (Fig. 2).

The New World settlements grew rapidly. Town meetinghouses, centrally located and singularly important centers for the congregation and community, were periodically replaced with larger edifices. In 1687 the people of Wenham, Massachusetts, sitting in their second and outgrown structure, voted to "build a new meeting howse & Admit our Ipswich neighb^rs to Joyne. . . ."

Of the Wenham meetinghouse completed the next year, only the weathervane (Fig. 3) survives. Like much that remains of colonial America, it has been ruined by repair or "improvement." It once radiated decorations like those which characterize the 1673 and 1711 flags. Telltale rivets, remnants of these features, can still be distinguished.

Unlike the Concord and Salem flags, Wenham's vane is not iron but brass. Its size (15 inches in its present unadorned length) is imposing for a meetinghouse vane and is especially impressive because brass was rare and a rich man's metal.

Iron, too, was costly in the seventeenth century and was sparingly used. The very use of metal for the manufacture of colonial meetinghouse vanes is a tribute to the importance of these architectural decorations. The 1682 banner (Fig. 4), made for the meetinghouse in Lynn, Massachusetts, achieved noble bearing with a mere 6½-inch width of iron.

The durability of metal helped these colonial armored flags to survive. The wooden meetinghouses (Concord's 1673, Salem's 1711, Wenham's 1688, and Lynn's 1682, all in Massachusetts) are long gone, their medieval styles of architecture almost forgotten. Only one Puritan meetinghouse still stands—the Old Ship in Hingham, Massachusetts —a restoration, whose vane unfortunately is of later origin, of a size and shape never meant for a medieval-style meetinghouse.

The Puritan house of prayer and politics was a square, or nearly square, structure whose pyramidal hipped roof supported a central belfry topped with a spire and vane. The 1682 meetinghouse, which stood on the common in Lynn until 1827, was known as the Old Tunnel. ("Tunnel" meant funnel-shaped and referred to the roof as seen from within.) This drawing of that hip-roofed building evinces the Puritan style of meetinghouse architecture that flourished until 1712. Small diamond-shaped panes admitted light through leaded-glass windows. Within, enormous unconcealed oak beams traversed the roof in all directions. A bell rope descended in the center of the room between the rows of unadorned benches.

Above the bell tower, a dignified vane turned in the wind. The decorative feature was an integral part of the stark and severe architectural style, an imposing part of a plain and practical design.

In the Puritan meetinghouses, men gathered to pray together and govern themselves. Slowly, as the Puritan theocracy gave way, the functions of the meetinghouse were assumed by church and town house. In Boston's Town House, Americans gathered to govern but found themselves increasingly ruled from abroad.

Boston's second Town House was erected in 1712–13, a brick replacement for a wooden medieval-style Town House which had been destroyed by fire. Known today as the Old State House, it is New England's oldest existing public building.

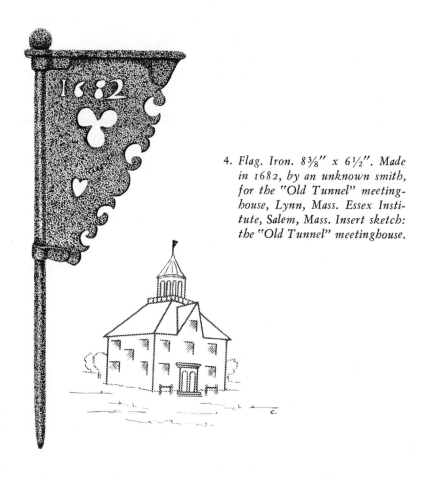

4. *Flag. Iron. 8⅜″ x 6½″. Made in 1682, by an unknown smith, for the "Old Tunnel" meeting-house, Lynn, Mass. Essex Institute, Salem, Mass. Insert sketch: the "Old Tunnel" meetinghouse.*

The structure's stepped gables are adorned with lion and unicorn, for it was designed to serve King George's colonial government as well as the town and the county. The architecture is vigorous English-Georgian, crowned with a weathervane (Fig. 5) of a type then most common in England and possibly imported from there.

The vane closely resembles a cloth banner with an arrow aiming at the wind. As the breeze blows the streamerlike tail away, the pointed end turns to indicate the direction from which the wind comes. Vanes point into the wind, although later we shall see a notable exception.

Bostonians could glance at the Town House cupola and tell the direction of the wind. But within the building it was often impossible to tell which way the wind was blowing. The popularly chosen representatives of the colonists, meeting in their hall, came increasingly into conflict with the crown's representatives, meeting across the passageway in the council chambers. In 1766 the Provincial House of Representatives took a giant step in democratic government. A visitors' gallery was installed and the public invited to view the legislative procedures (and hear the impassioned speeches of the fiery revolutionary, Samuel Adams).

In the council, matters were moving away from the people. There, the British governor labored to enforce the unpopular duties on imports that Parliament had imposed.

On the very day (March 5, 1770) that the Parliament in England repealed the repugnant Townshend duties, an incident flared in America of greater historic importance. The scene was the street beneath the Town House banner. About twenty of the king's soldiers, menaced by a mob of hundreds, fired on the crowd, more in fear and self-defense than in malice. They were branded mass murderers. Boston's radicals thus won a cause célèbre; for years, they periodically led revelers in memorializing as martyrs the five victims of the Boston Massacre.

5.
Swallow-tailed Banner. Probably copper, gilded. L. about 5'. Made in 1714, probably in America but possibly in England, for the Old State House, Boston, Mass. Maker unknown. Still atop the Old State House.

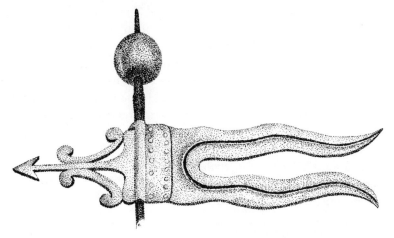

General Gage was the last British military governor sworn in at the Town House. After assuming office in 1774 he promply moved the government to Salem, away from the brawling, boiling port city of Boston.

Boston had not only an English government, but an English church. By 1723 the growing non-Puritan Anglican community required a second parish for the once detested Church of England. As a fitting setting for their elaborate religious ritual, the Anglicans built an elegant edifice. Christ Church is eminently American, yet distinctly English. Its dual characteristics are reflected in its gilded vane (Fig. 6).

This oldest of Boston's church structures survives because of its place in American history and verse. It is the Old North, cherished by Americans as the landmark where, on April 18, 1775, lanterns were hung in the belfry to warn of the English expedition. Paul Revere arranged for (but neither hung nor saw) the "two if by sea," as Longfellow dubbed the first of many signals which alerted the countryside on the eve of the Revolution.

The Old North, standing high on Copp's Hill, was clearly visible to patriots across the river in Charlestown. The steeple dominated the skyline, served as a landmark to ships at sea, and, indeed, had been donated by merchants from Honduras whose ships needed a sighting when they approached Boston harbor. So, although its worshippers were among the most ardent supporters of the English crown, Christ Church was logically chosen to flash the first light of freedom.

The Old North's historical significance is American, but its architectural magnificence is English.

The men who founded Christ Church had always looked to London for inspiration. After the fire of 1666 devastated medieval London, Sir Christopher Wren designed fifty-two new churches. Boston's Christ Church is of Wren's renaissance style. Its exterior of English bond brickwork is a simplified version of a Wren design, its interior is markedly similar to St. James's, Piccadilly, and its weathervane could have been copied from the building plans for St. James's. (When an architect designed a building, he also designed its vane.)

The vane's shape and size suited the new architecture. Wren's churches were built on small city lots. Each featured a tower surmounted with several wooden stories of diminishing size culminating in a slender spire lifting a vane toward heaven. At such an elevation, only a vane of great size could be seen, so the banners on such churches are much larger than medieval meetinghouse flags. At great distance, the front of a square or rectangular flag is indistinguishable from the rear. The added arrow and particularly the

6. *Swallow-tailed Banner. Copper. L. over 6'. 160 lbs. Made by Shem Drowne, August 15, 1740, for Christ Church, Boston, Mass. Spindle, with scrolls and letters, by Edward Lack. Still atop Christ Church.*

split tail of the standard made direction easily discernible. Like the Wren-style churches they crown, swallow-tailed vanes became widely popular in New England.

Christ Church's vane has stood on three steeples. The first was destroyed by a hurricane in 1804; the second, designed by Boston's master architect Charles Bulfinch, was downed by another ill wind in 1954. The old twice-spared vane helped raise funds for the building of the present steeple, a restoration of the colonial spire. The banner toured coast to coast, making "in person" pleas for money and appearing as a "guest" on television.

When the Christ Church weathervane returned to its elevated position in 1955, it was 215 years old, having been made for the 1740 steeple by Boston craftsman Shem Drowne. So although the vane's design is English, it is celebrated as the work of an American.

Shem Drowne (1683–1774) had previously made an unusual vane for the governor's mansion and a weathercock for another Boston congregation. His account books show that he was a tinsmith. Nathaniel Hawthorne's tale, "Drowne's Wooden Image," immortalized him as a figurehead carver (which he was not). Hawthorne, a century after Drowne's death, wrote of his reputation and creations.

> He became noted for carving ornamental pump heads, and wooden urns for gate posts, and decorations, more grotesque than fanciful, for mantelpieces. No apothecary would have deemed himself in the way of obtaining custom without setting up a gilded mortar, if not a head of Galen or Hippocrates, from the skilful hand of Drowne.

All that remain of Drowne's handicraft are four copper vanes. One of these, the grasshopper vane atop Faneuil Hall, Boston (Fig. 7), is America's most renowned weathervane, famous for its strange shape and historic situation. Today, it is recognized as Drowne's masterpiece, and fame has made it secure. (Even when it was temporarily snatched in 1974 (see page 206), it was for ransom, not for resale.) But in 1742, when the gilded grasshopper was raised to its perch atop Boston's new market, its fate seemed uncertain. The grasshopper headed into the wind at Dock Square, where his glass eyes seemed to survey the whole of the bustling colonial port. Sailing ships docked at his door; the wharf was teeming with men and cargo. The town was green with herb and vegetable gardens. Swine roamed the crooked streets; cattle grazed on the common. In the narrow lanes, street hawkers noisily peddled their produce.

These hawkers were dismayed by the grasshopper, the all-too-visible reminder

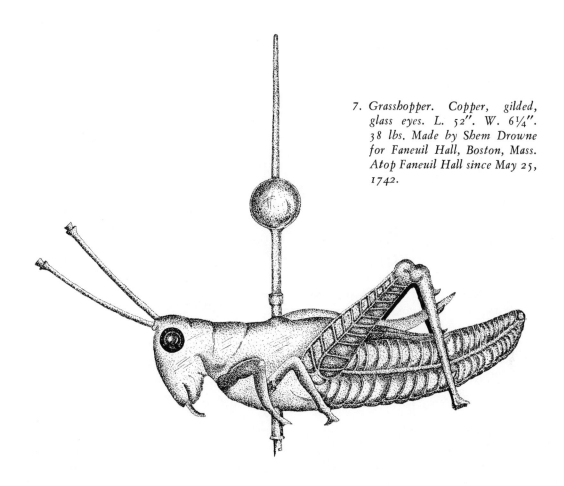

7. *Grasshopper. Copper, gilded, glass eyes. L. 52″. W. 6¼″. 38 lbs. Made by Shem Drowne for Faneuil Hall, Boston, Mass. Atop Faneuil Hall since May 25, 1742.*

of the building it crowned—the town's new market. Peddlers had been ordered to stop their house-to-house selling, rent a market stall, and submit to the competition of a central marketplace.

     For decades, the gentry had tried to establish a market, "a place to sett dry in and warme, both in cold raine and durty weather." A central market would benefit shipping merchants like Peter Faneuil, who complained about "the disadvantage under which trade was conducted with no market house as a centre of exchange." The peddlers, however, had long fought against a permanent market and had caused the failure of earlier market houses, including one in this very square.

Finally the authorities reluctantly allowed Faneuil to build a market at his own expense and to donate it to the town. Many people, however, still actively disapproved of a central market. Would they react to the new one as they had to the previous one in Dock Square? That market had been torn down on a dark night in 1737 by a group of anti-market men disguised as clergymen. (Dressing up for destruction remained popular in Boston. The 1773 Tea Party called for Indian garb.)

Faneuil's brick building had an added attraction to make it acceptable. Above the ground-floor market was a town meeting hall. There, Bostonians eagerly gathered to debate the issues of the day. In the years preceding the Revolution, the grasshopper over-heard the rumblings of colonial resentment against the crown. Faneuil Hall, resounding to cries for American self-government, was christened the Cradle of Liberty. The proud grasshopper was assured of a permanent pedestal.

But pedestals are perilous. When an earthquake tremor hit Boston in 1755, the grasshopper was shaken from his stand, and in 1761 . . . but let us continue with the grass-hopper's own account, as recorded on a paper found within the vane.

> Again Like to have Met with my Utter Ruin by Fire but hopping Timely from my Publick Scituation Came of With Broken bones, & much Bruised.—Cured and fixed [by] . . . Old Master's Son, Thomas Drowne June 28th 1768 And Though I [will] promise to . . . Discharge my Office, yet [I shall] vary as ye Wind.

The faithful service and patriotic significance of Drowne's grasshopper were appreciated by Charles Bulfinch, who designed the enlargement of Faneuil Hall in 1805. Bulfinch moved the cupola from the middle of the roof to the east end, thus creating a more imposing perch for the gilded insect.

Generations of Bostonians and visitors have wondered why a grasshopper was chosen as the vane for Faneuil Hall. Legends developed which purported to explain the emblem. In one, Shem Drowne is said to have been asleep in a field when awakened by a boy chasing a grasshopper. This chance meeting supposedly led the child's wealthy parents to become Shem's benefactors, and he honored this episode with a commemorative vane. A charming story, but it is unlikely that Faneuil would have left the choice of the subject of the vane to craftsman Drowne.

Faneuil himself selected the grasshopper, which was the mark of an exchange just as a mortar and pestle designated a pharmacy. Faneuil's trade sign was 4 feet 4 inches long, a copy of the 11-foot grasshopper weathervane on top of the Royal Exchange in London. (Another grasshopper marked Martin's Bank, London.) Boston's exchange, surmounted by the gilded grasshopper, could be readily identified by shipping merchants and seamen, all well acquainted with London, the world center of trade.

The London origin of this market symbol is also wrapped in legend. Sir Thomas Gresham, the founder of the Royal Exchange, was said to have been a foundling abandoned in a field where he surely would have died had not a chirping grasshopper called attention to his plight.

Actually, a grasshopper appears on Sir Thomas's heraldic crest. The insect is a rebus of his name. "Gresham" is of German origin (*Gras Heim*), the diminutive of which (*Gras Heimchen*) means grass, or field, cricket. Sir Thomas marked his building with his family crest. Peter Faneuil, a man of commerce, copied the sign which by then had become synonymous with exchange. On Faneuil Hall the grasshopper, emblem of Old World finance, became an honored symbol of New World politics.

Weathercocks are far older than weathervanes; that is, wind pointers were made in the shape of cocks long before they were made in the shape of fanes. Yet not until the eighteenth century did weathercocks appear in New England. One of the earliest (Fig. 8), imported from England in 1723, is still in use on the meetinghouse in the Cape Cod village of West Barnstable, Massachusetts.

Weathercocks were used in the seventeenth century in the other American colonies. But the Puritans, familiar with the weathercocks of old England, preferred fanes on their meetinghouses, probably because they honored the biblical admonitions about "graven images" and "gods of gold" and disapproved of the cock's long and strong associations with papal and episcopal churches.

The earliest weathercock of record was the bronze bird on the church bell tower in Brescia, northern Italy. It bore a Latin inscription saying that Rambert, Bishop of Brescia, *gallum hunc fieri praecepit* ("ordered this cock made") in A.D. 820. The wording of the inscription indicates that Brescia's cock was not then unique, but rather that such cocks were probably customary by the ninth century. In 980 Swithin, Bishop of Winchester, England, placed a cock on his church. It was probably one of the earliest weathercocks in England judging by the way Bishop Wulfstan, of a neighboring see, lauded it in Latin

8. *Weathercock. Copper, gilded. L. 5'. About 200 lbs. Made in England in 1723 for the newly expanded meetinghouse, West Barnstable, Cape Cod, Mass. Maker unknown. Still atop the meetinghouse in West Barnstable.*

eloquence—*ornatu grandis; regit; superbus; nobilis imperium*—and compared it to celestial splendors.

The Bayeux tapestry illustrates the elevation, in 1065, of the weathercock on Westminster Abbey. In 1091 a storm damaged the cathedral at Coutances, France, and there is a record that an English metalworker was summoned to repair or replace its cock. From that time on, church cocks of record are too numerous to list here.

When the Coutances cock was damaged, it probably was not referred to as *coq* ("cock"), for that word was just entering the French language. Originally the gilded effigies of roosters were called *galli* (Latin for "roosters") and later *coqs* ("cocks"), the same as the birds themselves. Then, in English, they became "weathercocks," a word older than "weathervanes," and for centuries a generic term for vanes of any shape.

The French distinguished the tower-topper from living fowl with the term *le coq du clocher* ("the cock of the bell tower"). Indeed, even when the cock was placed on a flèche, a bell-less spire, it was *le coq du clocher*. Not until the fifteenth or sixteenth century was there a French word which could refer to a vane of any shape: *girouette*.

The phrase *le coq du clocher* is most appropriate for weathercocks. The original practice was to place the effigies on bell towers. Why? Over the centuries that has been a matter for scholarly research, speculation, and sheer hokum.

A twentieth-century writer on English weathervanes, Albert Needham, alleged that a ninth-century papal bull ordered weathercocks to be placed on all church belfries. His assertion has been repeated ever since, but it is not so. No papal order originated or perpetuated the custom.

Another Englishman, J. Starkie Gardner, in his book on English ironwork, claimed that weathercocks originated in England and reached the Continent only after the Norman invasion (1066). He cited the English metalworker summoned to Coutances in 1091 as evidence that weathercocks were then new to the Continent. Chauvinistically, he ignored the recorded cock at Brescia (820).

In fact, where or when the weathercock began cannot be documented, and likely never will be. Much information, however, was gathered by Catholic clerical scholars who sought for centuries to explain the customary cock on the campanile. They noted that the idea of a wind-turned figure was ancient, a bronze Triton having been made to point the wind atop the Greek horologium of the first century B.C. in Athens. (Its story is on pages 188–189.) The scholars acknowledged possible Roman copies, but could not trace a transition from Tritons to cocks. Some noted that where knowledge was lacking, legend appeared.

Most of the legends concern St. Peter. In the words of the Gospel according to John, Peter was told by Jesus, "The cock shall not crow, til thou hast denied me thrice." The legend says that from the moment the cock crowed that morning, Peter bore a grudge against every cock he heard. Occasionally he impaled those which dared to crow near him, and to discourage other cocks, he exhibited the impaled birds in visible lofty places.

Legend sufficed for many, but not for scholars. Catholic clerical researchers acknowledged that the Christian significance of the cock—as a symbol of Peter's denial, as an easily recognizable warning to the faithful, as an emblem of the hour of resurrection—gave justification for the custom. But, they wrote, its Christian meaning did not explain the origins of the weathercock. Even before the Christian era, the cock was a familiar symbol of vigilance. The ubiquitous early riser was known to all as the alert herald of the dawn, who called the end of the fearful night with its imagined demons and real thieves. (The cock's call was so much the essence of the bird that men named it *coq* and "cock," in imitation of the bird's sound.) Acknowledging the cock's ancient symbolism, the scholars let the matter rest there.

Symbolism is probably the key to the origin of weathercocks. As nature's town crier, the cock was a logical emblem for campaniles, which since at least the fifth century served the same purpose as the cock. The campaniles sounded in the morning signaling the end of night, the time to arise for the day's labors, the time for morning prayers. If a bell tower was to have a symbol, what better symbol than the cock?

Of all the finials commonly used on Christian buildings—the cross, the star, the cock—only the asymmetrical cock offered resistance to the wind. It had to swivel in order to survive. So the cock was fashioned to turn in the wind like the ancient Triton, and because it was wind-blown, the English called it *"weather*cock." Because its earliest perches were bell towers, the French said "coq *du clocher.*" Always it was "cock," the vigilant bird, the first voice of the morning.

In 1754, when the people of Manchester, Massachusetts, decided to give their meetinghouse a steepled bell tower, they did as people had done for a millennium—they placed a weathercock (Fig. 9) upon it.

The cockerel that appears in Figure 10, however, is the oldest New England-made weathercock of record. Once a symbol of revenge and derision, it became a renowned and dignfied landmark. The story of this cockerel, which Shem Drowne made in 1721 for Boston's New Brick Church, actually began three years earlier in the New North Meetinghouse, Boston. A group within the New North objected to the ordination of Mr. Peter Thacher as their pastor. They deemed it wrong for the minister to forsake his flock in Weymouth, Massachusetts, where he was already solemnly ordained. The righteously indignant minority walked out of the New North.

In revenge they organized another religious society. On May 10, 1721, the New Brick Church on Hanover Street was dedicated as the home of the new society. As the cockerel, a symbol of Peter's denial of Christ, was raised to its perch on the New Brick's steeple, a fortuitous wind turned the bird's head in the direction of the New North. A merry fellow straddled the cock's back and crowed three times in the direction of Mr. Thacher's church, in derision of this preacher named Peter.

9. *Weathercock. Copper, gilded. 2'8" x 2'5". 15 lbs. Made in 1754 for the new steeple on the meetinghouse, Manchester, Mass., at a cost of £7/10/8. Maker unknown. On its original perch, 115 feet up.*

The New Brick, at times called the Revenge Church, was also referred to as the Cockerel Church (probably indicating that for a time this was Boston's only church weathercock). To the triple-named Congregational church came, in 1779, the displaced members of the Second Church in Boston. Their meetinghouse had been demolished, under British General Howe's orders, and used as fuel for his soldiers.

In 1817 the Cockerel Church, like many other Congregational societies, became Unitarian. Weathercocks are accustomed to turning with the prevailing wind, so the cockerel continued in office as a Unitarian and served upon the new edifice built in 1845.

With the shifting of the city's population, the Unitarians moved uptown, and Methodists bought the building and its changeable weathercock. In September 1869 a severe gale blew the spire down, sending the Methodists' cockerel through a neighbor's

10. *Weathercock. Copper, gilded, glass eyes. 5'5" x 5'4" x 9". 172 lbs. Made by Shem Drowne in 1721 for the New Brick Church, Boston, Mass. Now on spire of First Church, Congregational, Cambridge, Mass.*

roof. The 172-pound bird arrived as dinner was being prepared but was in no shape to stay and feast; he was seriously damaged. After being repaired, the cock was carefully housed inside the church until 1871 when Hanover Street was widened and the building was torn down.

In 1873 the Shepard Congregational Society (the First Church in Cambridge, Congregational) restored the cock to his original denomination. Impressed by his interesting past, the Cambridge Congregationalists bought him for seventy-five dollars and gave him a post on their new stone church. From the 170-foot-high perch, he gazed on the Washington Elm, beneath whose branches General Washington had stood as he assumed command of the American Army on July 3, 1775. By 1938 structural weakness of the spire made his position hazardous. He was removed, the spire dismantled, and just in time. The hurricane that September could have sent him through another roof.

The cockerel's glass eyes have surveyed Cambridge ever since from atop a new, shorter steeple. Great age and faithful service have given him dignity; historic associations have brought him renown. Revenge and derision are for younger hearts; this weathercock has mellowed.

The cheerful weathercock depicted in Figure 11 is a beloved landmark in Ipswich, Massachusetts. In 1643, after adopting the name from old England, the founders of Ipswich settled on three important sites: a mill, for the nurture of their bodies; a meetinghouse, for the nurture of their souls; and a burying ground. The location chosen for the meetinghouse was a lofty hilltop known ever since as Meeting House Green.

Five successive religious structures have stood on that patch of high ground. The fourth (built in 1749 to replace an old four-square) was a "new"-style meetinghouse whose adjoining tower had a slender spire and the great gilded weathercock in the illustration. After rotating for nearly a century, the vane fell while being taken down for the construction of the new, fifth, church. Rejoined, replaced, and regilded, it returned to the hilltop upon the Victorian-Gothic church completed in 1847 and held that perch until 1965.

The old cock pictured here stood above Meeting House Green from 1749 on, but his Lincoln-head-penny eyes are obviously much more recent. Sometime in his long history of repairs and regildings began a tradition of replacing his eyes with new coins. The Lincoln-heads set beneath his eyelids in 1957 replaced Indian-head cents. We do not know what eyes first surveyed the splendid view from the towering perch on the lofty knoll.

While the cock faithfully and attentively watched over Ipswich, the townsfolk frequently and admiringly glanced up at him. On June 16, 1965, they stood and stared. Ipswich's First Congregational Church, on its visible and vulnerable hilltop, had been struck by lightning and was burning.

The weathercock seemed doomed as flames reached up the steeple. But the fire receded and the gathered crowd caught glimpses of the cock through the smoke and flames. Repeatedly, flames attacked the spire. In less than two hours it became evident that the building was a total loss. The cock, continuing to ride out the holocaust, seemed to many to be kept aloft by more than the flame-wracked steeple.

11. *Weathercock. Copper, gilded. L. 53". H. 44". Made in 1749 for the meetinghouse, Ipswich, Mass. Maker unknown. Still owned by the First Congregational Church, Ipswich, Mass.*

The fire smoldered for hours through a steady rain. People went home for dry clothes and returned to keep the vigil for the cock. If the steeple collapsed, the copper bird would be lost. Finally, the fire was extinguished; the steeple—a charred shell—stood; the cock was saved.

When the ruin was dismantled, the first task was to remove the rooster. A workman, cradling the cock in his arms, brought him down to a cheering crowd.

People have a special attitude toward weathervanes. Partly because of their lofty position, often because they are part of a church, sometimes because of their great age, and particularly when they have the shape of creatures, real or imaginary, weathervanes are objects of admiration, affection, and awe.

Novelist John Updike, an Ipswich resident, describes this enduring weathercock in his novel *Couples*. The weathercock, a recurrent symbol in the story, survives the fire and is brought down after a career of centuries in which it

> turned in the wind and flashed in the sun and served as a landmark to fishermen. . . . Children in the town grew up with the sense that the bird was God. That is, if God were physically present in Tarbox [read Ipswich], it was in the form of this unreachable weathercock visible from everywhere. And if its penny could see, it saw everything.

The novel ends with the rescue of the cock. After the fire the old bird had a new problem: would it return to Meeting House Green? The members of the church were anxious to rebuild and to place the rooster on the new edifice. The era was past when the men of the parish built their own church, so they needed a mortgage. They could not get one, for they had no deed to the land on which their church had stood.

Meeting House Green had always been theirs, yet it wasn't. It was Ipswich's common, but the town had no deed either. Town and parish had ceased to be one, but the separation of church and state property had never been completed.

While the Massachusetts Land Court pondered the ownership of Meeting House Green, the Lincoln-head eyes saw only the inside of a cramped, dark basement. To spend long years in basements is sometimes the fate of weathervanes, although they are designed for lofty places. The old rooster illustrated in Figure 12 lay in a Waltham, Massachusetts, cellar for a quarter of a century while the gentleman who owned it pondered the problem: to whom should he give an old Puritan rooster? Were the Unitarians or Congregationalists truer descendants of the cock's first owner—the Puritan parish in Waltham?

The first humble meetinghouse built in 1720 was replaced in 1767 by a weathercock-topped meetinghouse which stood until 1840. The rooster, salvaged when that building was demolished, stood for a while atop a barn and then disappeared. About 1898 Charles F. Stone, the gentleman who later would deliberate upon the genealogy of religious societies, found what he felt certain to be Waltham's missing vane in the Wayside Inn, Sudbury, Massachusetts. The inn, made famous by Longfellow's tales, was then owned by an antique dealer. Mr. Stone bought the rooster and, returning it to its home town, placed it in his cellar.

Twenty-six years later, Mr. Stone decided to give the vane to the First Congregational Church, which seemed to him the lineal descendant of the first parish, although the church which retained the name "First Parish in Waltham" was the Unitarian Church.

12. *Weathercock. Copper, gilded. L. about 4′4″. Made by Thomas Drowne in 1767 for the First Parish, Waltham, Mass. On the spire of the First Congregational Church of Waltham, Mass.*

Unitarians noted that the Congregational Society had been formed in 1820 while the rooster was still on its original perch. But Mr. Stone called churches as he saw them.

Shortly after the rooster was raised to its spire top, the Congregational Church was partially destroyed by fire. "The ancient bird perched on top of the steeple" was blamed for the burning. An anonymous letter writer to the local paper called it "a Jinx." The donor was denounced for his ill-advised gift.

Perhaps, when the Unitarians saw what an ill wind blew this weathervane, they were less disturbed by Mr. Stone's decision. At any rate, resentment was assuaged when another historic vane was given to the Unitarians.

Part of the interest shown in the Waltham rooster came from the belief that it had been made by the patriot Paul Revere. Although no evidence supported the tradition, no evidence—until now—refuted it. Waltham's "Revere rooster," as it was called, had been made at the time Revere was working. The patriot, however, was a silversmith, working in finer metals. When he worked on copper, he did the finer work of engraving. In later life, Revere manufactured rolled copper, but he never was a coppersmith.

Paul Revere did not make the Waltham weathercock. The so-called "Revere

13. *Weathercock. Copper, glass eyes. L. 4'4". Made by Thomas Drowne in 1771 for East Meetinghouse, Salem, Mass., for £12. Essex Institute, Salem, Mass.*

rooster" is the work of another artistic craftsman, whose identity is revealed by the vane we see on page 23, the Waltham rooster's younger brother, a resident of Salem, Massachusetts.

On June 23, 1771, "a Cock . . . gilt in the best manner" (Fig. 13), costing twelve pounds, was delivered to the East Meetinghouse in Salem from the Boston shop of Thomas Drowne.

Thomas (1715–96), Shem's son, pursued his father's trade. In 1768, as we have seen, he had repaired the grasshopper, his eighty-five-year-old father's masterpiece (Shem lived to be ninety-one). A year earlier, 1767, the Waltham rooster was made, no doubt by Thomas, a creator as well as repairer of vanes. The Waltham and Salem cocks appear to be by the same hand. Indeed they may have been formed on the same wooden pattern. The Drownes, father and son, most likely formed their three-dimensional copper vanes on such patterns. Shem, according to Hawthorne, was a woodcarver. A coppersmith either carved a wood model in the round or dug out of wood concave negatives of each side of the design. Then he hammered the sheet copper against the wood until it assumed the pattern's form. Joining left and right copper sides, a pipe for the spindle, flat metal details (e.g., tail, cockscomb), and glass eyes, he gave the vane its final form.

The Salem and Waltham vanes have discernible differences. Waltham's rooster is now legless. The difference in tail feathers may be explained by the fact that the Salem bird was once tailless.

The history of the Salem rooster's tail is recorded in the diary of William Bentley, minister of the East Parish.

September 10, 1789

The vane . . . seen most easily at the Wharves, & in the Harbour as well as by the Inhabitants of the Eastern Part of the Town . . . was injured by a storm of wind, which broke off the hinder part, and prevented its motions otherwise than broad to the wind. It is now liable to be forced off by exposing its whole side to the wind, & to bend the Spindle, & besides being useless as a Vane, & dangerous to the Spire, it is a Public mark of inattention, & neglect.

Neglect continued for six years until:

August 20, 1795

This day at noon the Weather Cock was . . . sent on to the blacksmith's for a new Tail or to take the old Tail which was blown off . . . in March 1783.

August 25, 1795

This day the Weather Cock ascended the Spire, with his Coat of Gold.

But:

June 23, 1814

Wind high at North West. Vane . . . broken off . . . fell upon the House & thence into the adjacent field.

July 1, 1814

Erected stages to replace the Cock Vane. . . . The post was found rotten one foot from suffering the vane to be suspended for a long time after it lost its tail and could not traverse. It had opened the wood and suffered the water to get in.

Here the recorded adventures of the cock end. (Mr. Bentley died in 1819.) In 1861 the cock began a second hitch in weathervane service atop the Bentley School, named for the revered minister, renowned scholar, and recorder of New England life during the early years of our new nation. In 1953 the cock was given to the Essex Institute, Salem.

The hazards of weathercock existence related in Bentley's diary occurred in less than a half century. Considering the alterations that a vane sustains in two centuries of repeated damage and subsequent repair, it seems remarkable that ancient vanes retain so much that is old and original. The Salem cock and his Waltham brother, however, apparently have kept their original essential character. Damage did not destroy their basic quality. Repairers always respected their essence and spirit, restoring them with careful craftsmanship so the cocks retain their family resemblance.

Thomas Drowne's weathercocks are far handsomer than old master Shem's Revenge cockerel (Fig. 10). The older bird is parrotlike; the younger ones are true regal rulers of the roost. Thomas's roosters reveal that the son inherited his father's ability, acquired his father's craftsmanship, and enriched the skill with an artistry of his own.

2.

From Englishmen to Americans

And they ate the white kernels, parched in the sun,
And they knew it not, but they'd not be English again.

STEPHEN VINCENT BENÉT
Western Star

In 1716 the Province of Massachusetts acquired Peter Sergeant's handsome Boston mansion as a residence for colonial governors and shortly thereafter marked the three-story brick building as an official American edifice by placing upon its large octagonal cupola an Indian weathervane (Fig. 14).

The Indian had been an official American symbol since the Massachusetts Bay Colony had a seal designed in 1629 featuring an Indian exclaiming, "Come over and help us!"

The motto is believed to refer to the Christian conversion of the aborigines, supposedly the prime reason for the European settlement in America. This line of talk was the rationale for Charles I's signing of the compact allowing the establishment of a New England community based upon Puritan precepts. Actually, the colonists were not very zealous about converting and "elevating" the Indians. The English treated them with kindness but as inferiors.

To Europeans, the strange American savages made an ideal symbol for the

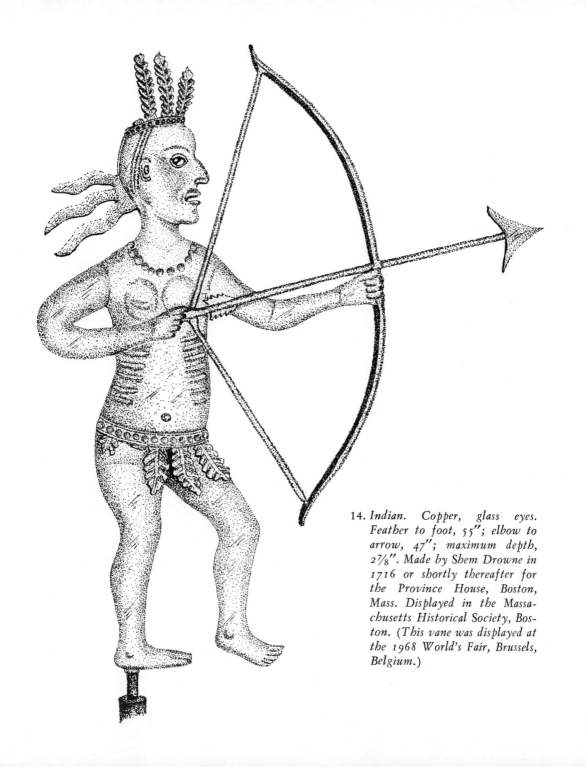

14. *Indian. Copper, glass eyes. Feather to foot, 55″; elbow to arrow, 47″; maximum depth, 2⅞″. Made by Shem Drowne in 1716 or shortly thereafter for the Province House, Boston, Mass. Displayed in the Massachusetts Historical Society, Boston. (This vane was displayed at the 1968 World's Fair, Brussels, Belgium.)*

strange and savage land. Visually, the Indian was a good symbol, readily identifiable as non-European by his dress, or lack of it. It is in this "unelevated" state that the Indian appears on the seals of Massachusetts and on the seal of the earlier settlement of New Plymouth.

The Pilgrims at Plymouth and the Puritans at Massachusetts Bay found the Indians friendly and helpful. Most of New England's approximately fifteen thousand red men were willing to share America with the settlers and were glad to gain some of the fruits of European civilization. Some were converted, and there were perhaps twenty-five hundred praying Indians by 1675.

Then, some unconverted tribes made a belated attempt to dislodge the English settlements. The Indians who had accepted the Europeans' religion and society became victims of the white man's prejudice and distrust. Although many aided the settlers, some converted Indians were slain and hundreds were restricted and then compounded on an island in Boston harbor. Although mistrusted and mistreated, the Indian remained the symbol for America, an appropriate subject for the weathervane on a governor's mansion.

Shem Drowne made the gilded Indian which, as Hawthorne wrote in "Drowne's Wooden Image"

> stood during the better part of a century on the cupola of the Province House, bedazzling the eyes of those who looked upward.

Actually, this vane is an oddity among wind indicators, because the Province House Indian points his arrow with the wind. Pointers on other vanes face into the wind.

The Indian, the earliest of Drowne's four known vanes, is a transitional piece. This is perhaps the first American-made vane with a shape other than a flag. The armored flags (Figs. 1–4) that were popular in the early 1700s had no arrows to point into the wind. The flags, of course, turned away from the wind. So did Drowne's Indian. In time, Shem Drowne learned the pointing style. His 1721 cockerel, 1740 swallow-tailed banner, and 1742 grasshopper all face into the wind.

One can imagine, however, that Drowne's Indian was turning his back on the winds of change which, in less than a century of European migration and prosperity, of Indian disease and war, had solidly entrenched the settlers in New England and made the Indian a minority in his own land.

The land which the Indians shared with the settlers was abundant in blessings

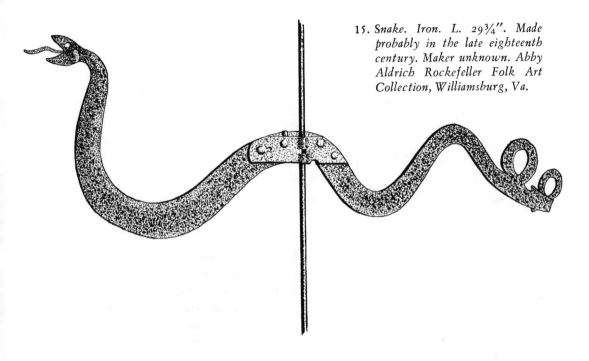

15. Snake. Iron. L. 29¾″. Made probably in the late eighteenth century. Maker unknown. Abby Aldrich Rockefeller Folk Art Collection, Williamsburg, Va.

and woes. New England's rivers were of delightfully pure, drinkable water; her streams were so full of fish at spawning time that one could gather them "with a scoupe, or a boule, or a peece of barke." Within her forests grew 200-foot-high trees whose magnificent trunks served as masts and broad planking for the ships which tied the New World to the Old.

    Wildlife abounded. Thirty-five-pound turkeys strolled past tepees never noticing the loss of one of their number to the pot. Grouse and heath hen were so prevalent that even the haphazard firing of the settler's crude matchlock provided a feast for the table.

    Abundant, too, were the "annoyances of woolves, Rattle-snakes, and Musketoes." Wolves and mosquitoes were found elsewhere in the world, but rattlers were indigenous to America. These exotic creatures creeping out of the soil of an exotic land became another symbol for the New World. And any symbol for America was certain to become the subject of an American weathervane. The graceful snake shown in Figure 15 was easily yet cleverly made, being simply cut of sheet iron, with a pierced eye and protruding tongue to give verve to the silhouette. The 3-foot-2-inch-long snake illustrated in Figure

16. *Snake. Wood (pine), painted brown on greenish yellow. L. 38″. Made by an unknown artisan in the late eighteenth century, Concord Antiquarian Society, Concord, Mass.*

16 would be 8 feet long if it could uncoil. It charms and impresses those who see it, but is seldom recognized for what it is—a patriotic emblem, a symbolic E Pluribus Unum.

England's New World provinces were separate, distinct, and distrustful of one another when the rattlesnake first urged union in 1754. The war against the French and Indians was greatly hindered by colonial disunity, so Benjamin Franklin formulated a Plan of Union. To popularize the idea, he designed a cartoon entitled "Join, or Die," depicting a rattlesnake with its long body cut into pieces, each labeled with a regional name (southernmost Georgia was the rattler's tail; northernmost New England, its head). The emblem for American unity was born; the reality of union had to wait. The colonies, cherishing their individuality and jealous of their rights, refused to join.

Eleven years later, when the Stamp Act produced anti-British feelings, the rattlesnake symbol was resurrected. Patriotic newspapers adopted the emblem for their mastheads, and widely circulated political cartoons of dismembered rattlers again pleaded for union.

By 1775 independence-minded Americans came to think of the rattlesnake as a perfect symbol for their cause. On December 27 of that year, the *Pennsylvania Journal* wrote:

> The rattlesnake is found in no other quarter of the globe than America. . . . Her eye exceeds in brightness that of any other animal, and she has no eyelids. She may therefore be esteemed an emblem of vigilance. She never begins an attack, nor, once engaged, ever surrenders. She is therefore an emblem of magnanimity and true courage. . . . She never wounds until she has generously given notice, even to her enemy. . . . One of her rattles, singly, is incapable of producing sound; but the ringing of thirteen together is sufficient to alarm the boldest.

The symbolic serpent had changed. It no longer reclined; it was alert. Its once fragmented body was united. The legend was not a plea to Americans but defiance to Britain: Don't Tread on Me. Such a rattler emblazoned on the flag presented to the Continental Congress in February 1776 seemed about to shake its tail, clamor its rattles, and strike.

On July fourth, it struck. The patriotic snake went to war displayed on martial drums and banners. On flags, rattlesnakes stretched across thirteen stripes, symbolizing unity. In one cartoon, the snake coiled around the Magna Carta, symbolizing the union embracing liberty.

Another cartoon rattlesnake coiled his powerful body into three loops. Two loops encircled British armies. The third and empty loop confidently advertised for more military gentlemen. By then the war was drawing to a close; the American rattlesnake was proud and victorious.

But in the years following the Revolutionary War, the young nation sought a new symbol—one which would not slither along the ground, but would soar in the skies above. The rattlesnake never became the emblem of the new unified nation. It remains, instead, the almost forgotten symbol of thirteen colonies gradually becoming united and free.

In 1774, when Paul Revere engraved a serpentine "Join or Die" for the masthead of Isaiah Thomas's newspaper the *Massachusetts Spy,* he included an accompanying symbol. His snake, its tail and tongue tipped with arrowheads, menaced a crouching dragon. The dragon, a familiar device for a villain, represented Britian in many patriot-published cartoons. In Revere's engraving, the dragon cowered before the symbol of the united colonies.

17. *Dragon and Snake. Wood, painted black on gray. 18″. Made in the late eighteenth century by an unknown artisan. Concord Antiquarian Society, Concord, Mass.*

A weathervane of a snake and dragon locked in battle (Fig. 17) may also represent the colonies and Britain. Here, however, the dragon appears to be winning the battle. (It seems to have bitten the snake so hard that four screws and a tin strip were needed to mend the serpent.) This may be a Loyalist's vane, reflecting the Tory view of the war in progress. After all, not all Americans wished to be free of Britain. Many, especially those with wealth or official positions, wanted to remain Englishmen. The king's supporters in Britain and America accepted the rebel's symbol for the colonies—the rattler.

The lowly, loathsome serpents they depicted in political cartoons testified to their opinion of the rebels.

Possibly they accepted the dragon symbol as well. Traditionally, the dragon stood for authority as well as for despotism, cruelty, and evil. In this vane, authority seems secure, and the dragon looks agreeable in spite of a toothy hold on its adversary.

The Loyalist cause lost. The American army, unified under the command of General George Washington and aided immeasurably by French forces, succeeded at Yorktown (1781). Washington, the Hero of Freedom, became a symbol of freedom. After his inauguration as president of the new constitutional government (1789), the likeness of the Father of His Country became a ubiquitous emblem of America.

No American home in the early 1800s was without its likeness of the Pater Patriae. George Washington appeared in statues of bronze, in figures of pottery, on teapots made in China, and on clocks made in France. Transfer prints of Washington decorated English pottery exported to America. Painted portraits of Washington enhanced Chinese porcelain and glass made for the American market. Women in the United States stitched Washington's likeness and name on handkerchiefs and, after his death, on mourning pictures, as they did for members of their families. Craftsmen in America embellished their work with likenesses of Washington, and an unknown craftsman made the Washington weathervane seen in Figure 18. Weathervanes were virtually never portraits of particular men, but this vane portrayed the Illustrious Washington, perhaps as the vane maker remembered seeing him as he rode through town.

In 1789 hundreds of thousands of Americans met or saw the Atlas of America. That April, the president-elect traveled from Virginia to the inauguration in New York; and six months later, as president, he traveled through New England. People lined every fence, field, and avenue to hail their hero. He rode by carriage or on horseback acknowledging again and again salutes, cheers, applause, and shouts of welcome.

Bands played, cannons boomed, bells rang. In teach town Washington was met and escorted by brightly costumed militiamen, many of whom had followed him a decade before in rags and barefoot. Flowers were strewn in his path and arched in bowers overhead. Odes were composed and sung, orations were delivered. Skyrockets illuminated night skies. At official dinners, he dined with hundreds. At balls, he danced with ladies who for a lifetime would recall the glorious moment with Columbia's Favorite Son.

Many wanted President Washington to be given a title. Isaiah Thomas's *Massachusetts Spy* advocated "His Highness, the President General." Reporting on the triumphal postinaugural journey during which the president stayed at inns, the *Massachusetts Spy* (November 12, 1789) printed an "inn-cident" to enhance its plea for a title.

> The President . . . towards the close of one day last week, sent forward a messenger to an inn to bespeak a lodging, etc. The innkeeper was absent; and the landlady, supposing by "the President" was meant the President of Rhode Island College . . . and being unwell, said . . . that he must go on to the next tavern. When the landlady found it was the great Washington who had intended to be her guest, "Bless me," exclaimed she, "the sight of him would have cured my illness. . . ." Does not this show the necessity of a title to distinguish our first magistrate from the chairman of a common tavern club?

But "The Man Who United All Hearts" remained in title simply Mr. President while he was lauded at celebrations, given honorific nicknames, and memorialized in art. Even in the diminutive Washington vane, there is much of the majesty of a life-sized equestrian statue. For decades after his death (1799), the figure who was "First in war, first in peace, and first in the hearts of his countrymen" continued to be a favorite symbol of America and a frequent subject of her fine and folk art.

In 1782 the bald eagle was designated as the emblem for the American Union. What had been until then just a bird of prey became an astonishingly effective spokesman for that quality without which the young nation could not survive—a national spirit.

Successful nationhood grows from a people's history and traditions. But the people of the new Union considered themselves primarily citizens of the several states. Virginians, Pennsylvanians, and New Englanders shared neither a common past nor a single American culture. The nation's history had begun but a half-dozen years before the emblematic eagle, with the Declaration of Independence.

On July 4, 1776, after declaring independence, the Continental Congress had "resolved that Dr. Franklin, Mr. J. Adams and Mr. Jefferson be a committee to prepare a device for a seal of the United States of North America." The design submitted by that august committee, a shield supported by a pair of allegorical figures, was rejected. Congress wanted something more than just a seal to authenticate government documents.

Six years and several committees later, Charles Thomson, Secretary of Congress, suggested a dynamic seal dominated by the figure of an American eagle. The eagle bore the shield on his breast. He held the olive branch in his right talon and thirteen arrows in his left, symbolizing peace and war. In his beak he held aloft a scroll with the motto E Pluribus

18. *Washington on Horseback. Sheet iron. H. 16½". W. 13½". Probably made in the late eighteenth or early nineteenth century. Maker unknown. Found in Connecticut. On display at the Shelburne Museum, Shelburne, Vt. A similar Washington vane is in the Mabel Brady Garvan Galleries at Yale University, New Haven, Conn.*

Unum. Here was what Congress wanted—a national symbol of courage and sovereignty for the fledgling Union.

The eagle, an emblem of ancient Rome, appealed to the classical fervor of the time. Americans, rejecting the traditions of European monarchies, sought inspiration from the Roman republic. But the Great Seal's eagle was no Roman bird. America had an eagle of its own. It built its lofty eyrie in every state of the Union. Its white-feathered head never soared through European skies. Congress specifically designated the American bald-headed species (bald meant white) as the eagle of the Great Seal.

19. *Eagle. Copper, some lead. H. 27¼". Made in the second quarter of the nineteenth century. Maker unknown. Found on shoe factory, Rockland, Mass. Displayed for sale by Hirschl & Adler Galleries, New York, in 1970.*

While chroniclers compiled an American history from the separate histories of the several states, patriots put to use the American emblem from the nation's seal. "To encourage a national spirit and to foster the national pride," Congress placed the eagle on the ballots and coins of the "more perfect union" formed when the Constitution was ratified (1788).

Artisans found the federal emblem a fine decorative motif. They featured the eagle wherever possible. Builders carved eagles over mantels and doorways. Cabinetmakers made chair rails look like eagles' wings, and bookcase pediments served as eagles' perches. Makers of weathervanes like that in Figure 19 prized the eagle as a handsome patriotic emblem. Foreign manufacturers appealed to the new and growing patriotism by incorporating the eagle design into their wares. Textile and wallpaper designers here and abroad wove and printed eagles in innumerable poses and patterns. The deft fingers of American women sewed, hooked, and embroidered eagles into quilts, rugs, and personal ornaments. The eagle was the most popular patriotic motif in an era when federal symbols were so common that the prevailing style is called federal design.

The eagles, dignifying government buildings, tavern signs, gilded mirrors, baking molds, ship figureheads, and down pillows, gave federalism an aura of permanence.

The traditionless Americans relied heavily on symbols, which at times were labored and ostentatious. Nevertheless, their sentiments were genuine and the symbols were effective. Americans and newcomers to America sloughed off their separate customs and allegiances and became a united people. The most potent emblem in the effort for Americanization was the popular eagle.

The history of the Union and the evolution of its principal symbol are intertwined. The Union's history reveals the triumph of the symbolic eagle; the eagle's design reflects the triumph of the Union. The eagle of 1782 looked like a chicken. Slight and scrawny, its beak could nip but not tear; its wings were wide but not powerful; its neck was slender; its chest was hidden by the shield. Its thin featherless legs had claws which could hold but could not seize.

Benjamin Franklin is often quoted as having preferred the turkey to the eagle as the national emblem. The gobbler was mentioned by Franklin only because the emblem's figure was not recognizable "as a Bald Eagle, but looks more like a Turk'y."

As the years passed, American patriotism and the patriotic eagle changed. The people, once merely tolerant of union, accepted it, grew intolerant of opposition to it, and in the Civil War fought to preserve it. By then a vigorous and powerful Union was depicted by a vigorous and powerful eagle. The national bird had grown from a scrawny nestling to a magnificent eagle with broad head, impressive beak, proud chest, powerful wings, fully feathered legs, and talons of mighty grasp.

By the time of the War Between the States, the federal period of American design had ended. Its patriotic motifs were seen less and less; many were seen no more. But the eagle, the official emblem, remained popular. In the 1860s Alvin Jewell, a weathervane manufacturer in Waltham, Massachusetts, featured an eagle (Fig. 20) in five sizes, from 17 inches to 51 inches in length.

The emblem was by then an octogenarian. Generations had passed since mighty words had been intoned about the desirability of a majestic eagle as a symbol of strength. At last the American eagle was the embodiment of "superior courage, power and authority," a bird who "defied storms and commanded the air," who "had no equal in keenness of vision and in strength." Nation and emblem, together, had become established, mature, and strong.

20. *Eagle. Copper, cast lead head. L. 51". Mass produced by A. L. Jewell & Co., Waltham, Mass., about 1855–67, in 17", 24", 29", 40", and 51" models. Stolen in 1966 from a Bolton, Mass., barn (not its original perch).*

For twenty-seven centuries the symbolic cap pictured on page 38 of J. W. Fiske's weathervane catalogue (Fig. 21) stood for liberty. Yet, in the twentieth century, in this land promising liberty for all, the emblem is all but forgotten.

In classical times the Phrygians of Asia Minor wore caps to distinguish themselves from their slaves. As early as 750 B.C., they impressed the image of the cap on their coins and seals. Romans adopted the cap and used it to distinguish emancipated slaves from those still in servitude. In the third century B.C., the liberty cap held high on a spear formed

METAL BALLS FOR FLAG POLES.

On Stems, gilded with best gold leaf.

No. 226,	3 inches,	-	each,	$0 70
" 227,	4 "	-	"	1 10
" 228,	5 "	-	"	1 42
" 229,	6 "	-	"	2 00
" 230,	7 "	-	"	3 00
" 231,	8 "	-	"	3 50
" 232,	9 "	-	"	6 00
" 233,	10 "	-	"	7 75
" 234,	12 "	-	"	12 00

Not on Stems, gilded with best gold leaf for Vanes or other purposes.

No. 235,	1 inch,	-	each,	$0 25
" 236,	2 inches,	-	"	36
" 237,	2½ "	-	"	46
" 238,	3 "	-	"	60
" 239,	4 "	-	"	96
" 240,	5 "	-	"	1 25
" 241,	6 "	-	"	1 57
" 242,	7 "	-	"	2 60
" 243,	8 "	-	"	3 08
" 244,	9 "	-	"	4 50
" 245,	10 "	-	"	5 00
" 246,	12 "	-	"	7 50
" 247,	15 "	-	"	18 70
" 248,	18 "	-	"	25 25

FLAG POLE BALLS OF BEST SEASONED WHITE WOOD.

2 in. diameter,	-	-	-	each,	$0 30
2½ " "	-	-	-	"	50
3 " "	-	-	-	"	65
4 " "	-	-	-	"	1 30
5 " "	-	-	-	"	1 80

6 in. diameter,	-	-	-	each,	$2 50
7 " "	-	-	-	"	3 50
8 " "	-	-	-	"	4 50
9 " "	-	-	-	"	5 50
10 " "	-	-	-	"	6 75

STARS.

LIBERTY CAP.

	9 in.	12 in.	15 in.	18 in.	24 in.
No. 106, 5 points,	$4 00	$5 50	$7 50	$10 00	$16 00
" 107, 6 "	5 00	6 50	8 50	11 00	17 00
" 108, 9 "	10 00	13 00	17 00	22 00	34 00
" 109, 10 "	12 00	15 00	19 00	25 00	37 00
" 110, 12 "	14 00	17 00	21 00	28 00	40 00
" 111, 14 "	16 00	18 00	25 00	33 00	50 00

No. 94,	6 inches high,	$7 50
" 95,	9 " "	12 00
" 96,	12 " "	15 00
" 97,	15 " "	20 00
" 98,	18 " "	30 00
" 99,	24 " "	40 00

☞All my Vanes are of copper, and gilded with gold leaf.

21.

Page 38 of a post-1885 issue of the Illustrated Vane Catalogue of J. W. Fiske, New York, N.Y. Phrygian Cap or Liberty Cap appears as Nos. 94–99.

part of the official insignia of the Saturnalia, the festival during which slaves were allowed temporary freedom.

The Phrygian cap, a brimless, soft-bodied hat worn with its pointed top tilted forward, was employed by Samuel Adams in his propaganda designed to stir Americans with a desire for freedom from England. Although most people knew nothing of Phrygia and little of ancient Rome, the classical symbol was recognized by all as the emblem of a poor but free man.

The cap appeared in political cartoons before and during the American Revolution. It was used by French revolutionists, who donned the *bonnet rouge*. During the early days of the American republic, it was a popular patriotic emblem in folk art and official seals.

The liberty cap is the second most frequently used symbol on state seals (the eagle is first). Iowa's emblem shows a citizen soldier with a liberty cap in hand. On West Virginia's seal, the cap is held aloft by two crossed guns—symbolizing the arms which obtained, and stand ready to maintain, liberty. On six other state seals the liberty cap tops a spear or pole held as an attribute by the Goddess of Liberty. Liberty could not present herself without her Phrygian cap any more than Justice could hold court without her scales.

The widespread use of the Phrygian cap and the numerous other patriotic symbols in American folk art of the early nineteenth century reveals the fervor with which Americans received and cherished their newly won freedom. But by the end of the century the emblematic cap was seldom seen. It rarely appears in the late-nineteenth-century weathervane manufacturers' trade catalogues through which vanes were sold. The weathervane catalogues of J. W. Fiske are exceptions.

The page shown here from Fiske's post-1885 catalogue illustrates three finials for flag poles: the liberty cap, which turned in the wind, and the ball and the star, which did not. In Fiske's 1893 catalogue the gilded copper liberty cap was illustrated on the page following a much more popular weathervane and flag-pole finial—an eagle standing on a ball. Earlier, in 1875, when Fiske's liberty caps were lower priced ($6.50 to $36.00), the cap was illustrated just before the copper American flag and just following the Goddess of Liberty.

The Goddess of Liberty (Fig. 22), with the Phrygian cap on her head, was the most popular liberty symbol in the nineteenth century and was a featured pattern in the catalogues of many weathervane manufacturers. This vane has been referred to as Columbia in recent years because of the American flag she carries. But in the nineteenth

22. *Goddess of Liberty. Gilded with painted copper flag. H. 60". Upper body cast in half-round lead, lower part hollow, partly-round copper. Mass produced by Cushing & White, later L. W. Cushing & Sons, Waltham, Mass., since 1869. Similar, but inferior, 22" and 30" models had been mass produced by Cushing and predecessor, A. L. Jewell & Co., Waltham, Mass., since about 1860 (see Figs. 86 and 90).*

century when she was made, she was listed as Liberty. With a cap—on a pole, in hand, or on her head—a female figure could be nothing but Liberty.

The printer of the *Boston Gazette* created Liberty in 1770. Taking courage from the rival *Massachusetts Spy,* which had adopted the rattlesnake as its emblem, he revolutionized his newspaper's masthead. He replaced the female figure of Britannia with a new lady. Her left hand held a spear surmounted with a Phrygian cap. She sat beside a bird cage which her right hand held open, releasing the bird shown flying toward the tree of liberty. With a liberty cap, a liberty tree, and a freed bird, the lady was quickly named Liberty.

Liberty at first held the cap on a spear, maintaining liberty with arms, upholding freedom with security. Americans always were aware that liberty and order went together. Order was the means; liberty was the goal. So Liberty was the goddess. She decorated furniture of the federal period, appeared in political cartoons of the new nation, and posed in patriotic paintings. In time the Goddess of Liberty placed the cap upon her head, freeing her hand of the spear and enabling her to carry the American flag.

The flag which the Liberty in Figure 22 carries has pierced stars and was realistically painted red, white, and blue when it came from the Waltham, Massachusetts, shop of Cushing & White. Leonard Cushing took particular pleasure in painting the finishing touches on the first Liberty vane made after he and White acquired the weathervane business. He noted in his journal on May 9, 1868:

> Work[ed] all forenoon on painting the Goddess of Liberty and in the P.M. sat it in the [store] Window of H. C. Sawyer where in the evening it attracted a thousand people.

Through a century of independence, the lady of liberty became so popular that her cap of liberty lost significance. Sculptor Frédéric Auguste Bartholdi replaced it with a radiating crown on his colossal Statue of Liberty. The memorial was presented to Americans by the people, not the government, of France. It commemorated the centennial of the surrender at Yorktown in 1781, a victory made possible by the French fleet.

The bronze figure, named "Liberty Enlightening the World," honored the American people's fight for freedom because it had set an example for the whole world, one which the French people had quickly followed. To most nineteenth-century Europeans, America seemed utopian.

The Old World learned about the New largely through letters from immigrants. For example, letters from Minnesota's Swedes to their homeland, cited by George M. Stevenson in "Typical 'America Letters,' " include these passages:

> We are so exceedingly well satisfied with our emigration from the fatherland that my pen is powerless to express it.
>
> This being a better country, I will do even better here.
>
> There is such an abundance of pasturage and prairie.
>
> Our circumstances are as happy as we could wish. I feel thoroughly at home with the Americans.
>
> There is one thing I dislike about America. The summers are exceedingly hot and the winters are the other extreme. . . . I am thinking of going to California . . . the climate out there is much better.
>
> Many have departed for the gold fields, where they make lots of money—at least some do. Jonas August . . . returned sometime ago with four thousand dollars in gold.
>
> We wish you would write as soon as possible whether you have any thoughts of going to America. . . . I do not believe that I will leave this place until death takes me away. We live better than people in Sweden, and we are not wanting in spiritual food. When I compare conditions here with those in Sweden, we are fortunate. We have good bread and wheat flour and as much beef and pork as we desire for each meal. We have all the butter, eggs and milk we need. Last summer I sold twenty dozen eggs every two weeks. . . . We have an abundance of various kinds of apples. In fact, we have so many things that make for comfort and happiness that, when I compare Sweden with this country, I have no desire to return.
>
> We are glad to know America is in your thoughts.
>
> If anyone intends to go to America in the spring, I recommend the Anchor line—I believe it is best.
>
> I bid you a hearty welcome to this free country.

Bartholdi's Statue of Liberty held her lamp beside the open door to this paradise. She welcomed 34 million Europeans who came to the land of liberty with an imperfect understanding of what lay ahead in America, but with a complete knowledge of what they left behind.

Many Americans objected to the cultures and skin tones of the immigrants, particularly those from southern and eastern Europe and those from Asia. The babble of foreign tongues was decried; the rabble in the crowded streets was despised; the immigrants' willingness to work for little pay was denounced. But America was so spacious that immigrants were admitted through a wide-open door.

The hardships, deprivations, and discrimination which followed settlement in America seldom obliterated from the immigrants' thoughts the destiny that they would have faced had they remained in Europe. To the millions who saw the lady with the lamp from steerage decks, the statue symbolized their rescue from poverty and oppression. They had come, as Liberty understood so well, "yearning to breathe free."

Miniature Statues of Liberty sold in the millions, but few weathervanes of the Statue of Liberty were made. Goddess of Liberty vanes, which enjoyed a limited popularity, were more common than statue vanes. Certainly, the goddess made a more effective wind indicator. She, herself, could point direction; the statue had to rely on an arrow beneath her feet. But perhaps the primary reason for the limited sale of Statue of Liberty vanes such as that illustrated in Figure 23 was that in an era when most mass-produced vanes were placed as finials on top of carriage houses, the Statue of Liberty symbol had its strongest appeal to those Americans—the new Americans—who had not, as yet, carriage houses.

Throughout the nineteenth century, while the new Americans were finding freedom, the original Americans were losing it. The Caucasian population was exploding, but the American Indian was being chased across the continent, ruthlessly boxed into reserved territories, and then repeatedly dislodged by the expanding white population.

Ironically, while the Indian's very existence was being threatened, the Indian motif in art was flourishing. Monumental bronze Indians were unveiled in city squares where bronze-skinned men walked no more. Although, or perhaps because, Americans were treating Indians with disrespect or disregard, American artists were creating imaginary Indians of two contrasting types—the regal and the ridiculous.

Academic artists created regal red men. James Fenimore Cooper's Indians, masters of nature, were majestic but unreal. Longfellow's Hiawatha was based on Indian legend but not on Indian life. George Catlin's portraits of red men captured authentic appearances and activities but were colored by the artist's Rousseau-like philosophy that Indians were noble savages as long as they remained outside the corrupting circle of civilization.

23. *Statue of Liberty. Copper. H. 41", quarter-round. Mass produced after 1886. Maker unknown. Abby Aldrich Rockefeller Folk Art Collection, Williamsburg, Va., and probably elsewhere.*

The Indians honored by Catlin were, in his eyes, "proud clear-eyed men who roamed the plains far from the white man's influence, . . . with poise of royalty. . . ." They were not like those "along the eastern shores, dirty and ignorant."

Few Indians remained in the Northeast. To most New Englanders, red men were strange unknown creatures of the western plains. Yankee folk artists freely created a race of fanciful and ridiculous red men.

24. *Massasoit. Copper, originally gilded. H. 30″. Mass produced by Harris & Co., Boston, Mass., in Harris's 1879 catalogue at $40. After 1883 mass produced (probably by W. A. Snow, Boston, Mass.), with slight variations (e.g., non-twisted base tube, larger arrow feathers). In several collections. The Shelburne Museum, Shelburne, Vt., owns a Massasoit on non-twisted base.*

Wooden cigar-store Indians belonged to no particular tribe. They had none of the authentic trappings of Catlin's subjects, were without even the legendary basis of Longfellow's Hiawatha, and were devoid of the vitality of Cooper's Mohicans. Silent, static, unnatural, and even grotesque, the folk artist's Indian was merely picturesque.

The Indian weathervane depicted in Figure 24 is part of that fanciful folk-art tradition. Harris & Co., a Boston weathervane manufacturer, gave him a real name, however. He was listed in their catalogue as "Massasoit," named after the chief of the Wampanogs, who had befriended and aided the settlers at Plymouth. Massasoit was a white man's idea of a good Indian. The barely three-dimensional Massasoit embodied in copper the white man's attitude toward the red race, an attitude verbally expressed by Henry Clay.

> Let us treat with the utmost kindness and the most perfect justice the aborigines whom providence has committed to our guardianship. Let us confer upon them, if we can, the inestimable blessings of Christianity and civilization, and then, if they must sink beneath the progressive wave, we are free from all reproach, and stand acquitted in the sight of God and man.

Clay's was a "liberal" view in the United States Congress. Most congressmen preferred to forget that recurrent inconvenience, the American Indian.

By the end of the nineteenth century, white men acknowledged that they had failed to save the Indian. Many set out zealously to preserve something of the Indian race before it vanished. Scholars sought to record accumulated data; missionaries tried to save a few souls; artists attempted to preserve a colorful savage image; the common man embraced the Indian motif, making it the vogue. America would save the image if not the race.

The Indian image was always a popular subject for American weathervanes. In contrast, the black man was not the subject of American vanes. His image was symbolic of servitude and remained so for decades after emancipation. Wooden Negroes stood at storefronts, although they were not nearly as popular as wooden Indians. Negro hitching posts were commonplace.

The same companies which made the hitching posts made weathervanes, but blacks seemed apt symbols for one and not the other. Weathervanes are insignia of dignity. A weathervane of servitude would have been a contradiction in terms.

The Indian image, however, always seemed appropriate for weathervanes, initially as a symbol for America, and later as an emblem of "man in his natural state." Indian weathervanes were particularly popular in the early 1800s in upper New York State where James Fenimore Cooper's literary Indians roamed. Perhaps the idea of a man at nature's mercy seemed an appropriate subject for a wind indicator. Certainly the form of a hunter with an arrow in his bow makes an effective pointer.

The primary direction indicator in the weathervane pictured in Figure 25, however, is not the hunter's arrow. The forceful directional form is the running horse itself.

25.
Indian on horseback. Horse of wood, Indian of sheet iron. L. 39″. Indian added in late 1800s. Maker unknown. Abby Aldrich Rockefeller Folk Art Collection, Williamsburg, Va.

Originally, this horse ran riderless. Somebody, caught up in the save-the-Indian-image-from-extinction-by-fashioning-fanciful-red-men fad, added an iron Indian to his wooden horse weathervane. Vanes were often altered; details were commonly added; unrelated objects were joined to form a vane. And so this horse received a rider.

The combination of an Indian with a horse is a fitting one. This iron Indian and his wooden horse did not start out together, but neither did the Plains Indian and the horse he mounted after the animals were introduced to this hemisphere by Europeans. Once together, the Plains Indian and his horse formed an excellent hunting and fighting duo. The union in this vane is somewhat less successful.

Different materials were at times combined in a single vane. When two materials were brought together in the original creation, however, the individual characteristics of each could be more effectively and imaginatively utilized (see Figs. 51, 101). This vane lacks full unity of design but nevertheless has vitality. The Indian seems precariously perched, but the horse is surefooted and enjoys the chase.

3.

Codfish, Sails, and Daring Men

For two hundred years the Bible was the spiritual, the sea the material sustenance of Massachusetts.

SAMUEL ELIOT MORISON
*The Maritime History of
Massachusetts 1783–1860*

Before there was a New England, Bretons and Normans fished North Atlantic waters from Labrador to Massachusetts Bay for cod. Mapmakers named the land from Newfoundland south *Bacalaos,* Spanish (and Greek) for cod. Explorers searching for gold and spice found seas swarming with cod. John Cabot, who reached these shores in 1497, reported that cod were caught in baskets equipped merely with stones to weigh them down.

In 1602 the arm of land with which New England clings to the Atlantic was given the first English name to designate any part of the Northeast—Cape Cod. Captain Bartholomew Gosnold left his ship *Concord* anchored in the bay to explore the cape on foot. He returned to find her decks thick with cod caught by his crew while he was ashore. Impressed by the abundant catch, Gosnold named the cape after the fish.

The codfish off Cape Cod, reported George Weymouth in 1605, were 4 and 5 feet long and so plentiful that they were hauled aboard as fast as the men could bait hooks. The fantastic winter codfishing in these waters became fabled in Europe and brought Western civilization to New England. In 1880 C. L. Woodbury wrote in *The Relation of the Fisheries to the Discovery and Settlement of North America:*

> Let me be clear, neither Pilgrims nor Puritans were its pioneers; neither the axe, the plough, nor the hoe led it to these shores; neither the devices of the chartered companies nor the commands of royalty. It was the discovery of the winter fishery on its shores that led New England to civilization.

New England's soil could be tilled, but summers were short. Without winter fishing, settlement would have been impossible.

The codfish, "the beef of the sea," was fleshy but not fatty and was readily cured by salting and sun-drying. Thus preserved, codfish sustained Americans, nourished Englishmen, and helped fill the heavy demands of Catholic Europe. The European market stimulated a steady trade in dried fish. Exported fish was traded for everything the New World needed. This trade was the source of almost all of New England's revenue. The transportation of fish required merchant ships, crews to sail them, shipwrights to build them, lumbermen to supply the shipbuilders, and so on. America's colossal economy began with the cod.

The House of Representatives of Massachusetts acknowledged the impact of the cod on colonial life when, on March 17, 1748, it voted "to hang a representation of a Cod Fish in the room where the House sits, as a memorial of the importance of the Cod Fishery to the welfare of the nation." A carved wooden cod, dubbed the "Sacred Cod," was installed. In 1795 it was wrapped in a United States flag and thus reverently removed to the new State House where it hangs to this day.

In the same spirit, the cod is honored in the old fish weathervane illustrated in Figure 26. Russell Hawes Kettell, who collected old pine objects during the early years of this century, bought this weathervane, concluded that it was meant to be a cod, and painted it accordingly. The 1-foot-6-inch-long fish, cut from 1¼-inch board, is much smaller than the seventeenth-century fisherman's cod, which measured over 4 feet in length and a yard around. But, after three centuries, the size of codfish, as well as the importance of codfishery, was diminished. The weathervane is a minuscule monument to a once mammoth industry and the munificent economy which sprang from the sea in the shape of a cod.

Paul Revere—renowned as the patriots' messenger, famous as a fine silversmith, and esteemed as a pioneer of America's rolled-copper industry—owned a weathervane. Above his copper-rolling mill flew the wooden fish vane shown in Figure 27.

26.

Codfish. Wood, painted. L. 18". W. 5½". D. 1¼". Maker and date unknown. Painted by Russell Hawes Kettell. Concord Antiquarian Society, Concord, Mass.

Was a copper mill properly served by a wooden vane? Certainly. The mill buildings were wood. Most weathervanes then were wood. Churches and public buildings might require, and could afford, durable but costly metal vanes, but for a family's place of business, a wooden vane was crown enough.

Revere's wooden fish, whose tail is now covered with painted cloth, has a body studded with shiny dots of black paint. The carved fin, gill, and mouth were also enhanced with paint, but only the eye and scales shine with thick glossy paint. Revere, that artistic and imaginative smith, might have created it himself. He certainly was capable of making a weathervane, and many men at that time made their own vanes. However, this is mere speculation. All we know is that the vane belonged to Revere.

Most mill vanes were trade signs. But the silversmith and industrialist was properly served by a fish vane. He was a patriot; the fish was a patriotic symbol. The fish emblem appealed to a New Englander whatever his trade. The Sacred Cod was already hanging in the new State House when Revere's mill was rolling the copper to sheathe that building's unfinished dome. Furthermore, the shape of a fish made an effective vane. Its sleek form had an arrowlike head for a pointer and a broad tail, similar to the forked tail of cloth streamers and swallow-tailed banner vanes. Although nature shaped the fish for travel in the sea, no other natural form is so well suited to catch a breeze on its tail, turn in the air, and point at the wind.

Although the fish is widely recognized in Christian art as a symbol for Jesus (the five letters of the Greek word for fish [Ιχθύς] are the initials of the five Greek words

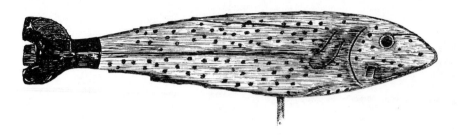

27.

Fish. Wood and cloth, painted. L. 30¾". 1" thick. Made about 1800. Maker unknown. Stood on Paul Revere's copper mill, Canton, Mass. Paul Revere House, 19 North Square, Boston, Mass.

for "Jesus Christ, God's Son, Savior"), and a fish is an attribute of St. Peter, the fisherman, the church weathervane shown in Figure 28 is not upon its post as a religious symbol. The illustrated cod is atop the Old North church in the Massachusetts coastal town of Marblehead primarily as a symbol of that town, described in 1660 as "the greatest Towne for fishing in New England."

The settlement, known originally as Marble Harbor (named for both its asset, the harbor, and its liability, the rocks), was begun in 1629 by fisherfolk who sought not to escape from religious persecution but to gain a livelihood. These English fishermen, from the Guernsey and Jersey islands, were rough and illiterate. Accustomed to toil and hardship, they were able to survive on the edge of a wilderness on a coast of rocks.

Marble Harbor fishermen were far from being religious people and built no church. In 1635, however, they invited the Reverend Mr. Avery to reside there as minister. He refused at first, possibly because of the fishermen's reputation as a godless people. Or perhaps that was the challenge which caused him to reconsider. He was on his way to Marblehead when he was lost at sea.

In 1638 schoolteacher and missionary William Walton came to Marblehead. He served as friend, counselor, and clergyman without ordination until his death thirty years later. Members of his flock traveled to Salem to receive communion or to be married.

Walton's successor, Samuel Cheever, similarly served for sixteen years until in 1682 a church was finally formed and Cheever was ordained. Marblehead, a thriving fishing community, had been without a church for over a half century. Puritan law did not usually allow any but church members to be freemen; nevertheless, Marblehead had been a self-governing town for thirty-seven years.

The members of the First Church of Christ in Marblehead originally worshipped in the town meetinghouse. About 1700 they built a church with tower, spire, and codfish vane (Fig. 28). The copper cod was moved in 1824 to the present church structure from which this trade symbol for an entire town overlooks the once "ungodly" community.

In May 1967 the vane happened to be removed for regilding just before a severe nor'easter blew through town. Some Marbleheaders, noticing that the vane was gone, feared the worst. Codfish are so important to Marbleheaders, weathervanes are so cherished by New Englanders, that when the regilded cod was returned to its spire, a nonparishioner neighbor sent the church five dollars to help defray the expense of what was assumed to be a replacement vane.

A popular subject for weathervanes on Cape Cod—where weathervanes are popular objects—is the swordfish, *Xiphias gladius* (Fig. 29). The Latin name seems to suit this weathervane sculpture, which is as accurate as an ichthyologist's model.

The story of the swordfish, on the cape of the cod, begins with the mackerel. In the early nineteenth century, mackerel fishing became as important as the codfishery. Mackerel annually visit the deep sea waters off the Cape from June to September. Swordfish feed on mackerel and come and disappear with them. Fishermen knew mackerel were about when they saw swordfish.

Mackerel were more sportive and elusive than cod, but more sportive and

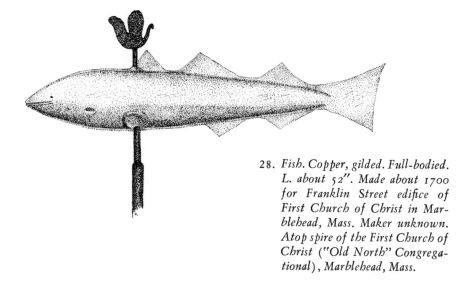

28. *Fish. Copper, gilded. Full-bodied. L. about 52". Made about 1700 for Franklin Street edifice of First Church of Christ in Marblehead, Mass. Maker unknown. Atop spire of the First Church of Christ ("Old North" Congregational), Marblehead, Mass.*

29. *Swordfish. Wood, painted, glass eyes. L. over 4'. Made probably in the late nineteenth century for Cape Cod barn. Maker unknown. Privately owned.*

elusive still were the swordfish. Considerable special gear was needed to harpoon swordfish, which were sighted and taken individually. Nevertheless, during the late 1800s, almost all mackerel vessels were prepared for swordfishing.

Cruising for "the most challenging fish in the sea," was an exciting adventure, especially for the harpooner, who stood in a special "pulpit" at the bowsprit. Men found the pursuit akin to hunting big game on land. Swordfishing became a favorite recreation of fishermen engaged in other work.

Part of swordfishing's fascination came from the danger involved. The powerful, infuriated fish could harm vessel and men. G. Brown Goode in a report on American fisheries, *Materials for a History of the Sword-Fish,* recorded the adventures of the vessels *Redhot* and *Fortune.*

> In 1871 the little yacht "Redhot", of New Bedford, was out swordfishing, and a Swordfish had been hauled in to be lanced, and it attacked the vessel and pierced the side so as to sink the vessel.

Since the swordfish kills its food by rising perpendicularly out of the water through a school of fish, some swordfish attacks on boats may have occurred inadvertently.

On the return of the whale-ship "Fortune" to Plymouth, Mass., in 1827, the stump of a sword-blade of this fish was noticed projecting like a cog outside, which, on being traced, had been driven through the copper sheathing, an inch-board undersheathing, a three-inch plank of hard wood, the solid white-oak timber twelve inches thick, then through another two-and-a-half-inch hard-oak ceiling, and lastly penetrated the head of an oil cask, where it stuck, not a drop of the oil having escaped.

Eighteenth- and early-nineteenth-century historical references to swordfish are few; usually they tell of incidents similar to the *Fortune*'s, with outcomes less fortunate.

The swordfishery grew in importance in the mid-1880s while Cape Cod's other maritime activities declined and its population fell. The Cape's harbors proved too shallow for many fishing vessels; midwestern salt deposits ended the saltwater-to-salt industry; the sandy soil yielded only berries.

Early in the twentieth century, the thinly populated, picturesque seaside area developed a new industry—tourism. Weathervanes, which had long accented the horizon, proliferated. Vanes of swordfish, "the ultimate gamefish," seemed particularly appropriate; the sea was the Cape's principal lure.

The swordfish's shape is ideal for weathervaning. The sword, which gives the fish its name and distinctive profile, enhances the already fine fish silhouette. *Xiphias gladius* makes a handsomer vane than the more commonly caught mackerel, bass, or haddock, or the shad for which Chatham's fishermen seined. It obviously works far better than the oyster of Wellfleet fame, or the lowly clam of Orleans. Swordfish vanes were used everywhere on Cape Cod. They were almost commonplace.

The vane seen in Figure 29, however, is far from commonplace. Carved and constructed of several pieces of wood, protected and enhanced by a realistic coat of gray and white paint, it is the epitome of swordfish—an effective and charming wind pointer, and a fine emblem for a land where men fished for everything from herring to whales.

Few shapes lend themselves less to weathervane purposes than that of *Physeter catodon*, the sperm whale. It presents a square snout where a vane's pointer should be and tapers away to a narrow tail just where a vane should be broad. Nevertheless, whale vanes, particularly sperm whale vanes (Fig. 30), are quite common.

The huge mammals themselves were commonplace in the fish-filled Atlantic during the period of the exploration and settlement of New England. When the *Mayflower* Pilgrims considered Cape Cod as a permanent residence, they noted that "it is a place of

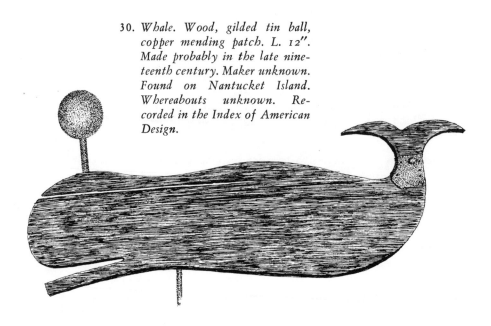

30. *Whale. Wood, gilded tin ball, copper mending patch. L. 12″. Made probably in the late nineteenth century. Maker unknown. Found on Nantucket Island. Whereabouts unknown. Recorded in the Index of American Design.*

profitable fishing: large whales of the best kind for oil and bone came daily alongside and played about the ship."

The treasure-laden giants were often stranded on shore, so often in fact that the early settlements in Massachusetts Bay, Plymouth, Cape Cod, and Long Island regulated the disposition of drift whales. Shares were alloted to colony, town, finder, and cutter. All benefited from the providential gift from the sea. Whales provided oil for lamps, bone whose strength and flexibility had innumerable uses, and spermaceti for candlemaking.

Before long the settlers, dissatisfied with only occasional, accidental treasure-troves, went in pursuit of whales. From virtually every northeastern seacoast village, whaleboats set sail to cruise near the coast and return to shore each night. Gradually they ventured farther and farther from land.

Seaports north of Cape Cod gave up the whalefishery in favor of codfishing and shipping. But on the southern New England coast and Long Island, men continued and expanded their whaling, improved their tools and technique, developed graceful and versatile whaleboats, and eventually constructed large whalers—vessels capable of carrying the whaleboats out over the oceans and of converting blubber to oil on deck.

The nineteenth century saw whalers sail to every watery corner of the globe.

Although ridiculed by most seamen for being unattractive, ungainly, slow, and smelly, these vessels brought wealth and culture to the whaling centers clustered about Buzzards Bay. The bay's ports all but monopolized the world's lighting-oil industry.

No wonder so many whale weathervanes turned in the sea breezes along the southern New England coast. A whale's shape is ill suited to vane work, but a whale symbol is well suited to New Bedford, Nantucket, and Cape Cod.

The whaling vane illustrated in Figure 31 is much more successful in design. The long trumpet, a welcome asset to the vane, gives thrust to the enchanting lines of the whaleman. Such horns were for speaking, not for music making. They were used for calling from one ship to another, "Ahoy there! Have y'seen whale?"

This joyful figure is actually the antithesis of the men who did the work of whaling. He flies free; they lived in a state of near slavery. He represents adventure and abandon; they endured exploitation and brutality. The weathervane reflects the romance, not the realities, of whaling. It is as fanciful as this shipping agent's advertisement:

LANDSMEN WANTED

One thousand stout young men, Americans, wanted for the fleet of whaleships, now fitting out for the North and South Pacific Fisheries. . . . None but industrious young men with good recommendations, taken. . . . Persons desirous to avail themselves of the present splendid opportunity of seeing the world and at the same time acquiring a profitable business, will do well to make early application.

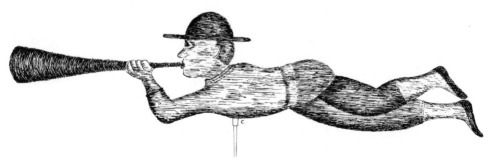

31.

Whaleman with Horn. Wood, painted. L. 47½". Made during the third quarter of nineteenth century. Maker unknown. Eleanor and Mabel Van Alstyne Collection, Smithsonian Institution, Washington, D.C.

The nineteenth century's giant whaling industry required many more hands than the local Buzzards Bay area could supply. While the shipping agent's lure might lead one to assume that only Americans need have applied, whaling crews had an international, interracial flavor that under better conditions would have been picturesque and exciting.

Immigrants without employment on shore signed up. At ports of call like the Azores and Cape Verde Islands, additional hands were procured. Portuguese, Spaniards, Swedes, Norwegians, Danes, Dutchmen, Germans, French and Englishmen, Scots and Irish, blacks from the West Indies and Africa as well as from the United States, New Zealand natives, Hawaiians, and South Sea Islanders added their foreign names to the false names given by Americans who signed on as a way to escape pursuing police. Not everyone on board had "good recommendations." Nor was "early application" necessary. Many were shanghaied or driven desperately into debt so that they would have to "avail themselves of the present splendid opportunity of seeing the world."

The opportunity offered about four years at sea, confined with sixteen other men to a 16- x 16-foot living space, a slimy, smoky, sweltering cell ironically named the forecastle. Wretched food and floggings were the whaleman's hiatuses during alternating periods of interminable idleness and unbelievably hazardous work. A rare visit to a foreign port was a debauched revel of deprived men.

And all did not end with the "acquiring of a profitable business." A whaleman on a long voyage might spend (buying from the shipmaster at his prices) all that he profited from his share of the proceeds. A seaman could debark, after four years, in debt or with little more than a ravenous appetite for food, grog, women, and running wild.

As a work of art and as a vane, the whaleman with horn is successful, but as a fact of life, the sailor with anchor in the vane shown in Figure 32 is more accurate. Instead of flying free, his feet are firmly on the ground and he is tied to the anchor in design and construction. How symbolic of his tether in life! The seaman's dour expression reflects his plight; his dapper clothes reveal his reason for being. This weathervane was probably a trade sign for a haberdashery. Repainting seems to have updated the sailor's costume. Holes and slits on the sides of the cloak remain from an earlier fashion. The allure of this clothier's trade-sign vane is clear: "Jack Tar, these dapper clothes are for you." Like so many seaport businesses, the shop specialized in the sailor's trade.

Whaling centers thrived and grew fat not only on the blubber of whales but also on the blood of whalemen. Like leeches the seaport establishments adhered to the sea-

32. *Sailor and Anchor. Copper, painted. L. 40¼". Made during the last half of nineteenth century. Maker unknown. Eleanor and Mabel Van Alstyne Collection, Smithsonian Institution, Washington, D.C.*

man and drained him of his share of the ship's profits. After four years at sea, niggardly earnings of $100 per year looked substantial as $400 in the pocket of a pleasure-starved whaleman.

Each incoming crew was eagerly awaited by grog houses, brothels, boarding-houses, and shopkeepers. In fact, the landsharks could not wait. They sent runners aboard

33.

Whaler. Painted wood, wire, and sheet metal. L. about 4'. Made in 1832 for Seamen's Bethel, New Bedford, Mass. Maker unknown. Owned by New Bedford Port Society and atop Seamen's Bethel.

each vessel as soon as, if not before, it anchored. These parasites welcomed the seamen and steered them toward their clients' establishments. The seamen were quickly separated from their money through an unbelievable commercial system which tempted whaling hands to indulge in every vice and dissipation. There were, as one nineteenth-century writer put it, "shoals, quicksands, and death pointed rocks upon the land as well as upon the ocean!"

The whaling centers' "respectable" institutions ignored the sailors' plight. Churchmen, regarding seamen as moral pariahs, did not welcome them at services. Their only refuge was the Seamen's Bethel, a mission-church where the discourses and decor had the smell of salt air.

The Seamen's Bethel of New Bedford, Massachusetts, built in 1832 and still standing, has, appropriately, a bowsprit pulpit and a whaler weathervane (Fig. 33). The Bethel was built and maintained by a citizens' group which christened itself "The New Bedford Port Society for the Moral Improvement of Seamen." It was a sop thrown to unfortunates by merchants who refused to alter the vicious system. Twenty-five years after the Bethel opened, a New Bedford citizen appealed for humanitarianism: "When the extent and value of the interests involved are thought of, it seems surprising that efforts are not made to improve the character and condition of the sailor. Millions of property are entrusted to his care."

But even a plea based on dollar practicality was futile. The harvest from the sea continued to be divided into disproportionate shares. The ship-owning aristocracy grew fat, the middle class grew; but the whaling hands reaped merely a brief and boisterous stay ashore.

Perhaps the carver of New Bedford's whaler weathervane was a seaman between voyages. He accurately, if crudely, depicted a whaler at sea, after her boats had left for the chase, as she appeared to the abused but brave men who rowed in pursuit of leviathans with their backs to the prey.

A whaleman was apt to fashion a weathervane; his occupation made him ever mindful of the wind. His songs often spoke of the whaleman's sorry lot. One of them, whose chorus calls upon the morning wind, has this stanza describing the men overhauling and harpooning the whale.

It's pull upon the oars, me boys,
Until your shoulders crack
And when she's fast she'll tow you, boys,
From here to Hell and back.

   Then blow ye winds in the morning
   And blow ye winds high-o!
   Clear away the morning dew
   And blow, winds, blow!

Swiveling vanes as well as sailing vessels depend on the wind for their motion and their fate. But this alone does not explain why weathervanes of sailing vessels such as those in Figures 33 and 34 are so much a part of New England.

New England's early settlers quickly learned that although the sea was bountiful, the boulder-strewn soil was stingy. To sustain life, they had to trade—to trade fish. "Fish is the only great stapple which the Country produceth for foraine parts and is so benifitiall for making returns for what wee need."

Poor-grade cod was shipped to the slave-populated West Indies in exchange for sugar, spices, and molasses. Catholic Europe bought the best-grade cod, trading for it wine, salt, iron, and pieces of eight. Fortunes were made, not from fish alone, but from its distribution.

Distribution required merchant ships. New England's many river mouths and coves were natural sites for shipyards. A plentiful supply of oak for hulls and pine for masts stood ready to meet the demand for fishing vessels and merchant ships. The art and industry of shipbuilding flourished at the mouths of the Merrimack, Mystic, Charles, and Connecticut, and in the bays and coves at Ipswich, Beverly, Salem, Charlestown, Boston, Weymouth, Scituate, Newport, New London, and New Haven.

Shipping was of such importance to Boston that in 1662 the city had one merchant ship for every fifty inhabitants. By 1700 the colonial merchant marine numbered some 1,000 ships, almost all from New England. The captains—seafaring Yankee peddlers —bought and sold fish and rum, whale oil and wine, naval stores and barrel staves, sugar, salt and spices, African slaves and European manufactures. At the outbreak of the Revolution, 2,343 ships, one third of the total English registry, were American, mostly Yankee.

Naturally, when New Englanders built weathervanes, sailing vessels were popular subjects. Ship vanes, symbols of the people's interests and investments, served as trade signs for individual business establishments and for entire seacoast communities. Where sailing is a business, wind direction is important, weathervanes are appropriate, and sailing vessel vanes particularly popular.

Early ship weathervanes, like their seaworthy originals, were made of wood. They were sometimes carved in three-dimensional form, full-bodied; sometimes merely cut out of flat board. Fragile masts held riggings and sails, often of copper or cloth. With paint to protect them, the wooden vanes were launched into the sea breezes.

The survival rate of wooden ship-vanes has been poor, but their production has been continual. Iron and copper ship-vanes have joined the wooden ones. Every type of sailing craft has been represented; many with imaginative riggings. (It seems doubtful that, in the days of sail, ship weathervanes were incorrectly rigged as often as they are today.)

A weathervane vessel usually has a fore-and-aft-rigged sail on the aftermost mast to catch the wind. Flat vanes can carry full sail. Full-bodied vanes which depict rigs with fore-and-aft sails only (e.g., sloops, schooners) can also display full sail. But full-bodied square-rigger vanes cannot carry full canvas. If they did, instead of swiveling, they would sail off their spires.

The vane illustrated in Figure 34 was safely rigged and lasted longer than the Cape Cod shipyard for which it was made. Neither winds nor money could take it from atop an antique dealer's roof. But a thief did. The vane soon showed up in Florida, and the Cape Codder who owned it flew south to identify it and—with two extra seats on the airplane for the old vane—carried it home.

The dignified and distinguished ship's officer represented in Figure 35 may have pursued a profession often regarded today as no better than thievery. The reputation of American privateersmen of the early nineteenth century has been tarnished by our misunderstanding. Privateering is often misinterpreted as piracy.

Piracy—theft on the high seas—was and is illegal, irresponsible, and dishonor-

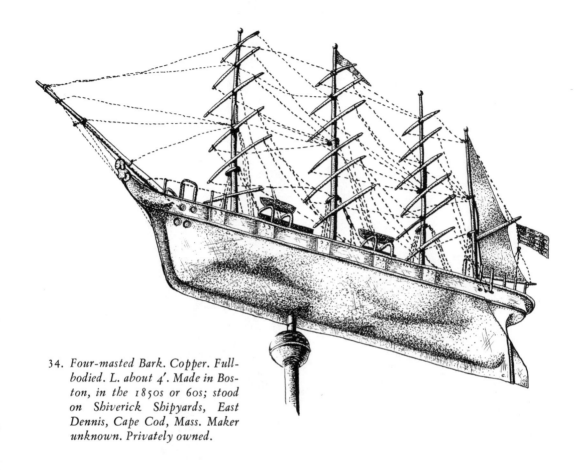

34. *Four-masted Bark. Copper. Full-bodied. L. about 4'. Made in Boston, in the 1850s or 60s; stood on Shiverick Shipyards, East Dennis, Cape Cod, Mass. Maker unknown. Privately owned.*

able. Privateering—war operations on the high seas by privately owned vessels—was enterprise in high style: legal, regulated, and respectable. Privateers carried letters of marque, governmental licenses to capture and confiscate foreign vessels.

Although privateering is no longer practiced (or practicable), it is still constitutional in the United States. Article I, section 8, clause 11, grants to Congress the power "To declare War, grant Letters of Marque. . . ." Letters of marque, granted by federal and state governments, restricted privateers as to who was fair game and where and when vessels could be taken. Privateering was a respected business. Its purpose was private gain; its target, the public enemy.

New England's greatest contribution to the winning of the Revolutionary War was in service at sea—not in the regular navy, which was embryonic, but in privateering.

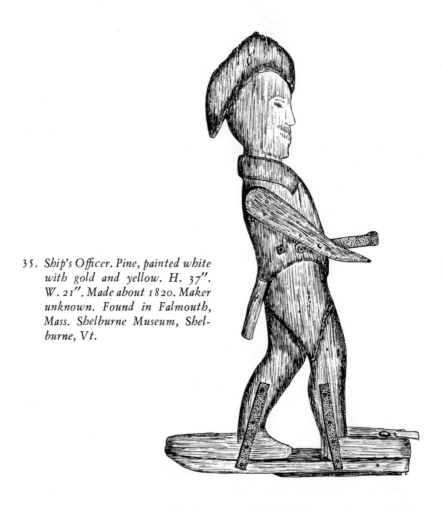

35. *Ship's Officer. Pine, painted white with gold and yellow. H. 37". W. 21". Made about 1820. Maker unknown. Found in Falmouth, Mass. Shelburne Museum, Shelburne, Vt.*

Privateers harassed the king's navy on both sides of the Atlantic and supplied the patriots with arms and stores at English expense.

When the Revolution and, later, the War of 1812 interrupted the normal pursuits of fishermen and merchant seamen, privateering more than took up the employment slack. Sailors and landsmen welcomed the opportunity for adventure and for a share in a possible bountiful booty. The *Yankee*, out of Rhode Island, America's most successful privateer, on her fifth cruise about 1814 brought almost $600,000—a quarter of a million to her owners, $15,789.69 to her captain, $1,121.89 and $738.19 to two ordinary seamen. (A workman on shore was earning about $12 a week.)

If potential profits in privateering were huge, so were the demands and risks. Speedy ships were required, so they were designed and built. Daring seamanship was needed and was developed. Courageous leadership was demanded and was achieved. Privateering was the school for the sailing men of America. They graduated with honors in independence, initiative, and imagination, well prepared for the business world of clipper ships and China trade. No wonder the weathervane's handsome officer seems so proud of his profession.

In 1784 a man from Worcester, Massachusetts, wrote a tune and named it after an exotic land—"China." In 1801 the words of a hymn were set to that tune and published under the same name. In 1818 some people in Maine honored their favorite hymn and renamed their town China. About 1830 an American from China, Maine, moved to nearby Warren, Maine, and placed over his barn the dragon shown in Figure 36, a symbol of remote China. Why was an Asian land influencing names and designs in New England?

Salem, Massachusetts, was a fishing port before the Revolution. Wartime privateering gave her seamen greater ambition, and they gave up fishing for merchant shipping and the riches of the Orient. Boston, always a trading port, lost its British markets when

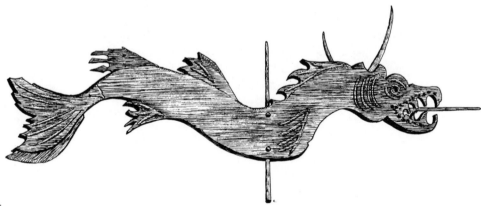

36.

Dragon. Pine board, red painted lips, flecks of yellow on fins. L. 6'3". Made by a Mr. Crane, about 1830, for a barn in Warren, Me. Recorded in the Index of American Design.

it gained independence. There, too, men looked to the Far East. China, however, wasn't interested in buying fish.

When in 1790 the ship *Columbia* entered Boston harbor after circumnavigating the globe, Bostonians found a way to the wealth of China. The *Columbia* (after which the river in Oregon, Washington, and British Columbia was named) had sailed westward, traded with the American Indians of the Northwest for fur, and sold the skins profitably in China.

Other Bostonians followed the *Columbia*'s route, trading for fur in the Northwest and for Chinese teas and textiles, spices and porcelains. The fortunes of many Boston families were founded in that Northwest and China trade. The Americanization of Hawaii began when the islands' sandalwood proved marketable in China. While Boston's ships sailed westward, Salem's ships sailed eastward, trading at ports in Africa, India, and the East Indies. Pepper, spices, and tin brought wealth to the former fishing port.

With their newly acquired wealth, New England merchants decorated their homes with the splendors of the Orient. Silks, porcelains, wallpaper, and carved figures brought Chinese design into Yankee homes. Prominent in that design was the Chinese dragon.

As Figure 36 shows, the popular oriental motif makes an exciting American weathervane. The Chinese influence is apparent. This is no English dragon such as might have fought with St. George or with an American rattler (see Fig. 17). This is a Chinese dragon. Art motifs as well as tea can be imported.

The China trade was of short duration. In the mid-nineteenth century, Salem turned to cloth manufacture, and Boston's China trade diminished as California-bound clipper ships brought shipping under sail to its zenith. Brief as it was, the period of the China trade was shipping's renaissance. As a bonus, it had brought Chinese objects into American homes and Chinese motifs into American folk art.

4.

For Lofty Steeples

Religious peace as well as religious freedom . . . contributes not a little to sweeten the lives of ordinary people.

JAMES BRYCE
The American Commonwealth

A flying figure, as we saw when we compared the sailors (Figs. 31 and 32), makes a remarkably effective vane. Craftsmen unwilling to portray the unlikely sight of a flying human had an acceptable and appropriate alternative—an angel. As the flying whaleman showed, the forward line is enhanced by a horn, and a horn is best blown by the angel Gabriel.

Gabriel, the herald angel, was an especially popular emblem in the early 1800s. The herald of good news was used in American decoration as herald of the new nation's newfound liberty. Patriotic Gabriels adorned porcelains, furniture, and rooftops. This subject, ideally suited to weathervaning, was also a marvelously meaningful symbol for church spires. Gabriel vanes were justifiably popular, and especially so on churches.

In New England's breezes, Gabriels of various shapes, all sizes, and assorted textures flew with differing degrees of agility and beauty. As variations occur in all themes, in all arts, they occur in weathervanes. Gabriel vanes were selected here as a case in point.

37. *Angel Gabriel. Pine board, painted white, black. L. about 4'6". Made by a Mr. Cook, Stepney, Conn. Reproduction of vane made about 1840. Recorded in the Index of American Design.*

The variety results from the individual contributions of the independent creators. Each craftsman of a Gabriel vane, after complying with the demands of good vane design and the conventions of Christian art, independently chose his construction material and freely created a product of his own particular skill and personality.

With a minimum of skill, the twentieth-century copy of an early-nineteenth-century vane shown in Figure 37 achieves considerable character. Reproduction of a wooden cutout vane is neither difficult nor unique; this is likely an accurate reproduction. Repainting, a common practice, can bring new charm to a vane. Much of this Gabriel's appeal comes from his painted features. No painter, however, could ever make of his crude form a handsome herald angel.

A more skillful artisan fashioned the Gabriel vane from Whiting, Vermont (Fig. 38). His horn is more graceful and his limbs are more substantial than the rubbery arms and legs of the preceding, wooden Gabriel. The skilled smith who made this vane cut two heavy, bulky iron sheets, rounded them ever so slightly, and joined them with hand-made rivets.

This sturdy Gabriel is a proud Baptist. In 1814 the members of that denomination in the town of Whiting, Vermont, could at last afford to build their own house of worship. (For years they had shared a church with Methodists and Congregationalists.) They crowned the tower of their new church with this mighty Gabriel. He remained blowing into the Vermont wind until 1930, when the church building became a public library. Now he blows into the Virginia wind in the garden of a folk-art museum in Colonial Williamsburg.

Being displayed in a museum garden seems prestigious for a weathervane, but that honor fades when compared to that of another Gabriel vane whose portrait was painted, and whose likeness was reproduced on some 1.2 billion miniatures which were sent around the world. The miniatures were distributed by the United States Post Office.

The graceful Gabriel (Fig. 39) was fashioned of flat sheet copper in 1840, in the Charlestown, Massachusetts, shop of Gould & Hazlett. The herald angel was furnished

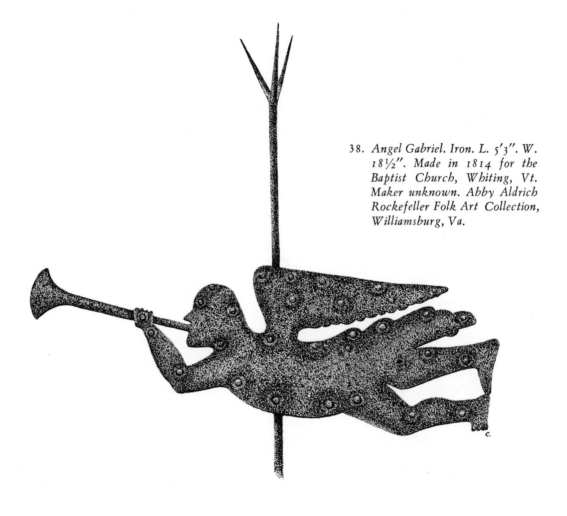

38. *Angel Gabriel. Iron. L. 5′3″. W. 18½″. Made in 1814 for the Baptist Church, Whiting, Vt. Maker unknown. Abby Aldrich Rockefeller Folk Art Collection, Williamsburg, Va.*

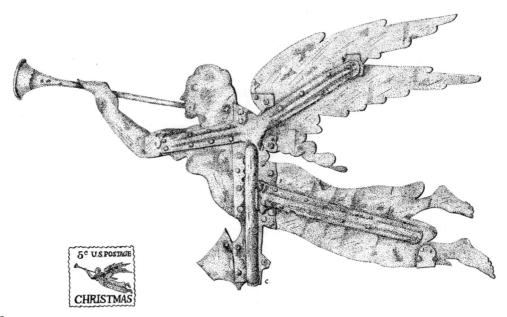

39.

Angel Gabriel. Copper, gilded. L. 6'2". H. 34". .075 thick. 38 lbs. Made by Gould & Hazlett, Charlestown, Mass., in 1840 for the Universalist Church, Newburyport, Mass. Atop People's Methodist Church, Newburyport, Mass.

with a three-dimensional trumpet, within which the coppersmiths left a note proudly signing their creation. (After seeing other Gabriel vanes, one can understand their pride.) The gilded vane was delivered to Newburyport, Massachusetts, and elevated to the spire of the Universalist Church.

Newburyport's Universalists had an outstanding vane, for while Gabriel weathervanes were not uncommon, the beauty of their Gabriel was. To its singularly handsome shape we may owe its survival as well as its fame. A less attractive vane might have been left on the spire when the Universalist building was abandoned and might have perished in the fire that consumed the old church. Gabriel, however, had been taken down and stored in a barn.

The People's Methodist Church stood down the street from the barn. One of its parishioners, having seen the salvaged vane, was determined that it grace his church's steeple. He knocked on doors up and down the street, raising the funds needed to buy the vane. Thanks to his efforts, Gabriel was again heading into the sea breezes above New-buryport as the nineteenth century ended.

In 1937 the United States government had the Newburyport Gabriel's portrait painted. During the depression artists needed employment. Also, in this age of mechanization, America needed a pictorial record of its vanishing decorative handicrafts. So the WPA Federal Art Project established the Index of American Design and set artists to work recording our folk and popular arts.

Index artist Lucille Chabot painted the portrait of the Gabriel as it appeared then, with little gold leaf remaining amid a coat of verdigris. The watercolor captured the vane's flowing contour and the subtle shadings of its weathered surface. When postal authorities sought a subject for the 1965 Christmas stamp, they looked through the index and were attracted by Miss Chabot's painting of Gabriel. They printed 1.2 billion tricolored copies.

Meanwhile, the vane had not fared as well as its portrait. The WPA had repaired it and returned it to its steeple, but in 1959 hurricane winds blew Gabriel's horn; that is, blew the horn down to the ground. The trumpet was tucked away in the minister's closet and forgotten. A new minister arrived and almost discarded the battered copper horn he found there. "What a way to begin a ministry," he later laughed, "condemning the trumpet of a heavenly herald!" By then, however, the old weathervane was hard to recognize as heavenly. With the fall of the trumpet, the archangel had lost its distinguishing attribute, and the vane's silhouette had lost much of its grace. Renovation of the church was being planned, but no arrangements had been made to refurbish the broken vane.

Then the Post Office released a photograph of its new stamp. A Connecticut man wrote the postmaster general, "The torso part of the figure is feminine. . . ." The Post Office dispatched a man to Newburyport; Miss Chabot's rendering proved accurate. The weathervane with the masculine name had a feminine form.

"GABRIELLE'S HORN?" queried the New York Times. The Pilot of Boston head-lined: "ANGEL BEDEVILS OBSERVERS." Theologians explained that, as spiritual beings, angels were sexless. Their visual shape was of artistic, not religious, concern.

Amid the confusion, the people of Newburyport looked up at the angel in their midst and noticed his/her/its sorry state. Gabriel was brought down. With renewed interest and pride in their weathervane, the people repaired, regilded, and restored Gabriel. Trumpet in hand, the angel was returned to radiant glory and lofty position.

If Gabriel can appear in feminine form, he certainly can materialize as a child-

40.
Angel Gabriel. Copper, gilded. L. 32″. Mass produced by Cushing & White, later L. W. Cushing & Sons, Waltham, Mass. Designed in 1869. Model carved by E. W. Hastings, Boston figurehead carver. Eleanor and Mabel Van Alstyne Collection, Smithsonian Institution, Washington, D.C., and elsewhere.

like cherub. He assumed this form in a vane (Fig. 40) listed as "Angel Gabriel" by Cushing & White (later L. W. Cushing & Sons) of Waltham, Massachusetts, and mass produced by them in copper for sale at twenty-five dollars. Cushing had the wooden model for this angel carved by E. Warren Hastings, a Boston figurehead and ornamental carver.

This angel, younger and smaller than the three previous heralds, was a product of the nineteenth-century revival of baroque and rococo styles. He is as cute as the Newburyport angel is graceful. His copper seems as soft as the Whiting Baptist's iron seems sturdy. He is as finely sculptured as the Stepney Gabriel is crudely cut. His plump curves suggest a roundness well beyond his 1⅜-inch thickness.

Picture him as he once was, completely covered in gold leaf. Never was there a more baroque weathervane. He is an angel snatched from a sentimental painting by Murillo, from a sumptuous fountain by Bernini, from the rococo walls of the Wies Church in Bavaria, or perhaps from the ornate carvings on a carousel's calliope.

Unlike Newburyport's Gabriel, distinguished by its elegant simplicity, Cushing's Gabriel was, simply, elegant.

The whims of men, as well as the whims of the wind, move weathervanes. Some have been removed when styles changed. Many have been relocated when needs changed. But few have traveled, as the vane in Figure 41 did, while still perched atop a steeple.

Dorchester, Massachusetts, had been growing since Puritans settled there in 1630 and built a meetinghouse "surrounded by pallisadoes." Three meetinghouses and a century later, a less fortified structure, the fourth meetinghouse, was built in typical eighteenth-century-meetinghouse style. Its adjoining bell tower was topped with a banner weathervane (Fig. 41). (Meetinghouse spires of the eighteenth century customarily bore either cockerel vanes or swallow-tailed banners.)

By 1795 the parish had outgrown its 68- x 46-foot meetinghouse. Rather than abandon it, they enlarged it in a curious but not uncommon procedure. The build-

41. Swallow-tailed Banner. Iron, gilded. L. 6'3". Made in 1743 for fourth meetinghouse (pictured in lower sketch) of First Parish in Dorchester, Mass. Maker unknown. Displayed on hall wall in the sixth meetinghouse, First Parish Church, Dorchester.

42. *Scroll. Probably copper. L. about 6'. Made in 1816 for fifth meetinghouse of the First Parish in Dorchester, Mass. Atop the spire of the sixth meetinghouse, First Parish Church, Dorchester.*

ing was sawed in half, divided along its ridge pole; one half was moved 14 feet and the addition was built between, uniting the two halves. The exterior evidence of the expansion was the meetinghouse's gambrel roof.

To complete the job, the vane-topped, 14-foot-square, 114-foot-tall tower had to be recentered. It was moved, standing, 7 feet "by means of screws, and with the strength of only four men."

The enlarged eighteenth-century meetinghouse and its eighteenth-century vane continued to serve the parish into the nineteenth century. With the new century came the classical revival in American design and a new vogue in church architecture. When the expanded meetinghouse was damaged by storm in 1815, the parishioners decided to build a new church in the new style with a vane to match (Fig. 42).

In the meetinghouse architecture of the old century, the entrance was placed in the middle of the long wall and the tower stood to one side. In the new classical revival churches, the entrance was on the short side of the structure, through the bell tower. Worshippers entered between stately columns, beneath an imposing many-storied steeple, below the gilded vane. The more elaborate entry and steeple demanded a more elaborate weathervane. Dorchester's old banner vane was retired. Swallow-tailed banners had been finials for eighteenth-century spires; scroll vanes became the finials for nineteenth-century steeples.

The scroll vanes descended from the earlier banner design just as the new church architecture evolved from the earlier meetinghouse style. Both retained the basic lines of the old style but enriched them with classical themes presented in delicate detail.

Among the classical motifs revived during the early nineteenth century, the federal period in American design, a most popular shape was that of the lyre. Stylized lyres decorated drawing rooms and rooftops, appearing on chair backs, table bases, wall clocks, and weathervanes as in Figure 43.

A classical symbol of song, a mythological instrument of the wind, the lyre was ideal as a church weathervane, a worthy competitor in heavenly music-making to Gabriel's horn.

The overall pattern of the vanes illustrated in Figure 44 (listed in manufacturers' catalogues as "scrolls") combines three basic design elements: an arrow, a scroll (or lyre) body, and a tail. Stars, sunbursts, and tulips commonly serve as tails. The placement of the lyre varies endlessly. One of the few scroll vanes without a lyre form, the Hamilton, Massachusetts, vane, has an exceeding felicitous design.

43.

Scroll. Copper. L. 34⅞". Mass produced by A. L. Jewell, Waltham, Mass.; designed before 1860. In the author's collection.

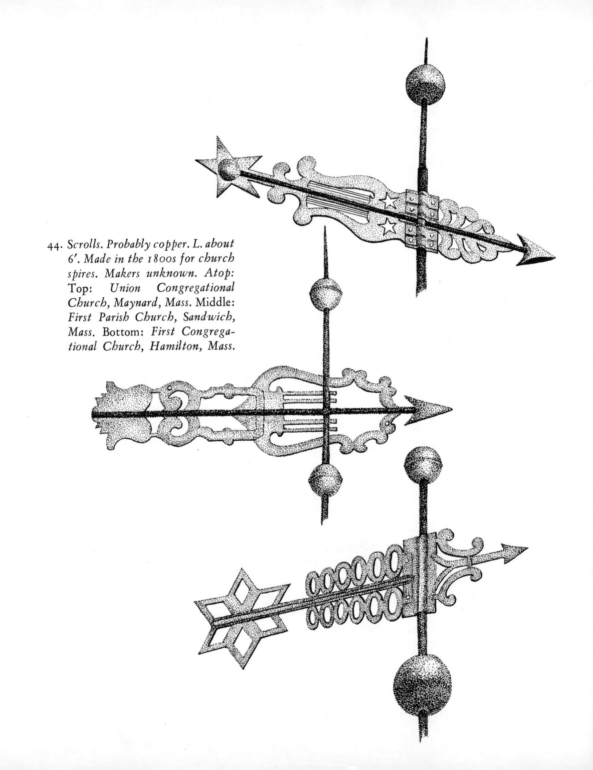

44. *Scrolls. Probably copper. L. about 6′. Made in the 1800s for church spires. Makers unknown. Atop:* Top: *Union Congregational Church, Maynard, Mass.* Middle: *First Parish Church, Sandwich, Mass.* Bottom: *First Congregational Church, Hamilton, Mass.*

Scroll vanes in their great variety are the most common of New England's church vanes. Scrolls are flat weathervanes, simple to construct and inexpensive to acquire. They were designed with classical motifs for the classical revival style of architecture, which flourished during the nineteenth-century religious revival and the boom in church construction.

Classical revival churches, unlike many of the earlier meetinghouses, continued in use for many years—often being reconstructed and preserved rather than sawed in half or replaced. To this day there are New England churches being constructed in the classical revival style, or as people often describe them, "you know, a New England church." Lyre-shaped vanes so often top this style of church that they are "you know, a church weathervane."

A most distinguished and graceful lyre vane (Fig. 45) crowns a most distinguished and beautiful church—the First Baptist Church of Providence, Rhode Island. Both the city and the parish were founded in freedom and were influential in the shaping of America's liberal traditions. Appropriately, the church and the vane were in their architectural design also trend setters. They are exquisite examples of what we have chosen to call the nineteenth-century style; yet they were created in the late eighteenth century.

New ideas in art and design were first accepted in southern New England and in urban centers, and only later adopted in the more conservative northern Yankee country and in rural communities. The classical revival which swept New England at the beginning of the nineteenth century found early expression in Providence. The new design was particularly appropriate for the Baptist parish. The style was one of church (i.e., religious) architecture as against meetinghouse (i.e., secular-religious) architecture, and the First Baptist Church, Providence, was a religious establishment in a city founded on the principle of religious separation from secular rule.

The Pilgrims of Plymouth, separatists from the Church of England, did not separate church from state. Neither did the Puritans of Massachusetts Bay, who sought to be reformers of the Church of England. But Roger Williams, who came to Massachusetts in 1631, quickly established himself as a separatist among separatists, a reformer of reformers.

Williams demanded strict separation of government and religion. For example, he held that no civil court had the right to punish breach of the Sabbath, that no government had the right to require loyalty oaths, for an oath was an act of worship. This champion of complete religious freedom for each individual was banished from Massachusetts in 1635 because his ideas seemed to threaten the very basis of the settlement. He

45. *Scroll. Probably copper. L. about 6'. Made by Samuel Hamlin in 1775 for First Baptist Church, Providence, R.I. (lower sketch). On the spire for which it was made.*

fled south and established the city of Providence (1636) as "a shelter for persons distressed in conscience."

There in 1639 Roger Williams repudiated the baptism of his infancy, was reimmersed, and in turn immersed eleven others, thus establishing the first Baptist church in America. Williams left the church a few months later to pursue his individual quest for religious truth, but the First Baptist Church of Providence continued, devoted to liberty of conscience and separation of church and state.

The Providence Baptists' third and present church was erected in 1774–75; both steeple and building were copied from London designs. The scroll vane was made for the 185-foot steeple by Samuel Hamlin (honored today for his pewter products). The vane was elevated to its station shortly after the battle at Lexington. The lovely scroll pointed the way for the new style of the coming century, for the new nation coming into being, based on the freedom first practiced in Providence.

Fashions come, go, and return. Medieval meetinghouse flags (Figs. 1–4) had

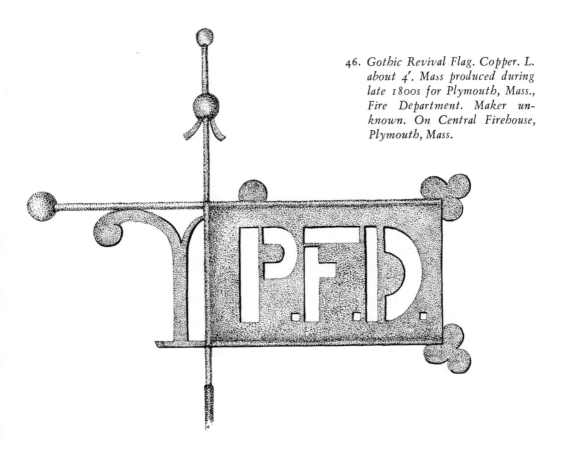

46. *Gothic Revival Flag. Copper. L. about 4'. Mass produced during late 1800s for Plymouth, Mass., Fire Department. Maker unknown. On Central Firehouse, Plymouth, Mass.*

47. *Victorian Banner. Copper. L. about 5'. Mass produced during late 1800s and purchased for West Topsham church. Maker unknown. Atop the spire of the Community Church, West Topsham, Vt.*

been succeeded by renaissance swallow-tailed banners (Figs. 5, 6, 41) which in turn had been followed by classical scrolls. And the classical scroll faded during the mid-nineteenth-century Gothic revival, which brought back medieval meetinghouse flags.

Of course, the nineteenth-century versions, such as that shown in Figure 46, were not quite the same as their medieval predecessors. Revival art never is. Gothic revival flags were larger than the old medieval vanes; they were generally mass produced (the originals, individually wrought) usually of copper construction (most originals, of iron). A few were fairly faithful to the ancient fane designs; others were imaginatively pseudo-Gothic. How well they suited the mock-castles from whose unfortified turrets they flew!

The Gothic revival was only one of the several ornate and elaborate styles commonly grouped together and called Victorian. The neo-Greek, neo-Egyptian, and neo-Gothic were followed by Victorian versions of Elizabethan and Jacobean decor.

As a protest against these neo-historic designs, a new style appeared in the last decade of the nineteenth century. Rather than imitate traditional styles, art nouveau imitated natural forms. The flowery style, sown by a Belgian architect, Victor Horta, was nourished in America by such craftsmen as Louis C. Tiffany and flourished in all the applied arts. Copper flowers and glass feathers undulated everywhere.

The once heraldic fleur-de-lis, so regal on old meetinghouse vanes (Fig. 1), reappeared on the church vane seen in Figure 47, with its flower more natural than noble, its form more dainty than dignified.

5.
On the Farm

Agriculture, within a few years, has been improved with a rapidity without precedent in the annals of art; . . . Every human being has an interest in that art which is the foundation of all the other arts, and the basis of all civilization.

New England Farmer
Boston, August 3, 1822

The old heraldic vanes of England suited the castle-centered medieval world. The golden banners on New England's meetinghouses, churches, and town halls suited the village-centered society of the seventeenth and eighteenth centuries. By 1800 American life was farm-centered: each farm was an economic unit; each homestead a social hub. So when weathervanes, accustomed to lofty steeples and stately domes, appeared on the humbler barn roofs, they were not coming down in the world, they were merely moving to new centers. In nineteenth-century agrarian America, weathervanes retained their place at the heart of the culture.

As a farming symbol, the plow (Fig. 48) was obvious; as a wind indicator, its shape was effective; and, as an emblem of America's scientific agricultural revolution, the plow vane was perfect.

Plows had long been used in the Old World, but the Pilgrims for their first twelve years in the New World had not even one plow. Fishing and hunting could not

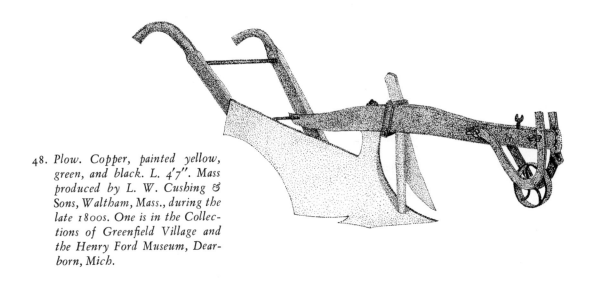

48. *Plow. Copper, painted yellow, green, and black. L. 4'7". Mass produced by L. W. Cushing & Sons, Waltham, Mass., during the late 1800s. One is in the Collections of Greenfield Village and the Henry Ford Museum, Dearborn, Mich.*

fill their food needs, so they adopted the Indian hoe culture. Hoe cultivation suited both the corn crop and the rocky New England soil. Many other crops needed more than hoe-made mounds, but still plows remained scarce for generations. All of a colonial village's arable lands would be plowed by the one plow owner in the village.

Through the eighteenth century, farmers struggled with clumsy, heavy, and inefficient plows which needed teams of two men and four or six oxen. As described by Josiah G. Holland in the *History of Western Massachusetts:*

> The old plough, composed almost entirely of wood, and of clumsy construction . . . [was] admirably adapted to load itself with earth, until its influence upon the soil was but little more than would result from drawing a log across it.

Repeated experimentation to improve plows brought results in the early nineteenth century. Thomas Jefferson was the first American to design a plow moldboard on mathematical principles. A flurry of new plow inventions followed. Between 1800 and 1830, 124 patents for plows were granted. These new plow designs shaped the moldboard scientifically, reduced the bulk of timber, and used iron to prevent clogging and to save wear. With the new plows, a smaller plowing team could make deeper furrows. The New England soils, depleted by a century and a half of poor farming practices, could be rehabilitated into new grasslands.

49. *Arrow. Oak, painted black. L. about 8'. Made in 1864 for Shaker barn, Hancock, Mass. Maker unknown. A facsimile is on the barn, the original is in storage.*

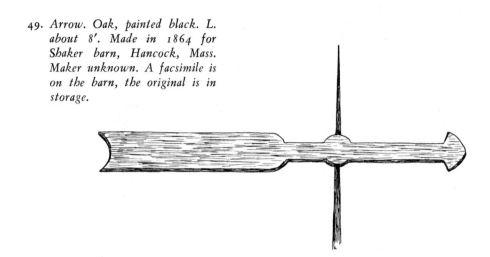

America's early-nineteenth-century agrarian awakening was the foundation of her great agricultural future. The era has no better symbol than a plow. Few, however, were as elaborately detailed as the one shown in Figure 48. It has been painted; others were purchased (for fifty dollars) wearing a coat of gold. What a fine heir to the tradition of heraldic fanes! Indeed, in heraldic times, the English poet Abraham Cowley (1618–67) had dubbed the plow "the Most Honorable of Ancient Arms."

The classic direction pointer, the arrow, is an ideal shape for a wind-direction pointer. Many farm weathervanes combined arrow and animal forms (Fig. 64), and arrows were often part of Indian vanes (Figs. 14, 24, 25). But sometimes a plain arrow stood alone.

The simple, functional pointer illustrated in Figure 49, adorning a simple functional barn, is most symbolic of the ideals of those who made it and used it. The plain and the useful, so characteristic of all farm life, was the special essence of life on the farms of the Shaker religious sect. In an age when each farm was a family community, the Shakers developed a different kind of family and a unique type of community.

The Shakers were noncombatant spiritualists who lived in celibate communities, held property in common, and considered the sexes equal. Each "family" elected leaders whose religious and civil duties included the planning of the economic life of the almost self-contained community. The "brothers" and "sisters" strictly regulated the routines of daily life but rejoiced in their religion. Their practice of dancing and marching at meeting earned them the name "Shakers."

The Shaker faith was founded by Ann Lee before she and her few followers came to America in 1774 to establish Shaker communities here. In the quarter century which followed, the Shakers grew to be one thousand strong. They settled mainly in New York and New England and established "families" based on their ideals of faith and ideals for living. From 1800 to 1850 their ranks swelled to six thousand dedicated souls, living on their distinctive but plain "family" farms, producing the plain but distinctive crafts so prized today for their simple beauty.

Beauty to Shakers meant order, regularity, harmony, and honesty of form. They eschewed the fancy because they regarded ornamental trim as useless. Utility and simplicity were their goals. A weathervane seemed useful; an arrow was simple.

The Shakers honored manual labor. They made virtually everything they used. So this arrow vane atop the round barn at the Hancock, Massachusetts, Shaker community was undoubtedly made by a "brother" of that "family."

Because America's ideals of religious freedom offered opportunity to independent sects, and because the Shaker ideals of faith dictated honesty in form, our American heritage includes the simply beauty of Shaker crafts and this plain, practical arrow vane.

The most popular subject for barn vanes (Fig. 50) was the most common animal of the barnyard, the chicken.

A typical eighteenth- or nineteenth-century farm might have 1 horse; 2 oxen; 15 cattle, of which 5 were dairy cows; 10 swine; 15 sheep; and 120 poultry. Such a barnyard population plus a balanced crop allowed a farmer and his family to be virtually self-sufficient, to require almost nothing from beyond their farm's boundaries except Sunday nourishment for their souls.

Self-sufficient farms dotted the countryside. Gone was the early type of settlement, where houses huddled securely about a meetinghouse with farmland (both common and individually owned) in outlying fields beyond the village. In the eighteenth century each farmer built his home in the midst of his one or two hundred acres, a mile or more from the village.

Between 1790 and 1840 most farms were almost totally self-sufficient. Gradually, farmers began to barter and buy, becoming less and less economically independent. But self-sufficiency in food lasted a long time. As late as 1930 a couple in northern Vermont boasted on their sixtieth anniversary of never having bought a pound of meat, flour, or

50. *Cock. Pine, painted; metal comb and wattles. L. 36″. Made in the early nineteenth century. Maker unknown. Nantucket Historical Association, Nantucket, Mass.*

sugar. They didn't even mention that they had never bought an egg. Self-sufficiency in eggs and poultry was just too commonplace.

In the eighteenth and early nineteenth centuries farmers recognized and called their animals by name. Only the ubiquitous chickens were nameless. Farmers sheltered and penned other animals, but hens and roosters ran loose. Other animals were specially fed; chickens scrounged. When livestock were counted and recorded, poultry were scarcely mentioned.

But the commonplace chicken was not overlooked in weathervane design. Ever present in the barnyard, he became emblematic of the farm.

Wind pointers in the shape of cocks, of course, were nothing new. For centuries, as we have seen, church weathercocks had vigilantly watched over noblemen and peasants in Europe's medieval towns and had alerted Americans with their Christian warning. Most farm cocks are distinctly different from church cockerels.

The cock shown in Figure 51, however, is similar in style to meetinghouse cocks; only his modest size and coat of paint distinguish him as a farm vane. His 28-inch length seems small for a tall meetinghouse spire. His wooden body was originally painted black, his iron wattles and comb painted red. Such realistic coloring was a practice with

51. *Cock. Wood, painted; iron tail and legs. L. 28″. Made possibly in the late eighteenth century. Found in Methuen, Mass. Maker unknown. Eleanor and Mabel Van Alstyne Collection, Smithsonian Institution, Washington, D.C.*

52. *Game cock. Wood, painted; iron legs. L. 45". Made, possibly in the late eighteenth century, for the barn of the Fitch Tavern, Bedford, Mass. Maker unknown. Displayed in Shelburne Museum, Shelburne, Vt.*

barn vanes. Golden vanes were customary on meetinghouses and churches. Usually church cocks were of gilded copper, but even a wooden one would be colored gold.

So this fine wood and metal sculpture, the very essence of a dignified lord of the roost, probably first roosted on a barn.

Of similar construction and of the same era, the weathercock in Figure 52 depicts a game cock, a scrappy fellow always ready for a fight. The vane came from a barn at a crossroads tavern made famous by scrappy Minutemen.

Since 1730 the Fitch Tavern has stood on Great Road in Bedford, Massachusetts, at the fork where two teamsters' routes joined on their way toward Boston. (It is not known when the barn and fighting cock were set up at the roadside.) Early in the morning of April 19, 1775, the men sitting down to breakfast at the tavern of Jeremiah Fitch, Jr., were not the usual assortment of teamsters. News had arrived from neighboring Lexington that the British were coming. Before Bedford's Minutemen set out for Concord's North Bridge, they breakfasted on what history records as a meal "hastily prepared." The captain reportedly rallied his men saying, "It was a cold breakfast, boys, but we'll give the British a hot dinner." With those words the victuals at Fitch's went down in history.

Much of the food served at Fitch's, as at other country taverns, was grown by the innkeeper-farmer. There were lawyer-farmers, physician-farmers, and minister-farmers. Everyone farmed—governors, presidents, and generations of Bedford's Fitches. The Fitch homestead continued to be farmed for another century.

When the barn came down, the cock moved across the road to the top of the tavern's woodshed where, in the 1930s, he caught the eye of the folk-art recorders of the Index of American Design. Like Gabriel (Fig. 39), he had his portrait done by index artist Lucille Chabot. Now he stands with other weathervanes in a folk-art museum—a place far quieter than the bustling tavern-farm with its fighting Minutemen, brawling teamsters, and scrappy live game cocks.

The Index of American Design also recorded the rooster shown in Figure 53, obviously of a different breed from Fitch's game cock.

Game birds, a highly nervous breed, were popular farm poultry because they were hardy, were good layers, and had tasty flesh; but other domestic fowl were fatter and less likely to maim and kill each other. Wanting a breed with all the best qualities, some farmers in the mid-nineteenth century began selectively crossbreeding chickens.

After years of scientific poultry breeding, farmers in the small community around Little Compton, Rhode Island, developed the Rhode Island Red. This breed, outstanding for its eggs and flesh, rapidly became the most popular breed in the nation. For many years, Rhode Island farmers supplied the entire United States with the celebrated Rhode Island Reds. Aptly, this rooster from Rhode Island (Fig. 53) was painted red.

Another red rooster (Fig. 54), whose form makes an effective silhouette against the sky, was simply sawed from board lumber. Many a self-sufficient farmer made his own wooden vane just that way and stood it on a bare spire. Forging cardinal points for the weathervane was a blacksmith's job.

Cardinal points, or "cardinals," were the four points of the compass, indicated by capital letters. They were commonly part of weathervane spires. Cardinal points desig-

53. *Cock. Wood, painted barn-red. L. about 24″. Made by a Mr. Gray about 1885. Privately owned in Little Compton, R.I., when recorded for the Index of American Design.*

nated the directions for most city vanes. On many early handcrafted ones the letters were joined to the spire by iron more elaborately wrought than the vane itself. On other spires the letters were merely held by metal straps. Cardinals were always sold with late-nineteenth-century manufactured vanes.

In the countryside a homemade weathervane mounted on the edge of a barn roof was likely to stand alone. The farmer knew what type of weather to expect from a certain quarter; he did not need to have that quarter labeled. And besides, it was not primarily wind direction that mattered as he made and mounted his vane; it was the dignity and grace with which it would distinguish his building.

Although weathervanes of sheet iron were common, tin (i.e., thin iron sheet coated with tin) was rarely used for weathervanes. Tin was, however, commonly used for household devices, and the weathercock depicted in Figure 55 was more a device than a vane.

The rotating bird turned the chimney cap, allowing the smoke to escape while keeping the wind from blowing down the flue.

The few household devices which the farmer did not make for himself were usually manufactured of tin in Connecticut—home of American tin manufacture—and brought to the farm on that mobile hardware store of the eighteenth and nineteenth centuries, the Yankee tin peddler's wagon, a jingling, clanging, varied collection of tinware. The variety of his wares is suggested in these lines from an old Connecticut verse, "A Yankee Lyric," by Hugh Peters:

> *They scour the country through and through*
> *Vending their wares, tin pots, tin pans,*
> *Tin ovens, dippers, wash-bowls, cans,*
> *Tin whistles, kettles, for to boil or stew,*
> *Tin cullenders, tin nutmeg graters,*
> *Tin warming-platters for your fish and 'taters!*

The tin peddler's assorted stock did not usually include weathervanes. It may have included chimney caps. This chimney cap may not have worked well and so it was

54. *Cock. Wood board, painted red. L. 28″. Maker and date unknown. Owned by the Concord Antiquarian Society, Concord, Mass. An identical vane was owned by Samuel Pennington of Waldoboro, Me., in 1966 and became the symbol of his periodical,* Maine Antique Digest.

55. *Cock on chimney cap. Tin. H.*
25". W. 20". Made probably in
the nineteenth century, for a
faulty flue. Cock may be older
than chimney cap. Maker un-
known. Displayed in Shelburne
Museum, Shelburne, Vt.

fitted by some tinker with a weathercock. The rooftop was surely enhanced. One can hope that the bothersome flue was also improved.

During the late nineteenth century, farmers became more and more dependent on the outside world for manufactured goods. An annual visit from the tin peddler no longer sufficed. Illustrated catalogues showed rural Americans a wider world of manufactured articles. Among the many supplies sold by catalogue were weathervanes.

Page 14 of L. W. Cushing & Sons' twenty-page weathervane catalogue No. 9

(1883), reproduced in Figure 56, listed several rooster vanes. A farmer ordering a copper cock was guided by the size of both his barn cupola and his budget. Whichever model he chose would be "Gilded with twenty-three carat Gold leaf . . . will not corrode or discolor, but remain bright and clean for many years." The farmer would receive it complete with a "Wrought Iron Spire With Steel Spindle; Cardinal Points, Gilt Letters, and Two Copper Balls." The catalogue also advises: "In ordering our Vanes, please describe each Design by the name, length and number in this Catalogue, and give distinct shipping instructions."

Even in the period when mass-produced copper vanes were most available (during the late nineteenth century), wooden weathercocks, many of which were highly individualistic creations, continued to be made. Occasionally a woodcarver won local recognition for his ability to make vanes. One such carver was James Lombard of Bridgton, Maine, a farmer and sometime furniture and weathervane maker. Lombard was born in Baldwin, Maine, in 1865, and probably was an active vane carver by the late 1880s. He had a distinctive style of carving a weathercock's tail feathers. His decorative pine hens and roosters (Fig. 57) must have appealed to his neighbors, for a number of his weathercocks have been found in the vicinity of Bridgton.

By the mid-twentieth century Lombard's cocks also appealed to folk-art collectors. Several of his vanes, including this one, were acquired by Jean Lipman, noted American art critic, and were later made part of the collection of the New York State Historical Association in Cooperstown.

Mrs. Lipman wrote of Lombard's "extremely stylized" rooster silhouettes: "the cut-out areas which indicate the arrangement of tail feathers greatly enhance the interest of the design." She admired Lombard's "flair for functional design" and his "natural vitality of execution" and considered the effect which Lombard achieved "hard to surpass in the most finished pieces of academic sculpture."

The cast-iron cock shown in Figure 58 (the last weathercock in this history) and many other fine weathercocks which perched on spires all over America embody the essence of the barnyard rooster. As Pablo Picasso observed to Xavier Gonzales (*New Masses,* December 19, 1944):

> Roosters, we always have roosters, but like everything else in life we must discover them. Just as Corot discovered the morning and Renoir discovered little girls. . . . Roosters have always been seen but seldom so well as in American weather vanes.

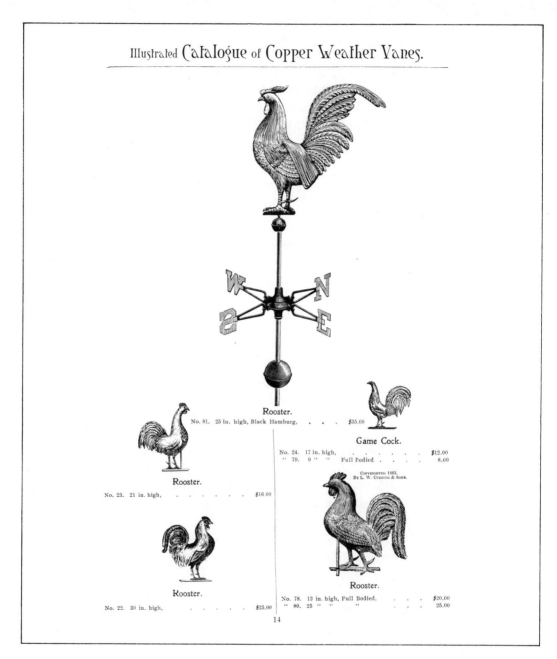

Rooster.
No. 81. 25 in. high, Black Hamburg, . . . $35.00

Game Cock.
No. 24. 17 in. high, ... $12.00
" 79.   9 "   "   Full Bodied 8.00

COPYRIGHTED 1883,
BY L. W. CUSHING & SONS.

Rooster.
No. 23. 21 in. high, ... $16.00

Rooster.
No. 78. 13 in. high, Full Bodied, . . . $20.00
" 80. 25 "   "   "   . . . 25.00

Rooster.
No. 22. 30 in. high, ... $25.00

14

56. *Page 14 of* Weathervane Catalogue No. 9. (*1883*), L. W. Cushing & Sons, Waltham, Mass.

57. Rooster. Pine, originally painted yellow. L. 20½". Made by James Lombard about 1890 for his barn in Bridgton, Me. Museum of the New York State Historical Association, Cooperstown, N.Y.

People seldom think of mass-produced objects as folk art, or of sheet copper and cast iron as artistic media. However, many manufactured weathervanes, most made of sheet copper, a few of cast iron, do qualify as art.

This haughty cast-iron herald of the dawn is a case in point. He stands—forever about to strut away—in a museum garden under the watchful eye of another iron herald, Gabriel (Fig. 38). Both are part of the museum's folk-art collection. The Gabriel, like many pre-1850 vanes, was individually cut and shaped of sheet iron. The mid-nineteenth-century cock was mass produced in cast iron.

The cock's fully rounded body was cast in two parts, right and left sides joined by screws. Each cock's sheet-iron tail, however, was individually cut so that the arrangement and number of feathers vary somewhat from one vane to another. Some are flat, others repoussé.

In 1970 one of the cast-iron cocks (a 31½-inch model removed from the carriage house of Château-sur-Mer, the Newport, Rhode Island, home of William S. Wetmore) appeared in an art gallery exhibition of folk art. In reviewing the show, Hilton

58. *Cock. Cast iron, sheet-iron tail. H. 22⅞". Mass produced during the mid-nineteenth century. Maker unknown. Abby Aldrich Rockefeller Folk Art Collection, Williamsburg, Va.*

Kramer, art critic of *The New York Times,* cited the cock and a copper eagle vane (Fig. 19) as proof that nineteenth-century American folk sculpture should "be taken seriously for its intrinsic esthetic quality. . . ." The art gallery was taking that quality quite seriously. The weathercock was priced at $3,500, the eagle at $4,500.

The exhibition was "rather thin on sculpture," wrote Kramer in *The New York Times,* May 10, 1970,

> but the "Cock" alone would be sufficient to establish the artistic superiority of American folk sculpture over its genteel "fine art" counterpart. There is not a single work

of sculpture in the Met show [a huge Metropolitan Museum retrospective of nineteenth-century American art] that can touch it for quality—not even the "Diana" of Augustus Saint-Gaudens, which comes closest.

The unknown weathervane manufacturer who captured the essence of the barnyard rooster in cast iron probably also made the vane shown in Figure 59, the epitome of horsepower. These two models and a similar but smaller cast-iron horse very likely composed the entire weathervane line of one unknown craftsman, perhaps America's sole nineteenth-century manufacturer of cast-iron vanes. He mass produced his vanes probably in the 1850s, 1860s, and 1870s, when America's iron industry flourished amid a mania for cast iron in almost any form: building façades, door stops, statuary, mirror frames, and furniture for garden and parlor.

The casting process (sculpting in clay, making a mold, and pouring molten metal) enabled the manufacturer to reproduce his designs exactly and repeatedly. The casting technique was often used by manufacturers of copper vanes, but they cast only

59. Horse. Cast iron, sheet-iron tail. L. 36″. Mass produced in the mid-nineteenth century. Maker unknown. M. and M. Karolik Collection, Museum of Fine Arts, Boston, Mass. Identical vanes have been found in Maine and Sturbridge, Mass.

detailed sections (e.g., animal heads) in bronze, lead, zinc, or iron, to be joined to primarily sheet-copper vanes.

Cast-iron vanes found tough competition in the late nineteenth century as the copper-vane industry proliferated and prospered. The sheet-copper vanes were lighter, easier to handle in manufacturing, easier to transport and install. The sheet copper's smooth surface held gold leaf longer—a great advantage because, traditionally, vanes were gilded, and customers wanted them to remain gold as long as possible. Cast iron's greatest advantage —that it was bulletproof—was not as apparent then as now when viewing century-old vanes. (More on this problem later when we discuss the damage done by gunshot.)

Most of these cast-iron vanes have been found in Maine; their creator may have been a down easter. He did not sign his work; artisans seldom did. He likely never thought of himself as an artist.

But he was. The horse he sculpted ideally matched his medium. Cast iron is a particularly appropriate material for the powerful animal portrayed. This horse (Fig. 59) is strong enough for the work of husbandry, powerful enough to be a draft animal, but too stocky to compete successfully in track and road races with lighter, sporting horses. (Compare him with the sporting horses portrayed in the lighter sheet-copper vanes, Figs. 103–111.) This horse of iron epitomizes that era in farming when manpower was merely an aid to horsepower.

The horse had not always been the power on the farm. A farmer of the seventeenth, eighteenth, and early nineteenth centuries might have kept a horse as (in terms of those days) a convenience—for going to church and to mill. But his farm vehicles were too heavy for horses to draw. His draft animals were oxen.

In the mid-nineteenth century, horse breeders began to improve the American draft horse. The era of the farm horse followed. The newly invented farm tools (e.g., the new plow) could be pulled by strong horses. In 1861 a farmer wrote for *Appleton's Cyclopedia:*

> Fifteen years ago the writer required twenty men to cultivate properly a garden of thirty acres; now, by the use of a few judiciously chosen horsetools, he cultivates many times that area, with but eight farm-hands, four of whom are boys.

The wooden mare on the vane illustrated in Figure 60 is a draft horse. She has none of the grace of a race horse. She seems strong enough to pull "horsetools" in spite of

60. *Mare and Foal. Wood, painted. L.
31". Made about 1850. Found in
Wakefield, Rhode Island. Maker
unknown. Museum of the New
York State Historical Association, Cooperstown, N.Y.*

rubbery looking legs. Her foal follows, as offspring do. The family resemblance is un-
mistakable.

The only horse in Plymouth Colony by 1632, twelve years after settlement,
was the mare which Governor Bradford rode. Swine, however, were so numerous by then
that historians assume that, although the original settlement had no horses, cattle, or sheep,
swine may have come over on the *Mayflower*. The scrawny, razor-backed pigs from England
thrived in New England on the corn and fish they were fed and on the acorns and beechnuts
they found in the woods.

Every eighteenth-century farmer raised swine. In winter, spring, and summer,
hogs roamed orchards and fields, kept from the grain by fences and prevented by rings in
their noses from ruining the land with their uprooting snouts. In autumn the farmer penned
four or five pigs, fattened them with grain, and as winter arrived, slaughtered them for the
family's yearly supply of pork.

Hogs were a most important source of food. Little pork was eaten fresh, but
cured pork, from barrels of brine or from sooty smokehouses, sustained New Englanders
from one autumn slaughter to the next.

The pig was one of the first animals in America to be improved by scientific breeding. In the early nineteenth century, new English breeds were imported and the razorbacks disappeared. (No American vane depicting a fat pig was made before 1800.)

By 1850 fresh meat was well distributed, and farmers were no longer dependent on their own pork barrels. Large-scale hog raising went west with the corn fields, so New England did not have pig farms in the nineteenth century when weathervane manufacturers widely distributed their copper vanes. Most Yankee farmers kept only enough hogs to consume the farm refuse.

Throughout the era when pigs and pork were vital to the farmer, pig weathervanes were whittled and carved; however, porker wind pointers were never as common as rooster or horse vanes. And later, although almost every weathervane catalogue listed a pig model, pig vanes were not as popular in New England as vanes of sheep or cattle, animals which were then being raised on many one-crop New England farms.

The nineteenth-century porker illustrated in Figure 61 is clearly not the old-type swine which by 1832 were merely a scornful memory, as the *New England Farmer* noted in that year:

> Formerly New England was over-run with a raw-boned lank-sided race of animals, which devoured the substance of the farmer and like Pharaoh's *lean kine* "were still ill-favored and lean as before."

Improvement of American pigs preceded that of cattle by a quarter of a century. In the mid-nineteenth century, wealthy farmers began to import magnificent cattle which yielded rich milk plentifully. They contrasted strongly with the small cattle which had been raised here since settlement days when a village cowherd tended everyone's cattle on common grazing land.

The cattle breeders were aware that their imported stock would revolutionize dairy farming. They knew that although the same breed of cattle had once met power, dairy, and beef needs, specialized husbandry was at hand. As the village herd had given way to small family-farm herds, so these would now yield to large-scale dairy farming.

A gentleman farmer, proud of his special breed of cattle, often had a portrait painted of his prize Jersey, Holstein, or Hereford. Animal portraiture was the rage among the wealthy in the late 1800s. Animal sculpture, in the form of weathervanes, was less expensive and even more popular.

61.
Pig. Painted iron. L. 32½". Made during nineteenth century. Maker unknown. Eleanor and Mabel Van Alstyne Collection, Smithsonian Institution, Washington, D.C.

Some of the copper vanes offered in manufacturers' catalogues were listed not merely as ox, bull, or cow but by breed. The vane shown in Figure 62 sold as a Jersey.

A contented cow, a fine symbol for the pastoral scene, is the weathervane subject (Fig. 63) most commonly seen in the pastureland of the Connecticut River valley.

The river, named by the Indians *Quonektacut* (Long River), runs through New England from near the Canadian border on the north to Long Island Sound on the south. It divides New Hampshire from Vermont, cuts through western Massachusetts, and bisects the state which was named after it.

The Connecticut's fertile valley became the heartland of the beef and, later, the dairy production which dominated New England's nineteenth-century agriculture. Where Indians once grew corn and hemp, where for a century before independence colonists farmed extensively, cattle still graze in great numbers and cow weathervanes still abound.

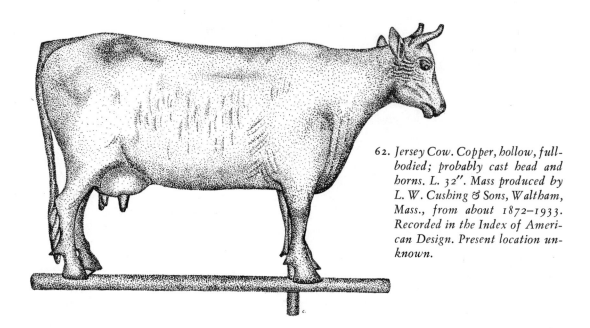

62. *Jersey Cow. Copper, hollow, full-bodied; probably cast head and horns. L. 32″. Mass produced by L. W. Cushing & Sons, Waltham, Mass., from about 1872–1933. Recorded in the Index of American Design. Present location unknown.*

Twentieth-century weathervanes are often mounted on the metal rooftop ventilators used for airing modern barns. In the nineteenth century, however, ventilation was usually achieved through wooden cupolas, whose louvered sides allowed air through and whose pointed roof was traditionally a perch for a vane.

Cupolas are small rooftop structures which since medieval times have been the architectural finials on many types of buildings. They have served several functions. Primarily, perhaps originally, they were belfries. Belfry-cupolas topped church towers and four-square meetinghouse roofs. Occasionally they were lanterns. Often they were belvederes (i.e., structures so situated as to provide excellent vistas). Belvedere-cupolas topped the seacoast mansions of shipping merchants who regularly scanned the horizon for incoming vessels.

A belvedere-cupola on a Middleford, Connecticut, barn was described in a late-nineteenth-century book on barn plans: "A long flight of stairs passes from the principal barn floor to the cupola, from which a magnificent view is obtained. . . ." Usually, however, barn cupolas were ventilators. Large barns needed two or more ventilating cupolas.

Each sat over an opening in the roof and above a hole or chute cut through the barn's upper floor. Hay from the loft could be tossed down through these chutes, but their primary function was to permit odors and heat to rise to the cupolas and exhaust.

Any farm outbuilding might have a cupola—even the icehouse, which needed a free flow of air under the roof. And if it was ventilated through a cupola, the icehouse likely had a vane. For whether cupolas were ventilators, belvederes, belfries, or lanterns (or, as they are today, mere architectural topping), they traditionally were finished with a finial. Occasionally the finial was a ball or acorn, on churches it was often a cross, but usually the cupola's finial was a weathervane. (Most of the weathervaneless old cupolas of today originally had vanes.)

Weathervanes were so much a part of cupola design that even when a nineteenth-century farm wagon house was designed to be "perfectly plain, in order to be the most economical," the building plans included a vane on the cupola. The Gothic-style

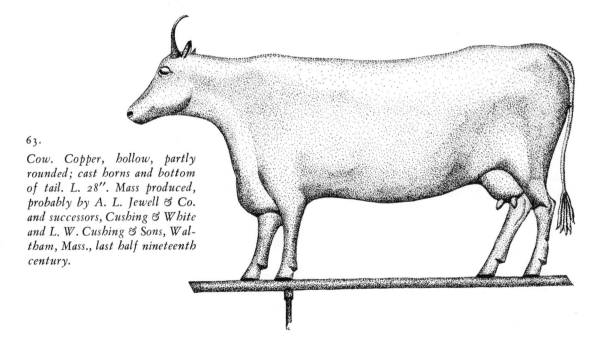

63.

Cow. Copper, hollow, partly rounded; cast horns and bottom of tail. L. 28". Mass produced, probably by A. L. Jewell & Co. and successors, Cushing & White and L. W. Cushing & Sons, Waltham, Mass., last half nineteenth century.

64. *Cow on Arrow. Cast aluminum finished to resemble iron. L. 36″. Mass produced by Whitehall Metal Studios, Montague, Mich., mid-twentieth century. Presently being produced. It can be seen on an ice-cream parlor in Belmont, Mass., as well as on numerous barns.*

flag designated was "plain" and "economical." If the architect ever considered omitting the vane for additional economy, he dismissed the idea. Plain was one thing, unfinished another.

As a result of the long association of vanes and cupolas, of cupolas and barns, modern metal barntop ventilators are often topped with weathervanes. Most are figure-on-arrow vanes, as in Figure 64, mass produced of cast iron or since mid-century of cast aluminum. Each features a small figure standing on an arrow's shaft. Some modern manufacturers center the figure over the spire, therefore requiring an oversized, wind-catching back on the arrow. Others mount the figure behind the spire where it can serve to catch the wind.

Horses, chickens, and cows are common figures on arrows. Whatever the subject, though, the cast form is usually uninteresting and adds little to the vane's pointing quality.

A type of cattle not seen in modern weathervane designs is the ox. The hardy animal itself is seldom seen today, but the ox was the mainstay of pioneer husbandry. These castrated cattle supplied both power and food. (A slaughtered ox yielded 770 pounds of edible meat and 80 pounds of suet for making 300 candles.) New Englanders preferred oxen as draft animals through the nineteenth century, while horses were replacing oxen in other states. In 1860 in New England, oxen were still as numerous as horses, with the Red Devon cattle the preferred breed.

In 1847 a stranger to New England was "attracted by the noble teams of oxen which are so frequently met with in the city of Boston . . . their spirited and lively air, and the brisk and springy walk with which they move along their heavy loads."

The stables and sheds which sheltered these remarkable beasts were ventilated through the slatted sides of a rooftop cupola. On the cupola roof was usually a vane, often, like that illustrated in Figure 65, in the form of an ox. Every nineteenth-century weathervane catalogue listed an ox vane.

Most catalogues also listed bull weathervanes. L. W. Cushing & Sons' catalogue listed bull and ox vanes of the same size, at the same price. J. W. Fiske's weathervane catalogue, however, illustrated only an ox and listed below it:

No. 35, new design, full bodied, Ox . . . 42 inches long
. . . . . $75.00

No. 37, new design, full bodied, Bull . . . 42 inches long
. . . . . $77.00

A breeder of cattle, having paid handsomely for the sire of his herd, would pay the two-dollar price of virility to get a suitable symbol for his barn's cupola. The mid-

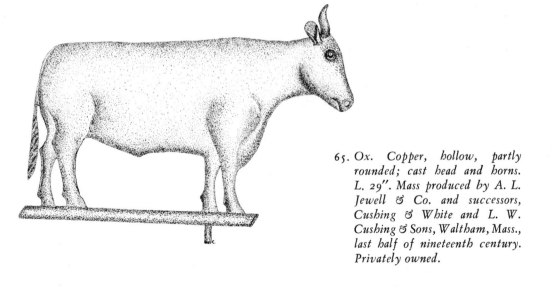

65. Ox. Copper, hollow, partly rounded; cast head and horns. L. 29″. Mass produced by A. L. Jewell & Co. and successors, Cushing & White and L. W. Cushing & Sons, Waltham, Mass., last half of nineteenth century. Privately owned.

66.

Model for Bull Vane. Wood carving, pattern for copper weathervanes. L. 45″. Modeled for unknown weathervane manufacturer in the mid-nineteenth century. Maker unknown. New York State Historical Association, Cooperstown, N.Y.

nineteenth-century bull shown in Figure 66 was carved in wood as a pattern for mass-produced copper vanes.

Not every farmer could afford a gilded copper vane. Even after manufactured vanes became commonplace, many barn vanes, like the one shown in Figure 67, were sawed and whittled at home, for the always busy farmer had an ever-ready knife.

Life on a New England farm was a continual round of chores. The habit of work and the influence of the Puritan ethic made idleness uncomfortable. Even in the house, the husbandman's hands were busy—often making things of wood—shaping bowls, grain shovels, and tool handles; fashioning hay forks and table spoons; whittling down rake and harrow teeth. A farmer was never without his knife. He became accustomed to reaching for it, much as a smoker today reaches for a cigarette, to occupy an empty hand, to fill an empty moment, as an aid in conversation, and as a necessity in haggling. The farmer was a whittler. Frederick Marryat observed in *A Diary in America:*

67. Bull. Wood, painted. L. about 36". Made for a New Hampshire barn. Maker unknown. Privately owned.

Whittling . . . is a habit, arising from the natural restlessness of the American when he is not employed, of cutting a piece of stick or anything else, with his knife. Some are so wedded to it from long custom, that they will whittle the backs of the chairs, or anything within their reach. A Yankee shown into a room to await the arrival of another, has been known to whittle away nearly the whole of the mantel-piece. Lawyers in court whittle away at the table before them; and the judges will cut through their own bench. In some courts they put sticks before noted whittlers to save the furniture. . . . Yankees . . . whittle when they are making a bargain, as it fills up the pauses, gives them time for reflection, and more over prevents any examination of the countenance.

Since most farms had whittlers, many barns had wooden vanes. These were realistically painted; the occasional exception had a coat of gold paint in imitation of gold leaf. Each wooden vane was as individualistic as the whittler himself.

In the struggle for sustenance from a self-sustaining farm, a farmer was thrifty not only with his time but also with materials. No product of husbandry was considered a by-product. Each resource was counted on and thoroughly utilized. The *American Farmer's Encyclopedia* of 1844 advised:

> The hair of the goat may be shorn, as it is of some value, making good linsey; that of the Welsh he-goat is in great request for making white wigs. Ropes are sometimes made from goats' hair. . . . Candles are manufactured from their fat . . . ; their horns afford excellent handles for knives and forks; and the skin, especially that of the kid, is in demand for gloves and other purposes. Goats' milk is sweet, nutritive, and medicinal. Cheese prepared from goats' milk is much esteemed.

Goats supplied milk for the first settlers at Plymouth, but soon cattle became the primary milk suppliers, making goats far less important. Self-sufficient farmers kept a few of these versatile animals, but goat raising, unlike cattle and sheep raising, never developed into a farming specialty in New England. Goat weathervanes (Fig. 68) were as rare as goat farms. Weathervane catalogues did not list any copper billies or nannies for sale.

Even if the subject had been commonplace, the vane in Figure 68 would be uncommon. It is one of the finest pieces of American folk sculpture at the Smithsonian Institution. Its unknown carver knew the various attributes of the goat. His appreciation of these characteristics was captured in the carving, in the distinctive textures of beard, horns, and hairy coat.

The same attention to significant detail was given to the fleece on the ewe and lamb in the vane shown in Figure 69. These creatures, smaller than the wooden goat, also have textured coats. Their carver was fully cognizant of the value of curly fleece.

Settlers brought sheep to the New World to be raised for their wool, and only secondarily for their meat. The transplanted Englishmen were willing to replace mutton with venison, but were unwilling to replace woolen clothes with animal skins. Wool was in great demand in New England. Because of the cold climate, more woolens were consumed there than in all the other American settlements.

Cold winters and hungry wolves brought heavy losses in sheep. Government regulations were enacted to increase the domestic wool supply. Under colonial laws sheep were protected, pampered, and positively unexportable. Finally, they thrived. During the eighteenth century wool became a commercial product, although most sheep were still part of self-sufficient farms, and most wool was still woven into homespun textiles.

68. *Goat. Wood, full-bodied. L. 34".
Made in the nineteenth century.
Found in Falmouth, Mass. Maker
unknown. Eleanor and Mabel
Van Alstyne Collection, Smith-
sonian Institution, Washington,
D.C.*

As early as 1760 attempts were made to improve the colonists' breed of scrawny "rat-tailed" sheep in order to increase the quality of their coarse, short-staple wool. The weathervane sheep in Figure 69 are obviously of the early "rat-tailed" variety. The lamb is surprisingly well preserved; he is probably two centuries old. His mother, however, shows signs of repair. Sometime during these two hundred years of being constantly followed by her lamb, she lost her head.

The large, copper mass-produced sheep in Figure 70 is obviously not of the "rat-tailed" native breed as are the little wooden ewe and lamb. His stately and dignified form was listed in weathervane manufacturers' catalogues by breed as a Merino.

Merinos, excellent wool-bearing Spanish sheep, were first imported into the

United States in the early nineteenth century when Spanish export restrictions crumbled under Napoleon's invasion. The United States ambassadors to France and Spain secured the valuable animals, taking advantage of the deteriorated European political situation to improve the American agricultural situation.

Merino breeding continued to be influenced by politics. American trade embargoes and the War of 1812 cut off woolen imports, forcing an expansion of domestic wool manufacture which required an increase in fine domestic production. A Merino craze resulted. In a few years, Merinos were the principal sheep in the country. All were raised for their wool, their mutton being inferior to that of the common native breed.

America's woolly Merinos were not only beneficial to the woolen industry, but also, by curious coincidence, to the art and science of agriculture. In 1807 Elkanah Watson of Pittsfield, Massachusetts (scholar, friend of the importing ambassadors, and businessman-turned-farmer) obtained the first pair of Merino sheep ever introduced into Berkshire County and possibly the first in Massachusetts. Elkanah Watson wrote (*Agricultural Societies*, 1820):

> As all who examined their wool, were delighted with its texture and fineness, I was induced to notify an exhibition under the great elm tree in the public square, in Pittsfield, of these two sheep, on a certain day. Many farmers, and even women, were ex-

69. *Ewe and Lamb. Wood and tin. L. 14½". Maker unknown. The wind-catching tailpiece and spinning front are later additions, giving the vane something of the character of a whirligig. Concord Antiquarian Society, Concord, Mass.*

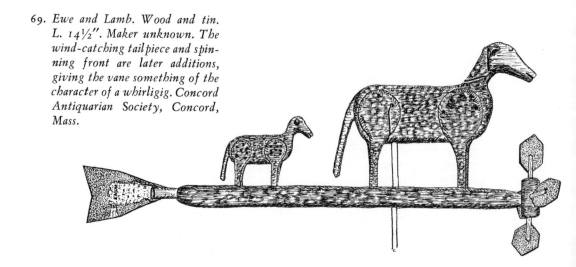

70. *Merino Ram. Copper, gilded. L.*
29". Mass produced during last
half of nineteenth century.
Maker unknown. Eleanor and
Mabel Van Alstyne Collection,
Smithsonian Institution, Wash-
ington, D.C.

cited by curiosity to attend this first novel, and humble exhibition. It was by this lucky accident, I reasoned thus,—If two animals are capable of exciting so much attention, what would be the effect on a larger scale, with larger animals?

Watson's answer to his own question was to establish livestock shows, county fairs, and agricultural societies. He organized the Berkshire Agricultural Society. It served as a model for others. These societies fostered scientific farming and selective breeding. County fairs offered opportunities for livestock comparison and competition.

By the mid-nineteenth century these farming institutions, born in the "novel and humble" exhibition of a pair of Merinos, had helped revolutionize agricultural methods and had so increased productivity that a part of the population was freed from work in the fields for employment in factories.

6.

Industrious Yankees and Their Glorious Machines

. . . the spirit and influence of free labor,
. . . the indomitable industry of a free people,
. . . the zealous determination to improve and profit by labor, have done it all.

DANIEL WEBSTER
"Opening of the Northern Railroad"

A sheep was as apt a vane for some mills as it was for some farms. Woolen mills and sheep farming thrived together. The Merino-importing American ambassador to Spain, David Humphreys, began a new career in 1806. Having been a wartime aide to General Washington, a legislator, a writer, and a diplomat, Humphreys became one of America's first successful wool processors. He built a mill at the waterfall on the Naugatuck River in Connecticut, creating the village of Humphreysville.

Humphreys' mill and village were soon followed by other mills and towns. In 1810 twenty-four woolen mills were operating in and about New England. Five more years brought fifty more mills. Improved machinery further stimulated the industry in the thirties and forties, and when the Civil War brought a demand for woolen uniforms and a dearth of raw cotton, woolen manufacturing flourished.

The textile industry brought the initial and most dramatic changes of the industrial revolution. Cotton mills and woolen mills ended what had been a home industry and gave a phenomenal impetus to the factory system, a system which put all production operations under one management, under one roof, next to one water wheel.

The mill's massive water wheel, its huge spokes and dripping rim slowly turning, rolled the broad cylinders prickled with wires to card fiber; moved the jennies and jacks which spun 140 times as much as spinning wheels; drove power looms whose flying shuttles were watched by a few girls (cheaply hired), replacing the experienced hands of many weavers; powered the machines—fullers, nappers, and shearers—which finished the cloth that clothed America.

While transforming clumps of cotton or greasy wool into finished fabrics, factories transformed the lives of Americans and the landscape of the nation. Woolen mills gave rise to new towns and dominated them. Cotton mills established entire cities overnight and created employment for all their inhabitants. Textile mills made rich men richer and clothed all men inexpensively.

These factories were focal points of a changing economy and society. As vane-topped meetinghouses had been centers of colonial settlements, mills were centers of their communities. Similarly, some factories had bell towers to toll the townsmen to their duties. Virtually every textile mill had its weathervane; a woolen mill, its gilded sheep (Fig. 71).

The sheep vanes of woolen mills are still seen in New England's hill country, in the many mill towns which nestle in the hills and straddle the streams. The region was suited to wool manufacturing; the power for manufacturing was available at the many waterfalls and running streams. The material for wool manufacturing was easily produced nearby, for the rocky soil, never well suited to general farming, was good for sheep raising.

As Merinos provided the raw material and water supplied power, so the trade embargo (1807) made money available. Jefferson's embargo and the War of 1812 sharply curtailed shipping, leaving the wealthy merchant-shippers of New England with idle capital. The men who had owned the ships built the mills. The fortunes amassed on the high seas harnessed the power of the rivers and streams. Yankee business interests were changing.

New England industry has continued to change. Early in the twentieth century the textile industry started shifting to the South and after World War II virtually deserted the Northeast. In Ludlow, Vermont, the old mill building became the home of General Electric's Jet Propulsion Laboratory, but remained the perch for a wind-propelled Merino (Fig. 72).

The textile mill weathervane illustrated in Figure 73 also proved more durable

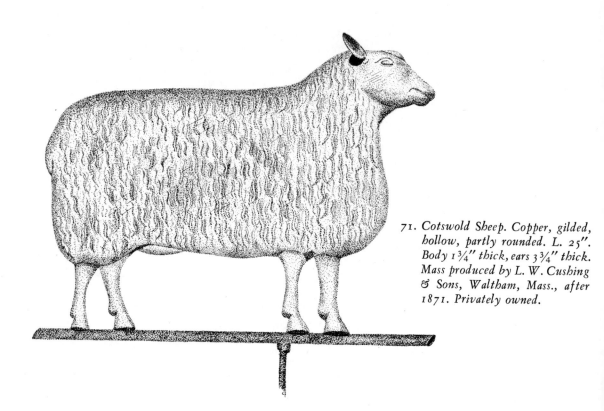

71. Cotswold Sheep. Copper, gilded, hollow, partly rounded. L. 25". Body 1¾" thick, ears 3¾" thick. Mass produced by L. W. Cushing & Sons, Waltham, Mass., after 1871. Privately owned.

than the textile industry. Jeremiah V. Murphy observed in a story in the *Boston Globe* in 1967, datelined Lowell, Massachusetts:

> High over the famous Boott Mills complex in this dreary mill city on the polluted Merrimack River stands a steeple, its white paint faded and peeling.
>
> At the top of the steeple is a unique* weathervane—it has been there since the 1870's—in the shape of a textile shuttle. It is symbolic of the city's long history as a textile center.

* Newsman Murphy's word; I know of no other shuttle vane but would not assume that this was unique.

"A textile museum has its eye on that weathervane," explained John R. Dickson, president of Boott Mills. "They want it for an exhibit."

The museum may not have long to wait, for there remains only one major textile mill in this old industrial city some 25 miles northwest of Boston.

The shuttle is the device on a loom which carries the weft thread back and forth through the warp threads—thus weaving. It was an ideal emblem for the Boott Mill, for the whole city of Lowell, and for the men for whom the mill and city were named.

Spinning in America had been mechanized and moved into mills early in the nineteenth century. The bottleneck in domestic cloth manufacture was weaving. Francis

72. *Merino Sheep. Copper, hollow, partly rounded. L. about 30".
Mass produced, possibly by the Cushing firm, Waltham, Mass., or the Harris firm, Boston, Mass., in late 1800s. Atop old mill building, Ludlow, Vt., which became G.E.'s Jet Propulsion Lab.*

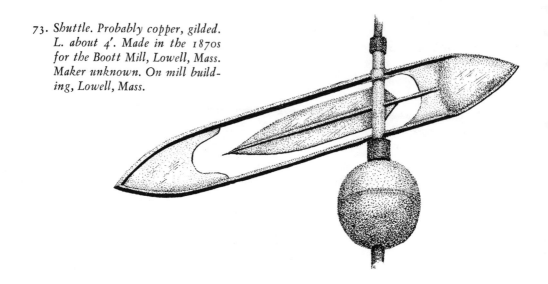

73. *Shuttle. Probably copper, gilded. L. about 4'. Made in the 1870s for the Boott Mill, Lowell, Mass. Maker unknown. On mill building, Lowell, Mass.*

Cabot Lowell, an American merchant, saw power looms in use in England and recreated the devices here. Since Britain forbade the export of machines or machine drawings, Lowell actually reinvented the power loom. He built a cotton mill on the Charles River, Waltham, Massachusetts. There in 1814 water-powered weaving joined water-powered spinning, making that mill America's first complete textile factory.

Lowell's water-powered shuttles flew. His cotton mill soon outgrew the power of the Charles. After Lowell died in 1817, his partners bought land at the Pawtucket Falls on the Merrimack and began manufacturing cotton cloth there in 1823 in a mill managed by Kirk Boott. Three years later, the growing mill community was incorporated as Lowell, Massachusetts.

Other mills followed, including the Boott Mill, incorporated in 1835. Cotton manufacturing boomed; Lowell, Massachusetts, thrived.

But the first city that textiles built became just one more city that textiles deserted. In 1967, of the forty firms in the Boott Mill complex, only one—a dye company—was in the textile trade. Not a single shuttle moved beneath the shuttle vane.

The age of factories began with the textile mills. But the era of artisans continued during the nineteenth century. Industry which relied upon power moved into factories. Hand trades which relied upon skill remained in small shops.

Among specialists, the blacksmith was of outstanding importance. He was often the only supplier to otherwise self-sufficient farmers. In the early settlements, his role was so vital that he worked under government regulation. In 1642 the Plymouth colony ordered smiths to "repair armes speedyly" and take corn as payment. A blacksmith was so important to the village of Derby, Connecticut, in 1711 that it granted

> John Smith of Milford, blacksmith, four acres of land for a home lot . . . anywhere within one mile of the meeting house . . . upon condition that he . . . set up the trade of a blacksmith, and follow it for the benefit of the inhabitants for the space of seven years.

As settlement towns grew larger, itinerant artisans no longer needed to travel for their trade. They settled down in village shops and hung out their shingles, trade signs, or trade vanes. Carpenters, hatters, tailors, and shoemakers also opened shops, but never far from the smithy. All were dependent upon the blacksmith who made and mended the tools of their trades. The *Boston News-Letter* carried this advertisement in July 1732:

> This is to give notice, that there is one William Bryant, Blacksmith, that now keeps a shop adjoining the presbyterian Meeting House in Long Lane, Boston, who makes and mends Glaziers' vises, . . . Cloathers' Shears, . . . Smiths' vises, Ship Carpenters', Blockmakers', Tanners', Glovers' and Coopers' Tools, Braziers' and Tinmen's Shears.

Blacksmith Bryant advertised to attract customers. A trade sign or trade-sign vane may also have brought business to his "shop adjoining the presbyterian Meeting House in Long Lane." Trade signs and trade vanes were everywhere, informing the public of the trade practiced within.

Blacksmiths far outnumbered other metalworkers. Boston in 1789 had two silversmiths, two coppersmiths, three braziers, four pewterers, five founders (makers of cast iron), seven tinsmiths, seven farriers (horseshoers), and twenty-five blacksmiths.

As populations and trade grew, urban blacksmithing split up into many specialties. A thriving city gave work to farriers, ornamental ironworkers, whitesmiths (who polished and finished ironware), coopers'-hoop makers, shipsmiths, boatsmiths, ax and

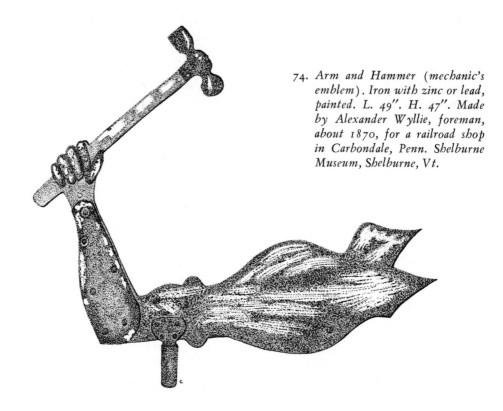

hoe makers, nailmakers, cutlers, pumpmakers, and, in colonial Boston's North End, even a fishhook maker. The arm and hammer vane in Figure 74 was made for a railroad shop. Now in the Shelburne Museum, Shelburne, Vermont, it is seldom recognized as the emblem of mechanics. However, it was universally recognized in nineteenth-century cities, where it designated many types of mechanics' shops.

In a small community, however, there was only one smithy. There farmers congregated, welcoming the change from the work and isolation on their farms. There the blacksmith's powerful arm wielded his hammer for all and varied tasks. He shoed horses and often treated their diseases. He crafted fireplace equipment (e.g., firedogs, cranes, skewers, toasters, spits), axheads, hoes, shovels, scythes, chains, hinges, latches, locks, boot-scrapers, weathervane spires, cardinals, and the vanes themselves. Many a smith must have made his own shop's vane, perhaps on a day when all his orders had been filled.

Little is known about individual smiths, their lives or their products. Few ever signed their work. In 1850 one hundred thousand American blacksmiths were handcrafting iron. With so many men making such commonplace articles, anonymity was the blacksmith's lot. Their story went unrecorded (Longfellow's lines merely sentimentalized the smith) except in the ingenious designs they evolved. Blacksmith-crafted weathervanes are illustrated in Figures 1, 2, 6, 15, 18, 38, 61, 97, 122.

The blacksmith not only shaped the iron but improved its quality with heat and vigorous hammering. His smithy had a forge in which to heat the iron, a water tank in which to cool it, and an anvil on which to hammer and shape it.

Through the ages, the anvil's shape has evolved into a masterpiece—a remarkably versatile yet compact work block. The flat top is a hammering base for the smiting smith. The blunt heel has a hole on top over which the work can be placed so punches can be driven clear through or into which the smith can insert a device for guiding the work or holding it in place. The horn, or pointed-cone end, is so shrewdly shaped that an innumerable variety of curvatures can be formed on it.

The wonderful iron shapes wrought on the anvil, and just the wonder of shaping iron, gave anvil smiters since ancient times an aura of magic. Some of that magic permeated their work. In the clanging at the anvil, good fortune seemed to be captured in the curve of each blacksmith-wrought horseshoe.

Horseshoes became an increasingly important part of the blacksmith's trade during the late nineteenth century. As roads developed, the need for tires on wheels and for shoes on horses increased. Much of the old hardware trade was lost to factory-made products, making farrier's work a most prominent part of general blacksmithing. In some smithies, men no longer fashioned things like weathervanes, not even for themselves.

For such smithies, an anvil vane could be ordered from any weathervane manufacturer. The anvil vane would be made of copper with only rare exceptions, one of which is illustrated here. The white-metal vane illustrated in Figure 75 and a white-metal dog at the Smithsonian (see Fig. 91) were likely made by W. A. Snow of Boston, Massachusetts.

Usually, an anvil would be a special order. However, the catalogue of copper weathervanes issued by J. W. Fiske in 1893 listed, as No. 529, a 20-inch anvil mounted over a 6-foot arrow vane, priced at $120, with the added offer: "Any Size Made To Order."

The paradox—a blacksmith's vane made of a metal other than iron—was probably unnoticed by the men who mass produced copper vanes in iron molds. Mass

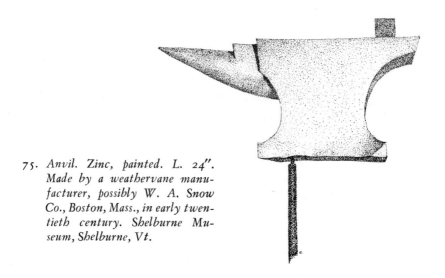

75. *Anvil. Zinc, painted. L. 24".*
Made by a weathervane manu-
facturer, possibly W. A. Snow
Co., Boston, Mass., in early twen-
tieth century. Shelburne Mu-
seum, Shelburne, Vt.

producers of copper vanes were usually mass producing ironware as well. J. W. Fiske, the manufacturer of copper vanes, was also a "Manufacturer of Ornamental Iron and Zinc Work." His metalworking trade was typical for his time.

Joseph Winn Fiske began his career as a cast-iron dealer. In 1853, when he was twenty-one, he left his home town, Chelmsford, Massachusetts, an ironworking center, and sought his fortune making and selling hardware in Australia. He returned home in 1858 and began manufacturing tools and decorative cast-iron ware in Massachusetts. Continuing to manufacture in Massachusetts, he moved his retail outlet to New York City in 1864. The then new practice of utilizing iron molds in the production of copper vanes brought Fiske, and other ironware dealers, into the copper weathervane business. By 1868 Fiske was prospering in New York, selling both copper vanes and the factory-made ironware which was radically changing the trade of the blacksmith.

The quill pen (Fig. 76) is an ideal vane for a school. The three Rs of early colonial education were Reading, 'Riting, and Religion. 'Rithmetic was introduced later at the insistence of a practical public which wanted its children to be able to "cipher." Religious study was, originally, of prime importance. New England took the lead in public

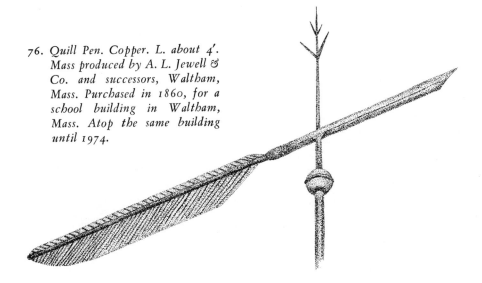

76. *Quill Pen. Copper. L. about 4'.*
Mass produced by A. L. Jewell &
Co. and successors, Waltham,
Mass. Purchased in 1860, for a
school building in Waltham,
Mass. Atop the same building
until 1974.

education because the Puritan theocracy needed to educate a ministry and to assure a public capable of reading Scripture. (Rhode Island, where church and state were separate, took little interest in public education until the nineteenth century.)

'Riting lessons included not only the use of the quill pen but the cutting of the goose quill. Every schoolboy learned to use the *pen*knife. Pupils supplied their own quills, usually from geese slaughtered at home. About two hours of each school day were spent cutting nibs and carefully penning the alphabet. 'Riting was a requisite—a distinct subject often taught by writing specialists, sometimes in separate schools.

But Reading and Religion were as completely combined as the flax fiber and wool yarn in the pupil's linsey-woolsey breeches.

> A   In *Adam's* Fall
>   We Sinned all,

began the *New England Primer*, for generations *the* book of primary education for Americans everywhere. During the two hundred years of its publication, its editions varied in religious tone. Other precepts varied too:

K   *King* Charles the Good
       No man of blood,

became "*King* William . . . ," then, for more permanent usefulness, "Our *King* . . . ," but, with strained relations between colonies and monarch, "*Kings* should be good not men of blood," and after the revolution, "The British *King* lost States thirteen" or "Queens and *Kings* are gaudy things."

    The new nation needed to educate its citizens to be their own rulers. Because the constitutional democracy had different educational needs from a theocratic colony, Americans adopted a new concept of education—universal, nonsectarian, and free. The public followed, if somewhat reluctantly, reformers like Horace Mann, who championed centralized control of local schools and initiated special training for teachers. Mann established America's first normal school in 1839 at a time when people assumed that anyone knowing a subject could teach it.

    Because of such "statesmen of the schools," the little red schoolhouse changed. The dilapidated shack of the early 1800s, sparsely if at all supplied by its local school district (even with wood for heat), became, in the mid-nineteenth century, the concern of all society—a structure worthy of wearing a weathervane.

    The quill vane illustrated in Figure 76 was for over a century atop the school building it was placed upon in 1860. Quill vanes must have adorned many schools then. The quill had been the principal writing instrument for centuries, and although the steel pen replaced it in the mid-nineteenth century, the quill remained the symbol of writing.

    The widely recognized symbol had a perfect pointing shape, was easily wrought of copper, and was consequently featured by all weathervane manufacturers. The pattern, listed in their catalogues simply as "pens," was appropriate not only for schools but for businesses employing many clerks or bookkeepers. Could an insurance company find a better emblem for under*writers?*

    There can be no doubt about what business the emblem illustrated in Figure 77 identified. The nautical folk in New Bedford, Massachusetts, and its sister city, Fairhaven, were too busy with the business of whaling to raise all the swine and cattle they needed for food. City dwellers throughout New England consumed more livestock than they could raise in their crowded city streets. So pork and beef, primarily from the Connecticut River valley, were brought into the cities on the hoof.

    During summer and fall (winter snows and spring mud made roads impass-

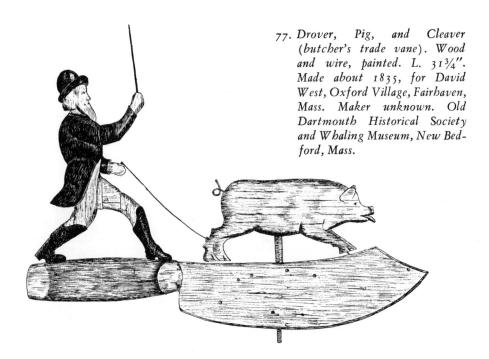

77. *Drover, Pig, and Cleaver (butcher's trade vane). Wood and wire, painted. L. 31¾″. Made about 1835, for David West, Oxford Village, Fairhaven, Mass. Maker unknown. Old Dartmouth Historical Society and Whaling Museum, New Bedford, Mass.*

able), drovers marched herds of cattle, swine, and sheep to eastern markets. At the outskirts of each city, the animals were sold—some to butchers for slaughtering, some to consumers who first fattened the animals slimmed by their long march to market.

In Fairhaven a man with a fattened hog or an order for meat could find David West's slaughterhouse beneath the vane of the porker, drover, and cleaver. An illiterate could identify West's business by its weathervane (Fig. 77).

West's slaughterhouse vane is everything a good trade vane should be. It is attractive and clearly descriptive of the trade (even though an attractive, graphic description of the slaughtering business seems a contradiction of terms). It is effective as a wind pointer—the striding pig, walking drover, and pointed knife direct the eye windward. And finally but foremost, it has that element of dignity, in the bearing of the drover, which weathervanes inherit from the days of knights and fanes.

The attractive vane shown in Figure 78 depicts a once familiar, although now forgotten symbol of fire fighting. The fireman's speaking trumpet vane from Fire Station

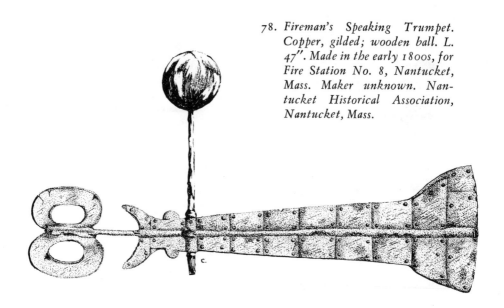

78. *Fireman's Speaking Trumpet. Copper, gilded; wooden ball. L. 47". Made in the early 1800s, for Fire Station No. 8, Nantucket, Mass. Maker unknown. Nantucket Historical Association, Nantucket, Mass.*

No. 8 on the island of Nantucket, Massachusetts, is effective as a proud emblem. Unfortunately, as a wind pointer, its shape is rather unsuccessful.

Much early American fire fighting was unsuccessful too. Colonial townsfolk struggled to fight fires on thatch-roofed wooden houses with buckets of water and 12-foot, swab-tipped poles. In 1678, after a damaging conflagration, Boston bought its first fire engine—a tub with a man-powered pump and a nozzle, which was man-pulled to the fire. The bucket brigade poured water into the tub while other men pumped the handles, supplying the pressure which shot a stream of water into the flames.

By 1707 other bad fires led Boston to outlaw thatched roofs and to buy two more engines. When one hundred buildings burned in 1711, the city added three more engines. That made six engines, six engine companies, six rival teams, each racing to the fire to win the five-pound prize awarded to the first company to get water onto the flames. By 1762 (after the fire in which Faneuil Hall burned and the grasshopper [Fig. 7] almost met with "Utter Ruin") Boston had ten fire-fighting companies.

In New England communities with more than one fire engine, rival engine companies fought each other almost as fiercely as they fought fires. Companies vied for prize money, but even more for honor. They dragged their tubs to the fire as fast as their manpower would permit and hosed down the flames as fast as their men could pump.

In the nineteenth century, hydrants and suction hoses made bucket brigades no longer necessary, but still each engine company needed from sixty to eighty men. A hand tub required fifteen men on a side, thirty men at a time, at the handles. Twenty minutes' pumping exhausted the thirty men, so each company had two alternating teams to man the handles.

The engine companies within each community were numbered. Fire fighters proclaimed these numbers with pride and christened their engines with appropriate appellations as well. A big fire might be quenched by Reliance 1, Protection 2, Alert 3, 4-Leaf Clover, Water Boy 5, Torrent 6, and Cataract 7.

An engine company also had its foreman. He stood beside or on top of the apparatus calling out through his speaking trumpet the rhythm for the pumping team. Sometimes a foreman beat out the rhythm, banging his brass speaking trumpet noisily on the engine. Sometimes a foreman waved the speaking trumpet in the air, marking the time like a conductor with a baton. Speaking trumpets were essential implements for the shouting, banging foremen; some were marked with the engine company's number.

In 1855 a hand tub, aptly named Mankiller, waged a fire-fighting contest with a newly developed device—a steam fire engine. The men on Mankiller outpumped the steamer. But when the contest ended, sixty men lay on the grass exhausted while the steamer puffed and pumped along. That year Boston acquired its first steamer. The hand tub's days were numbered.

After steam fire engines appeared, cities bought them as fast as they could afford them. Initially, they were dragged to the fire by teams of men as hand tubs had been. But men could not hustle with the heavy steam engines. Oxen were tried, a few self-propelled steamers were used, but these proved too slow. The strong and swift draft horses then becoming popular were pressed into the fire service. By the 1860s fire fighting in large cities was a steamer-and-horse business.

Three horses, driven abreast, sped steamers of six thousand and more pounds along city streets. For snow-clogged streets, two additional horses were hitched in front. In small cities and towns, two-horse steamers were common. As one Bostonian phrased it, "Two-horse steamers were for one-horse towns."

No one-horse town could afford a two-horse steamer vane like the 8-footer seen in Figure 79. It cost about four hundred dollars when that sum was the price of a working man's home or a prosperous man's two-horse, three-vehicle carriage house. Many cities, including Manchester, New Hampshire, where the illustrated vane was installed, and Concord and Nashua, New Hampshire, where smaller, similar vanes were used, sent

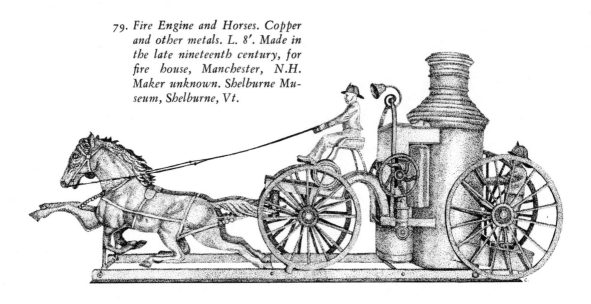

three-horse steamers to their fires but put two-horse steamer vanes on their engine-house cupolas. A third copper horse would have added little to the vane but additional cost.

Each fire house had a cupola, because fire horses were stabled in the engine house. When the alarm sounded the horses quickly took their places in front of the engine, beneath a complete harness, which dropped from the ceiling. With a snap of the horses' collars, they were ready to go. Thirty seconds after the alarm was received, the apparatus rolled.

As the steamer's horses charged out of the fire house, a driver held the reins and a stoker tended the boiler, making sure they reached the fire with a full head of steam. As this weathervane accurately shows, only these two men, of the steamer's three- to six-man crew, rode the engine to the fire. The others rode the hose wagon. At the fire, the horses were unhitched and led away from the excitement and danger.

The well-trained, well-cared-for fire horses had quickly become vital to first-class fire fighting.

When the fire horses were disabled, disaster struck. On November 9 and 10, 1872, Boston was devasted by her greatest fire: 65 acres, the mercantile heart of the city, burned; 776 buildings were gutted; $75,000,000 went up in smoke.

Two weeks before Boston was hit by the conflagration, her horses were stricken. Fire horses, streetcar horses, freight horses—almost all the horses in the horse-drawn city were laid low by an epizootic influenza-type disease. On October 26, because the fire horses were prostrate in their stalls, Boston's fire engineers decided to curtail service for the duration of the epidemic. They drastically cut the number of steamers responding to first and second alarms.

So when the alarms sounded that Saturday evening, November 9, fewer engines than usual responded at first. Eventually all of Boston's twenty-one steamers arrived— sixteen further slowed by having to be dragged by men and boys. Some engines were merely a few minutes late but the farthest Boston engine was forty minutes late. By then an uncontrollable conflagration was consuming downtown Boston.

Thirteen miles to the north in Wakefield, the men of a hand-tub company saw a red glow in the southern night sky. Thinking the fire was in the next town, they took up the drag ropes of their hand tub and ran three and a half miles to neighboring Melrose. Finding no fire there, they continued, more slowly no doubt, through the next town and the next. Two exhausting hours after starting out, they reached the fire's edge. There, on Boston's Broad Street, the tired Wakefield team, aided by men in the street, pumped a steady stream and helped hold the line on the north side of the fire.

Twenty-five out-of-town engines came to Boston's aid. Some were dragged by men summoned by the reddened sky. Some out-of-town and out-of-state steamers arrived by railroad in response to telegraphed alarms. Portsmouth, New Hampshire, sent its new, powerful steamer, Kearsarge No. 3, manufactured by the Amoskeag Company of Manchester, New Hampshire. Kearsarge arrived in Boston without horses and was dragged by men from the railroad station to Washington and Milk streets just an hour before daylight and not a second too soon.

There stood the Old South, a colonial brick meetinghouse with a towering wooden steeple. Across the intersection, the fire was furiously consuming the *Transcript* building. Flying brands had leaped to the meetinghouse belfry and started it smoking. Several fire engines were watering the Old South's roof but none was strong enough to reach the lofty steeple, already glowing against the predawn sky. Kearsarge No. 3 arrived with her steam up and soon sent water steaming into the belfry. The mighty Amoskeag from Portsmouth saved the church and stopped the fire at Washington and Milk.

The engine weathervane in Figure 80 is an amazingly accurate replica of a type which the Amoskeag Company began making in 1870. A powerful Amoskeag, like Kearsarge No. 3, was understandably the pride of any town which owned her. Perhaps her fire house deserved no less than a miniature Amoskeag as a vane. Still, it seems remark-

80. *Amoskeag Steamer and Horses. Copper, gilded. L. 4'. Mass produced by Cushing & White, later L. W. Cushing & Sons, Waltham, Mass. Designed about 1871, sold for $200. Purchased for fire house in Concord, N.H.*

able that weathervane manufacturers (such as L. W. Cushing & Sons, who made this diminutive Amoskeag) went to such great lengths for accuracy and detail, when weathervanes were perched at such lofty heights that accuracy and detail were lost to all but the birds. Who could tell from the street below that this vane was piece for piece, part for part, lantern for lantern, a faithful copy of a real Amoskeag?

Disease fighters, like fire fighters, relied upon horses. Doctors worked from homes or offices, but spent most of their time "going the rounds." Rural medicine in the eighteenth and nineteenth centuries was an in-the-saddle trade.

New England medicine had made progress since Puritan times, when disease was considered God's punishment for sin, to be treated more by a minister and prayer than by a physician and medicine. Prominent among Puritan preacher-physicians, men wont to "bleed and pray," was the Reverend Thomas Thacher of Weymouth and Boston, who wrote the first medical paper in America (1677), and whose grandson, the Reverend Peter Thacher, caused the copper cockerel to crow thrice (page 15). In that era, medical prescriptions might include "thre or 4 graines of unicornes horn" or "lyons hair, what he would let his keeper get off at this time, . . . to be aplyed under the armes."

By the nineteenth century unicorn's horn and lion's hair were passé, but bleeding was still accepted procedure. Doctors learned their trade from older practitioners, mastering the techniques of bleeding, cupping, dressing a wound, and cleansing the system.

The country doctor was physician, surgeon, pharmacist, and dentist, all in one. Singlehandedly, he fought epidemics of yellow fever and cholera. He was unbearably overworked and unbelievably underskilled. He made his rounds with cupping glass and homemade herb concoctions, with wisdom about human nature but ignorance of the medical science of that time, with devotion, mercy, and considerable courage. A surgical operation performed with his saddlebag's instrument kit, with his ignorance of anatomy, and without anesthesia, demanded courage on both sides of the knife.

The medicines in his saddlebags appealed little to his patients and even less to the scholar-physician Oliver Wendell Holmes. In 1861 Holmes suggested that if the medicines then used in America were "sunk to the bottom of the sea, it would be all the better for mankind,—and all the worse for the fishes."

Nevertheless, cures were wrought. Faith in the doctor cured some. The body's ability to fight disease cured others. Some patients survived because no doctor reached them in time to bleed them into weakness or to minister away nature's recuperative powers.

Doctors, trying to tend their many patients, spent long hours in the saddle, in sun and storms, by day and night. "I am going the round from sunrise to 9 or 10 o'clock at night," wrote a physician in 1849. By 9 or 10 at night, a country doctor and his horse may well have resembled the silhouette of the tired man and beast on the vane shown in Figure 81. The vane's origins are unknown, but by museum label and by reputation, this is the Country Doctor.

Some people traveled seated on a horse like the country doctor. More people traveled in horse-pulled vehicles. In the early nineteenth century, overland transportation usually meant horses. Horses dragged coaches through the dusty countryside, drew barges along canals, and, because early railroads were designed for horse-drawn cars, sped cars over iron tracks.

When the iron horse appeared, some New Englanders feared for their future. By 1830 stagecoach companies and wagon owners, horse breeders and roadside innkeepers

feared the loss of business that the steam locomotive would cause. They fought against railroads with dire warnings. Hens would be too frightened to lay eggs, and horses would be terrorized. Even a weathervane supposedly commemorates the horses' terror. An old gentleman from Hingham, Massachusetts, owned a horse-and-gate vane like the one in Figure 82 early in the twentieth century. It did not depict a steeplechase horse jumping a hurdle, he insisted, but a horse jumping the fence in fear of a passing locomotive.

Early in the nineteenth century, an Ipswich, Massachusetts, legislator in House debate seriously questioned how eggs, butter, and turkeys would look after coming over a railroad at thirty miles an hour. The people living near the ocean, the waterway to the world, saw little need for railroads. "A railroad from Boston to Albany . . . would be as useless as a railroad from Boston to the moon," admonished a Boston newspaper in 1827.

Inlanders scoffed at those who thought the locomotive would "set the whole world a-gadding" or "encourage flightiness of intellect." People living in the Berkshires and farther west saw virtues in a rapid railroad. The debate continued on Sundays with ministers actually preaching on the moral effects of railroads.

Nevertheless, the steam-powered railroad arrived. The 9-foot-long weather-vane of a locomotive and tender seen in Figure 83 captures some of the engine's impressive

82. *Horse and Gate. Copper. L. 40".*
H. 32½". 2" thick. Mass pro-
duced by A. L. Jewell & Co.,
Waltham, Mass., in the 1860s,
for sale at $20. One is in the Col-
lections of Greenfield Village and
the Henry Ford Museum, Dear-
born, Mich.

power and reveals some of the railroad's impact on America. Henry Thoreau wrote at Walden:

> When I meet the engine with its train of cars moving off with planetary motion,—or, rather, like a comet, for the beholder knows not if with that velocity and with that direction it will ever revisit this system, since its orbit does not look like a returning curve,—with its steam cloud like a banner streaming behind in golden and silver wreaths, . . .—as if this travelling demigod, this cloud-compeller, would ere long take the sunset sky for the livery of its train; when I hear the iron horse make the hills echo with his snort like thunder, shaking the earth with his feet, and breathing fire and smoke from his nostrils (what kind of winged horse or fiery dragon they will put into the new Mythology I don't know), it seems as if the earth had got a race now worthy to inhabit it.

The earth's new worthy "race" changed geography, shifted population, revamped economics, accelerated technology, and sent America steaming out of the nineteenth century at a far swifter speed than the horse-powered pace with which she had entered it.

Commuting, a phenomenon of mid-twentieth-century America, was born in mid-nineteenth-century Massachusetts when railroads first made possible an evening exodus from Boston. Upper-class Bostonians fled the city via seven railroad lines, which, because

83. *Locomotive and Tender. Copper, some brass and iron. L. 9'. Made by unknown weathervane company, during the late 1800s, possibly a special order. Models usually up to 6' or 7' long. Recorded in the Index of American Design. Collections of Greenfield Village and the Henry Ford Museum, Dearborn, Mich.*

84. *Locomotive and Tender. Tin, painted. L. 5′3″. Made by Otis B. Jepson, April 1886, for railroad station in West Medford, Mass. Collections of Greenfield Village and the Henry Ford Museum, Dearborn, Mich.*

they were not originally designed for metropolitan area service, bore such names as Boston and Lowell, Boston and Worcester, Boston and Providence, and Boston and Maine.

The Boston and Lowell, which had run through Medford, Massachusetts, since 1834, built an elegant passenger station in 1886 for the exurbanites of West Medford. One decorative feature of the elaborately appointed facility was a steam locomotive weathervane (Fig. 84) atop the cupola. The makers of the miniature engine proudly identified themselves in a note sealed within it:

> This vane was made by Otis B. Jepson,
> April 28, 1886. Assisted by E. J. Flynn.
> Painted by James C. Kelley, Boston, Mass.

Jepson's replica of an early type of coal-burning locomotive and tender became a landmark of West Medford. For seventy-one winters it carried a load of snow; in spring it held a nest for birds. Extremes of weather and years of neglect took their toll. In 1956 pleas went out to the Boston and Maine, by then the owners of the line, to rehabilitate the vane.

The railroad responded. It took the vane down and denounced it as a menace to safety. Local residents asked that it be repaired and restored to its old stand, but a railroad spokesman pronounced it "beyond salvage."

The dilapidated vane was not as far "beyond salvage" as was the railroad's commuter service. A year later, a Boston and Maine publication carried a picture of the rebuilt vane, flanked by the mechanics who had repaired it. The tiny locomotive sported a new coat of black paint, the name *Medford* on its cab, the number 23 on head and rear, and the initials B L & N RR (Boston, Lowell and Nashua Railroad) on the sides of the tender.

West Medford expected the renovated vane to be returned; instead it disappeared. The railroad denied knowledge of its whereabouts. Rumor placed it on a building on the estate of Patrick B. McGinnis, president of the railroad, but a newsman sent to the estate failed in his mission to locate the lost landmark. In 1959, while West Medford residents tried to track their train, the Boston and Maine sold the passenger station.

Eventually, the weathervane posed for another picture, this time for an auction catalogue. Parke-Bernet Galleries sold the Boston and Maine vane on March 26, 1964, for a party named McGinnis. It brought $625.

The vane, an antique, had become valuable. The antique railroad station, however, was useless; it was demolished that same year. Suburban commuters had transferred from railways to highways.

The tiny locomotive transferred too, from a railroading position to a new career in the heart of automobile-building country, suburban Detroit. In 1967, when Boston and Maine president Patrick McGinnis was incarcerated in a federal penitentiary for a kickback deal in the sale of full-sized locomotives, the little steam locomotive vane was on display, among other relics of America's past, in a museum founded and funded by Henry Ford.

Before Americans approved of steam-powered railways, they had accepted the idea of steam power on the waterways. In 1807 Robert Fulton's *Clermont* began steamboat service on the Hudson River, and slowly the service was expanded. Public acceptance of steamboats did not come without problems, but then neither did steamboats.

Boston's first steamboat, built for the Salem-Boston run (1817), failed mechanically on its first trip, met with financial disaster, and then while being taken to Charleston, South Carolina, was lost at sea. Rhode Island's first steamboat, Fulton's *Firefly,* could not successfully challenge the sailing packets for the Newport-Providence trade. Agents for the sailing vessels stood on the steamboat's wharf shouting that the packets would arrive before the *Firefly,* or the twenty-five-cent fare would be refunded. The *Fulton,* on the New York-Connecticut run, carried a mast and sails but nevertheless failed to attract passengers.

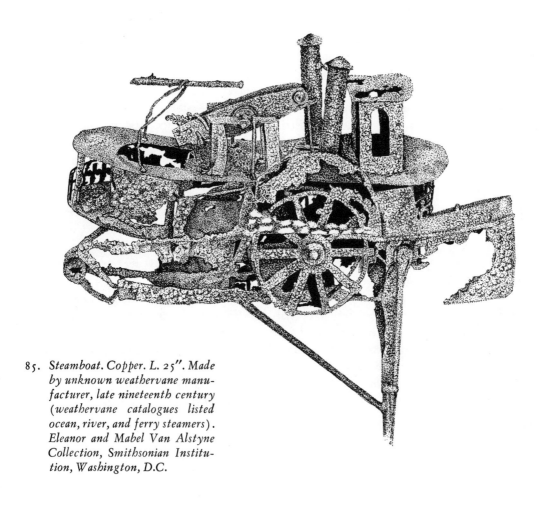

85. *Steamboat. Copper. L. 25". Made by unknown weathervane manufacturer, late nineteenth century (weathervane catalogues listed ocean, river, and ferry steamers). Eleanor and Mabel Van Alstyne Collection, Smithsonian Institution, Washington, D.C.*

There were, however, successes. Maine's first steamboat inspired the rhyme:

A fig for all your clumsy craft,
Your pleasure boats and packets;
The steamboat lands you safe and soon
At Manfield's, Trott's or Brackets'.

On the Connecticut River, the new steamboat *Oliver Ellsworth* attracted much favorable attention until in 1818 it exploded and burned.

After every steamboat disaster "catastrophe broadsides" were published to protest and warn against the dangers of steamboat travel. Throughout the first half of the nineteenth century (until the 1860s, an era of railroad disasters) people sought to make the wooden steamboats safer, but with little success. Steamboats blew up, burned, and were otherwise destroyed at a rate of over one hundred a year, and were just as rapidly replaced. Many travelers avoided them. Railroads were somewhat faster and far safer. Steamboats, however, were cheaper.

In 1834 a new service was inaugurated combining a Boston-Providence railroad and a Providence-New York steamboat. A splendid new boat, the *Lexington*, especially built for the run, steamed out of Providence for New York, where it arrived in twelve hours. Boston, suddenly, was a mere fifteen hours from New York; the fastest stagecoaches took forty-one sleepless hours. Five years after the start of the new service, on a wintry evening in 1840, the *Lexington* burned in Long Island Sound with the loss of 123 lives.

Time and time again, the fire and steam which powered the boats became the force that destroyed them. The fiery fate shared by so many of the new craft was shared by the steamboat weathervane illustrated in Figure 85. The vane would not have been part of an actual boat and probably burned in a dock or boathouse fire. Many weathervanes have been destroyed by fires, but this is the only badly burned vane preserved in the Smithsonian Institution, or in any other museum as far as I have been able to determine. The charred remnant is an excellent reminder of the perils of steamboat travel.

7.
The Weathervane Industry

In 1860 Alvin L. Jewell journeyed sixty miles from his shop in Waltham, Massachusetts (just outside Boston), to a fair in Springfield, Massachusetts, and in two days sold twenty-three gilded weathervanes. His display of wares was acclaimed the finest of the show. No wonder. Jewell was an exceptional craftsman in a fledgling industry.

Alvin Jewell pioneered in the manufacture of weathervanes. He used the latest business practices, working up an entire line of weathervane designs and publishing a catalogue of patterns and prices (Fig. 86). He used new production methods—making his copper vanes in iron molds, a method that yielded identical recreations time after time. Jewell's marketing and manufacturing methods (subsequently used by all copper weathervane manufacturers) enabled him to become probably the first craftsman to devote most of his business activities to vanes.

Jewell began in business in 1852, making "iron hat trees, umbrella stands, dentist's spittoons, . . . also lightening rods and vanes." His manufactory was in the same

building as the local lockup, in the center of a bustling manufacturing town. Jewell's weathervane trade thrived and became more and more important in his business. By 1865 the business outgrew·its quarters, and Jewell moved to a larger shop alongside the railroad.

Jewell's simple stylized figures made especially effective vanes. Each was cleverly modeled to appear full-bodied from afar, to look alive when viewed from almost any angle, and to point direction unambiguously. (See eagle, Fig. 20; pen, Fig. 76; horse-and-gate, Fig. 82; Ethan Allen, Fig. 104; and centaur, Fig. 119: Nos. 38, 45, 8, 2, and 28, respectively, as listed in Jewell's illustrated price list for 1867, pictured in Fig. 86 in its entirety.)

On June 26, 1867, while Jewell was erecting a sign on a building, the staging collapsed, and Jewell and an assistant were killed. Jewell's premature death, however, did not end the production of his weathervane patterns.

The auction of A. L. Jewell & Co.'s stock, patterns, and goodwill that September attracted Josephus Harris of Brattleboro, Vermont. Harris was high bidder at $7,975, but he failed to post the required security, so the next highest bidder, Leonard W. Cushing, a local man, and his partner, Stillman White, acquired Jewell's business. The Brattleboro bidder, however, was not finished with vanes. J. Harris and his son, Ansel J., established a weathervane and ornamental ironwork business in Boston in 1868. Their "Boston Weather Vanes" became the principal New England competition for what a business card of the Cushing & White partnership described as

The Celebrated Waltham Copper Weather Vanes,
Manufactured and Sold, Wholesale and Retail,
by CUSHING & WHITE (Successors to A. L. Jewell & Co.)

HORSES.

No. 1, 29 inches long, Ethan Allen,				$18 00
" 2, 42 " " " "				35 00
" 3, 35 " " Patchen,		-	-	25 00
" 4, 29 " " Flora Temple,		-	-	18 00
" 5, 35 " " Ethan and Sulkey,				35 00
" 6, 47 " " " "				50 00
" 7, 30 " " Horse and Hoop,			-	18 00
" 8, 30 " " " " Gate,				20 00
" 9, 30 " " " " Ball,				16 00
" 10, 30 " " " Plain,			-	15 00
" 12, 17 " " Arabian,				14 00
" 13, 27 " " Farm,		-	-	25 00
" 14, 35 " " "				35 00
" 28, 36 " " Centaur,		-	-	25 00
" 34, 30 " " Military,		-	-	35 00
" 35, 30 " " Civilian,		-	-	32 00
" 36, 30 " " Plain Horse,		-		22 00
" 70, 30 " " Dexter,		-	-	18 00

CATTLE, &c.

No. 15, 41 inches long, Ox,			-	$65 00
" 16, 30 " " "		-	-	35 00
" 17, 25 " " "		-		20 00
" 18, 41 " " Bull,		-	-	65 00
" 19, 30 " " "		-	-	35 00
" 20, 41 " " Cow,		-	-	65 00
" 21, 29 " " "		-	-	22 00
" 25, 28 " " Sheep,		-	-	22 00
" 27, 28 " " "		-	-	22 00
" 26, 29 " " Ram,		-	-	25 00
" 43, 33 " " 6 inch letters,				40 00
" " " " 7 1-2 "				45 00
" 68, 36 " " Pig, 6 inch letters,				35 00
" " " " 7 1-2 "				40 00
" 69, 25 " " Deer,		-	-	25 00

BIRDS.

No. 22, 30 inches high, Rooster,		-	-	$25 00
" 23, 21 " " "			-	16 00
" 24, 17 " " "				12 00
" 37, 33 " long, Peacock,		-		25 00
" 38, 51 " " Eagle,		-	-	100 00
" 39, 40 " " "		-	-	60 00
" 40, 29 " " "		-		35 00
" 41, 24 " " "		-	-	25 00
" 42, 17 " " "		-	-	20 00

VESSELS.

No. 29, 36 inches long, Ship,		-	-	$50 00
" 30, 30 " " "		-	-	40 00
" 31, 30 " " Brig,		-	-	40 00
" 32, 30 " " Schooner,		-	-	30 00
" 33, 45 " " Steamer,		-	-	65 00

MISCELLANEOUS.

No 11, 19 inches long, Flag,		-	-	$18 00
" 44, 17 " " Cannon,		-	-	18 00
" 45, 48 " " Pen,		-	-	22 00
" 46, 36 " " "		-	-	16 00
" 47, 48 " " Scroll,		-	-	25 00
" 48, 36 " " "		-	-	15 00
" 49, 26 " " "		-	-	12 00
" 57, 36 " " "		-	-	16 00
" 58, 28 " " "		-	-	12 00
" 59, 16 " " "		-	-	6 00
" 60, 34 " " "		-	-	14 00
" 61, 26 " " "		-	-	11 00
" 66, 40 " " "		-	-	18 00
" 67, 32 " " "		-	-	14 00
" 50, 48 " " Arrow,		-	-	18 00
" 51, 41 " " "		-	-	16 00
" 52, 35 " " "		-	-	13 00
" 53, 28 " " "		-	-	11 00
" 54, 20 " " "		-	-	8 00
" 55, 16 " " "		-	-	5 00
" 56, 12 " " "		-	-	4 00
" 62, 54 " " Plow,		-	-	40 00
" 63, 33 " " "		-	-	25 00
" 64, 22 " high, Goddess of Liberty,				25 00
" 65, 30 " " " "				40 00
" 71, 16 × 21 inches, Butterfly,		-	-	10 00
" 72, 5 feet long, Locomotive,		-	-	75 00
" " 3 " " " no Tender,				40 00
" " 2 " " "		-	-	25 00
" 73, 35 inches long, Cod Fish,		-	-	25 00

CHURCH VANES.

01, 8 feet long, 12 in. letter, 14 in. ball,				$90 00
02, 7 " " 10 1-2 " 12 "				75 00
03, 6 " " 9 " 10 "				60 00
04, 5 " " 7 1-2 " 8 "				50 00
05, 4 " " 6 " 6 "				40 00

ALL KINDS OF VANES MADE TO ORDER.
Illustrated Circulars sent free.

86. *Four-page Price List of A. L. Jewell & Co., Waltham, Mass.*

Leonard W. Cushing, a college-educated engineer and a descendant of Waltham's first and second ministers, was probably the principal financial partner. He had met Stillman White, a mechanic, while both worked in Waltham's watch factory. That factory, which in time made Waltham the Watch City, brought it prosperity—a fine stimulant to local weathervane sales—and a population that included many trained artisans and precision craftsmen. In the Watch City poor workmanship failed quickly. Cushing & White prospered.

In 1872 White sold out to his partner. Cushing took into the business his sons —Harry, who stayed only briefly, and Charles, who eventually inherited the firm of L. W. Cushing & Sons.

Leonard W. Cushing added to Jewell's weathervane designs his own equally excellent but decidedly different patterns. Some Jewell patterns were replaced, but many remained. Jewell's deer, as it appears in the 1867 listing, was still featured, with the same number and price, in Cushing's catalogue for 1883 (Fig. 87). The elegantly simple deer is Jewell's. The elaborately textured full-bodied leaping stag is Cushing's. The catalogue illustrations clearly show the different styles originated under Jewell and his successor. The vanes are so accurately depicted that they could be ordered satisfactorily, sight unseen, by Americans anywhere in the nation.

By 1880 steam transportation had welded the United States into an economic unit. The entire country had become one market, with a common standard of living and a singular sense of fashion. Craftsmen eager to serve a three-thousand-mile-long market were mass producing their wares and mass marketing them through catalogues.

Trade catalogues, many illustrated with artistic renderings of the wares, became a phenomenon of post-Civil War industry, though catalogues were not new. In 1760 John Tweedy had published

A Catalogue of Druggs, and of Chymical and Galenical Medicines; sold . . . at his shop in Newport, Rhode-Island. And For Him In New-York, At The Sign Of The Unicorn and Mortar.

Early catalogues usually were lists of "druggs," books, or seeds. By the late nineteenth century, however, virtually everything was available through catalogues—a few huge, miscellaneous ones (e.g., that of Sears, Roebuck & Co.) and a plethora of pamphlets of specialized trades.

Copyrighted Sept. 11, 1882,
By L. W. Cushing & Sons.

Deer.

No. 69. 25 in. long, . . . $25.00

English Setter Dog
McDona's "Ranger."

No. 320. 36 in. long, ... $35.00

Deer.
FULL BODIED

No. 85. 50 in. long, ... $100.00
" 86. 30 " " 35.00
" 87. 20 " " 20.00

Copyrighted 1883, by L. W. Cushing & Sons.

Fox Hound.

No. 88. 27 in. long, ... $20.00
" 90. 52 " " Hound chasing Fox, . . 35.00

Copyrighted 1883, by L. W. Cushing & Sons.

Grasshopper.

No. 410. 42 in. long, ... $60.00

Copyrighted 1883,
By L. W. Cushing & Sons.

Angel Gabriel.

No. 230. 32 in. long, ... $25.00

Fox.

No. 89. 22 in. long, ... $15.00

17

87.

*Page 17 of Catalogue No. 9 (1883), L. W. Cushing & Sons, Waltham, Mass. Note Cushing's cardinal
design.*

Weathervanes were listed and pictured in catalogues of building materials, of ironwork or garden furniture, among roofing, railings, hitching posts, or flower urns. For many businesses, vanes constituted only a small part of their trade. (Known weathervane vendors and an estimate of the extent of their trade in vanes are listed in Appendix I.)

A few companies specialized in weathervanes and published catalogues devoted primarily to them. The following weathervane catalogues, now collectors' items, are fun to look through:

SAMUEL BENT & SONS, NEW YORK, N.Y.:

1888   A catalogue of 42 pages, 39 devoted to vanes. This catalogue includes a vane, "Flora Temple and Mate," of two horses facing each other. The mare represented the well-known trotter, the stallion was unidentified.

L. W. CUSHING & SONS, WALTHAM, MASS.:

1883   Catalogue No. 9, 20 pages, all on vanes. This large, 8⅝″ x 12¼″ catalogue illustrates 69 vanes, lists another 9, and shows 2 styles of mortar-and-pestle emblems.

A 7⅛″ x 10⅛″ facsimile of this catalogue was printed in 1974 by Francis Andrews, Waltham.

J. W. FISKE, NEW YORK, N.Y.:

1875   Of this catalogue's 47 pages, 39 are devoted to vanes. On page 27 is an illustration of a brewer's vane, "Malt Shovel and Barrel."

A facsimile of this catalogue was published in 1964 by Gerald Kornblau Antiques, New York.

Post-1885   This is a catalogue of 100 pages, all on vanes. It lists 145 patterns, including a "Tobacco Leaf."

1893   A catalogue of 140 pages, 136 of which are devoted to vanes. A reproduction of this catalogue, entitled *J. W. Fiske 1893*, was published in 1971 by the Pyne Press, Princeton, N.J.

HARRIS & CO., BOSTON, MASS.:

1875   A catalogue of 40 pages, 24 pages devoted to vanes.

1879   Catalogue of 60 pages, 33 pages devoted to vanes. This small catalogue, 4¼″ x 5½″, also pictures finials and crestings (ornamental railings then very much in demand for Victorian mansard roofs).

A. L. JEWELL & CO., WALTHAM, MASS.:
1867   This four-page list of vanes is reproduced in its entirety as Figure 86.

A. B. & W. T. WESTERVELT CO., NEW YORK, N.Y.:
1883–84   This 100-page catalogue, all on vanes, includes a "Moose."

1890   Catalogue of 16 pages.

Many companies pirated catalogue illustrations from their competitors. Most of the illustrations in Westervelt's catalogue are identical to Fiske's; a few to Harris's. Businesses devoted mainly to other metal products usually reproduced in their catalogues weathervane illustrations from Cushing, Harris, Fiske, or Bent. Some firms were agents for these manufacturers; others merely pirated the pictures; others stole the designs of the vanes as well.

In addition to the many designs in their catalogues, weathervane manufacturers promised to produce vanes of any style, as Harris's catalogue states:

We also make Vanes of any desired pattern from Architects' plans or other drawings. Vanes carefully packed for exportation. Vanes for home trade are also packed with care and are shipped to all parts of the country.

Harris aimed at a broad market. Cushing had agents in various cities, taking orders for "Waltham Vanes." Steam transportation and catalogue selling had ended the time when the work or the style of a craftsman was confined to his own immediate locale.

All over America in the latter decades of the nineteenth century, roof-topping copper sculptures were in demand. During the years between the Civil War and World War I, many town houses had mansard roofs with iron crestings and weathervanes, while many public and private buildings had castlelike turrets bearing vanes. Private residences often had stables or carriage houses with cupolas and weathervanes, and larger farms meant larger barns with higher cupolas and large, store-bought vanes. As Charles C. Kessler, an old gentleman of E. G. Washburne & Co., a copper weathervane manufacturer, recalled for a reporter in *The New Yorker*, September 12, 1964:

. . . the big estates . . . were going up then [1908], and when I say big . . . besides the

88.

Model for Setter Vane. Wood (pine). L. 35⅝". Carved probably by H. Leach, for Cushing & White, Waltham, Mass., about 1871. Collection of Herbert W. Hemphill, Jr.

main house there would be a superintendent's house, a gardener's cottage, a laundry, a garage, and of course, a stable and carriage house—and they'd all have vanes. . . .

To fill the demand for hollow copper vanes, manufacturers used a method of mass (but handcrafted) production.

First the craftsman carved a wooden model. Alvin Jewell may have carved his models himself. Often the weathervane maker had his models "cut in" by ornamental woodcarvers or by ship and figurehead carvers. Harris probably used one of the many shipcarvers working along Boston's waterfront. Rarely can the carvers' names be traced today.

Of Henry Leach, who carved the models for almost all of the vanes Cushing & White added to the Jewell line, relatively little is known. We do know that Leach, an ornamental carver, lived and worked at 2 Indiana Street, Boston, having begun his short woodcarving career (1867–72) after trying map selling, book selling, and clothing selling, and working for six years as a pen dealer.

Cushing's business journals show that Leach carved the trotter Ethan Allen (Fig. 105), the trotter Dexter (Fig. 108), the 60-inch Goddess of Liberty (Fig. 22), the fox and hound (Fig. 100), and the squirrel (Fig. 124), among others. He probably carved the wooden model (Fig. 88) for Cushing's setter vane (Fig. 93). The same vane was listed as No. 320 and illustrated in the 1883 catalogue (Fig. 87). Leach's trotters and other designs reveal him as a superb sculptor of animals. But he may not have been experienced or skilled in carving the human form. When Cushing wanted his angel Gabriel carved, he went to E. Warren Hastings, a Boston figurehead carver.

The carver of the bull model (Fig. 66) is unknown, as is the company for which it was made. The wooden bull was among many weathervane effects acquired by E. G. Washburne & Co. early in this century from several weathervane manufacturers then going out of business. The bull and a matching calf model are now part of the collection of the New York State Historical Association, Cooperstown, New York. A matching cow is privately owned. Few wooden weathervane models are extant, and all are highly prized.

Colonial craftsmen making copper vanes could shape the sheet copper directly on a rounded wooden model or in a hollowed-out wooden form, since they made few vanes of each design. The mass producer of copper vanes, however, could not repeatedly reuse a pattern of even the hardest wood. Quantity production required much more durability. The answer was negative (concave) molds of cast iron or occasionally of bronze. The patterns auctioned with Jewell's goodwill were of cast iron.

A negative mold requires several sections—at least a body left and a body right; usually, additionally, a tail left and a tail right; often a left-foreleg left; a left-foreleg right; a right-foreleg left; a right-foreleg right; and so on. A swell-bodied (i.e., low-relief) animal might require only a few sections, perhaps eight—two sides (each including head, body, and the outsides of two legs); a tail left; a tail right; and the insides of four legs. Full-bodied vanes might require many more sections. (See wood carving, Fig. 66. The saw cuts denote separately molded sections.)

The molds illustrated in Figure 89 are five of the six needed for the dog shown in Figure 91. The right side of the body is not pictured here. These durable iron molds were designed about 1870 by Harris & Co. and used by them through 1881. Harris went out of business about 1882. By 1885 W. A. Snow Co., Boston, was producing vanes from Harris's molds, probably having acquired Harris's entire line. Snow used them for many years, but about 1940 Snow ceased operations and sold their molds to E. G. Washburne & Co., then of New York, now of Danvers, Massachusetts, where these molds are still in use.

The advent of iron molds made volume production possible, but the weathervane maker still had to handcraft each vane. After clamping sheet copper to the iron, he beat the copper into the mold with his mallet. Slowly the malleable copper assumed the shape of the cast iron. Weights held the work in place as the craftsman hammered, using a

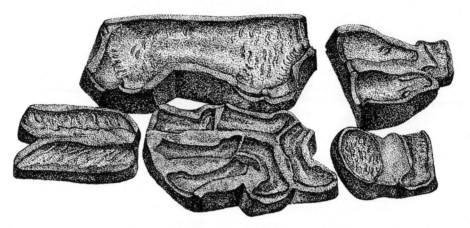

89.

Molds for Dog Vane illustrated in Fig. 91. Iron. Body mold, 21″ x 10½″ x 2½″. Weight approx. 50 lbs. Head mold, 11″ x 11″ x 2½″. Tail mold, 9¾″ x 7″ x 1½″. Leg mold, 15″ x 12″ x 1⅞″. Weight approx. 15 lbs. Designed and used by A. J. Harris & Sons, later Harris & Co., Boston, Mass., from about 1870 to 1881. Used by W. A. Snow, Boston, Mass., 1883–1940. Owned and used by E. G. Washburne & Co., New York and now Danvers, Mass., since about 1940.

hickory-wood set and lastly a metal set to emboss fine details such as the lines of the dog's fur.

Then the copper parts were trimmed, fitted, and soldered together, resembling at last the wooden original. Elaborate, full-bodied vanes had many parts to be smoothly seamed together. When seams are obvious on mass-produced copper vanes, they reveal either post-1940 production or recent repairs. The nineteenth-century craftsmen invisibly joined the numerous copper sections, at times adding some solid parts usually cast of a lead-zinc alloy, sometimes of bronze. Cast heads were common—Jewell used them even on low-relief patterns—and small details like oxen's horns, birds' legs and claws, and firemen on engines were almost always cast. Sometimes the weathervane maker affixed wire constructions (e.g., ships' rigging). The whole received a coat of gold leaf, and with iron spire, cardinals, and gilded copper balls, the handmade mass-produced vanes were shipped out.

Gradually, in the early decades of the twentieth century, the orders stopped coming in. Garages, which have no ventilating cupolas, replaced stables and carriage houses;

mansard roofs and castlelike turrets became passé; huge estates were seldom affordable, and skyscrapers were no places for vanes.

Through the 1920s Charles Cushing managed to continue his father's trade (Leonard had died in 1907). But when in 1933 the eighty-year-old Charles decided to lay down his mallet, there were no bidders vying for his "stock, patterns and goodwill." L. W. Cushing & Sons had no successor.

The stock on hand sold well, mainly to antique dealers. However, the molds for the cannon and the butterfly, the centaur and the setter, the cow and the grasshopper, the "patterns" from which thousands of Jewell and Cushing vanes had been produced, could not be given away. The local historical society refused Cushing's offer of a mold or two, seeing less value in having them than trouble in storing them. The weighty load of iron and brass molds went to a scrap-metal dealer in Chelsea, Massachusetts.

The junk dealer shrewdly claimed that the grasshopper mold he had acquired from Cushing was the one used to make Faneuil Hall's vane. He priced it accordingly and would not sell it without the rest of the lot. So, for years, Cushing's molds remained in a heap of scrap metal, the lot dwindling somewhat during World War II when the price of scrap metal soared.

Meanwhile Edith Gregor Halpert, founder of the Downtown Gallery and director of the American Folk Art Gallery, became convinced, and convinced others, that some weathervanes were fine folk-art sculptures. Mrs. Halpert had been buying up weathervanes since the 1920s and had, as *Time* magazine said "busily stripped the New England skyline of more than a hundred vanes" which she sold to folk-art collectors and museums.

In the 1940s, she became suspicious of vanes then appearing on the market as nineteenth-century originals. She asked her friend and fellow art dealer, Boris Mirski of Boston, if he could find their source. Mirski searched and found the Chelsea scrap-metal dealer carefully crafting vanes from Cushing's junked molds. In 1953 Mrs. Halpert and Mirski bought the entire load of Cushing's molds (they didn't fall for the Faneuil Hall story) and removed some 350 bulky pieces, most of iron, some of brass, from the junk dealer's. Mrs. Halpert then "arranged for a limited number of facsimiles to be made in the original hand manner and finished in patines [*sic*] exactly like the antique originals," according to the catalogue of the Halpert/Cushing vanes issued in 1954, a page of which is reproduced in Figure 90.

The antiquelike patina did not look exactly like that of the originals to Charles Cushing's daughter, Winifred. She attended the showing and, as she wrote in a letter to a

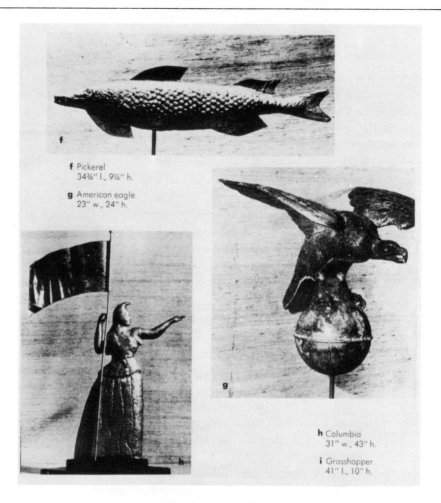

f Pickerel
34¾" l., 9¼" h.

g American eagle
23" w., 24" h.

h Columbia
31" w., 43" h.

i Grasshopper
41" l., 10" h.

90.
Page of the Catalog of Weather Vanes, *Associated American Artists Galleries, 711 Fifth Avenue, New York City* [1954]. *Vanes photographed were Edith Gregor Halpert's facsimiles of Cushing vanes.*

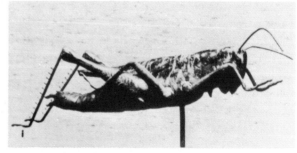

friend, "really didn't enjoy it so much. The arrangement was lovely, but the *vanes were not gilded,* just copper, sort of antiqued."

Mrs. Halpert produced limited editions (about twenty copies) of each of sixteen patterns, priced them at up to five hundred dollars, and reportedly intended to retire the molds and to donate them all to a museum. Mrs. Halpert never said where, and after the Halpert copies were made, the molds disappeared. None went to the Historical Society in Waltham, which had become eager to display that which it once could not manage to store.

Time magazine, in a glowing account of Mrs. Halpert's Cushing show, said in its issue of September 27, 1954: "Considering that they were meant to be seen atop a high perch, the figures were remarkably graceful close up . . . they had many touches of humor or pride." "Humor" and "pride" had been rescued from the scrap heap to be sold as sculpture on New York's Fifth Avenue.

While Cushing's surviving molds were producing "objets d'art," albeit folk art, other weathervane molds which had survived were being returned to production.

The dog vane illustrated in Figure 91 was made in the 1960s by E. G. Washburne & Co., originally of New York, now of Danvers, Massachusetts. But Washburne did not originally design this model. As the weathervane industry collapsed in the early years of the twentieth century and virtually died in the economic depression of the 1930s, the Washburne concern acquired molds from several weathervane manufacturers going out of business. About 1940 they took over W. A. Snow's molds, most of which had originally been Harris's. When the Washburne firm changed hands in 1956, the old molds from the defunct manufacturers, as well as the Washburne molds and name, moved to Danvers.

This dog is not quite identical, however, to the setter vanes produced by Harris in the 1870s. It is clearly a twentieth-century Washburne product. The seams where the several copper sections are joined together are wider and much more visible on new Washburne productions than on vanes made in the nineteenth century from these same molds. The shaping of the copper, however, is well done, hand-hammered in the old manner in the old molds. Curiously, Washburne has put this dog's ears on upside down. Harris and Snow placed the pointed ends down.

This setter vane was purchased from an antique dealer by a resident of the North Shore of Massachusetts, and it looked quite antique. Washburne's newly made old-mold vanes are sold in several finishes—gilded, polished copper, painted, or with an "antique verdigris patina," as the catalogue denoted an artificially induced copper corrosion.

91. *Dog. Copper. L. 34″. With Washburne's cardinals, following Mott's design. This style dog was originally mass produced by A. J. Harris & Co., later Harris & Co., Boston, Mass., from about 1870 to 1881, and sold for $25; it was then produced by W. A. Snow Co., Boston, Mass. from 1883 to 1940. (A white metal version owned by the Smithsonian was probably made by Snow in the twentieth century.) Currently mass produced in copper from Harris's old mold by E. G. Washburne & Co., Danvers, Mass.*

In the past customers wanted gilded vanes; a verdigrised vane was a sign of neglect. Today the verdigris finish, designed for customers seeking a "folk-art" look, enables some antique dealers to pass off the new vanes as antiques.

Another producer of newly made old-mold vanes is J. W. Fiske of Paterson,

New Jersey. A small percentage of the old molds of the J. W. Fiske firm, previously of New York, survive. Most were given to scrap-iron collections during World War II when it seemed that they would never be needed again. Then the postwar growth of suburbs brought "colonial" houses with garages, generally low rooftops on business establishments, and, consequently, a revival of interest in weathervanes. So Fiske's surviving molds are again in use, although weathervanes are but a small part of the architectural metalwork produced by J. W. Fiske in Paterson since 1956. Fiske's catalogue describes their vanes as

> full-bodied, three-quarter full-bodied or silhouette. The first two of these, hollow for lightness, are skillfully hand-hammered out of sheet copper, then given a beautiful and enduring weatherproof surfacing of 22K gold leaf. Silhouette vanes, as supplied by Fiske, are made of aluminum and finished in black.

Most post-World War II weathervanes are of the silhouette type. Either they are barely molded, cast in aluminum, and painted (usually black), or they are simple cut-out vanes, stamped out of flat metal and painted. One firm, Kenneth Lynch & Sons, Inc., of Wilton, Connecticut, adds to its silhouette vanes what the catalogue calls "antique reproductions"—not vanes made from old molds but copies of old vanes.

Twentieth-century silhouette vanes are sometimes used in business. Eighteenth- and nineteenth-century business vanes were usually signs of the trade conducted beneath the roof; twentieth-century commercial vanes seldom are. Most are decorative finials and not signs at all. Other commercial vanes are signs, not of the trade (they do not signify grocery, restaurant, fried chicken purveyor, or gasoline station) but of the company or chain conducting the trade. They are not trade vanes, but trademark vanes.

Trademark vanes are a switch on an old switch. Remember New England's oldest trade vane, Faneuil Hall's grasshopper (Fig. 7)? In Faneuil's time it was a trade sign, but it had descended from Gresham's grasshopper, originally a personal mark. Ancient castle vanes bore the mark of ownership. Trademark vanes do the same.

Ownership emblems, whether heraldic or corporate (Fig. 92), were not designed with weathervanes in mind and have to be adapted to weathervaning. The adaptation used by A & P is related to heraldic castle vanes, dated meetinghouse vanes, and the initialed flag vanes which were very popular for all types of buildings during the nineteenth-century Gothic revival (Fig. 46). Those vanes had emblems, dates, or initials pierced in a metal flag. Pierced vanes can be effective even though they have a wrong (mirror-image)

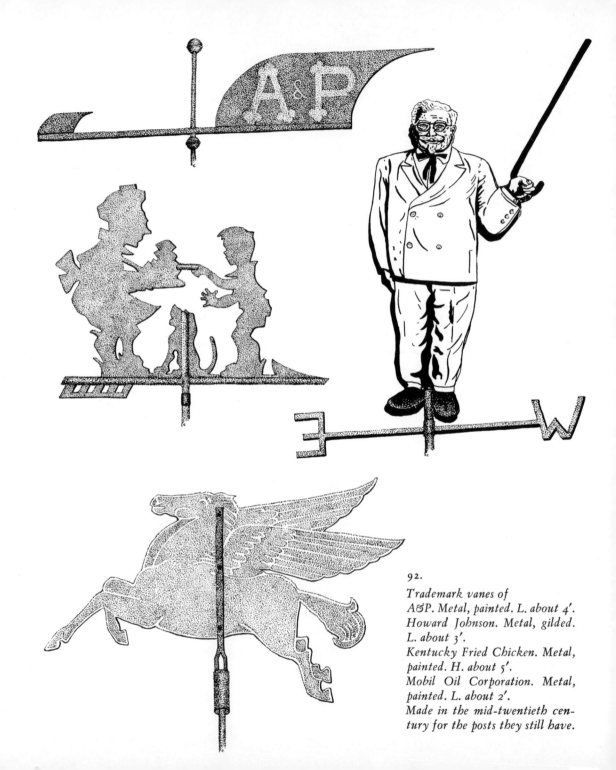

92.
Trademark vanes of
A&P. Metal, painted. L. about 4′.
Howard Johnson. Metal, gilded.
L. about 3′.
Kentucky Fried Chicken. Metal,
painted. H. about 5′.
Mobil Oil Corporation. Metal,
painted. L. about 2′.
Made in the mid-twentieth cen-
tury for the posts they still have.

side. The A & P flag has painted initials; it is spared the wrong-side problem but requires frequent repainting.

Using the corporate emblem itself as a vane does not always succeed. A good trademark need not point direction; a good weathervane does. Howard Johnson's child and pieman, facing opposite directions, only point inward. The Kentucky colonel's casually held cane does not provide a distinct and forceful forward thrust. In fact this "vane" was not built to rotate in the wind. Although supplied with cardinals, the colonel merely poses as a vane.

A flying horse has the potential of being a superb weathervane. But Mobil's flying horse was designed for stationary signs and displays less forward action than the wingless horses on sporting vanes. The emblem lacks the illusion of speed achieved by the wooden Pegasus (Fig. 118). Yet that illusion of speed is probably what the gasoline vendors desired when, searching for a corporate symbol, they selected the mythical Pegasus from the panoply of real and imaginary animals.

8.
Sports and Leisure

The reaction of an out-of-door people herded in a single generation into overgrown cities was the rise of sport.

RALPH H. GABRIEL
Annals of American Sport

In the late 1800s, the weathervane that a man chose for his carriage house usually reflected a sporting theme. The dogs shown in Figures 91 and 93 are sporting vanes; they honor the hunter's bird dog. The popularity and variety of weathervanes inspired by leisure activities attest to the importance of sport in late-nineteenth-century American life. The era's democratic and industrious Americans are remembered for scorning a leisure class and extolling the virtue of work, but they nevertheless found time for recreation. Even austere New Englanders learned to play.

The settlers who first arrived on America's shores were not sportsmen. In the Old World, hunting and other sports were pastimes of the aristocracy. As middle-class Englishmen, the settlers knew little of hunting or sportfishing. In the midst of the New World plenty, they would have starved (and almost did) had they not gone out to hunt. Driven by necessity, Americans were soon at home in field and forest.

Hunting was practical and therefore an acceptable sport. All of America's

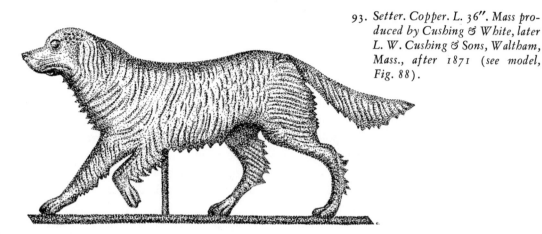

93. *Setter. Copper. L. 36". Mass produced by Cushing & White, later L. W. Cushing & Sons, Waltham, Mass., after 1871 (see model, Fig. 88).*

struggling settlements banned unproductive diversion. As the struggle to survive abated, bans on the pursuit of pleasure relaxed. But while southerners began to play at many pastimes, the Puritan ethic kept New Englanders from such sports as bearbaiting, cock-fighting, and horse racing. Hunting, in deference to its practical nature, remained an acceptable activity, even after it had become truly a sport, with the edible game merely a bonus.

From the start, New England's woodlands were an excellent source of fine-eating feathered game. In the late nineteenth century, however, game birds became scarcer and shyer. Fewer woodcock hid in tall grass, fern, and willows; fewer ruffed grouse (partridge to Yankees) rustled or drummed among spruce, pine, juniper, beech, and alder. The dense wooded retreat of the birds made a hunter rely on a dog who could flush and retrieve birds from the tangled growth. The English setter's heavy coat and furry legs ideally suited him to the rough New England uplands.

A hunter prized his setter for his marvelous pointing instinct and retrieving skill. The dog worked hard to give the hunter as many chances to shoot as possible, for not every flushed partridge presented a clear target, not every fallen bird was easy to retrieve. A hunter credited his canine companion with much of the weight in the gamebag, and he was likely to select as his vane one which honored his bird dog.

Even when the gamebag remained empty, a fowler enjoyed the day in grouse country. In the newly industrialized society, men spent long hours in mills and factories. They sought the pleasurable change of the out-of-doors. It was the hills and glens, the spruce and alder, the smell of ripened fruit and the panorama of painted leaves—not the need for food—that brought men and their dogs out to hunt.

All manner of canines helped in hunting. Pointers, short-haired bird dogs, were very popular, particularly in the South where thickets were less dense. Newfoundlands and the progenitors of Chesapeake Bays retrieved waterfowl. Dogs of assorted breeds harried furry game. A wooden hunting dog in Figure 94 seems to be a pointer. Unfortunately, as with so many other vanes, a hunter pointed at him: the wooden dog's missing tail was most likely cropped by gunshot. Besides his broken tail, one foreleg was broken (and has been repaired). The other foreleg is of lead (perhaps an original attachment to balance the vane better). Many vanes lost legs and tails, or were marked with holes and dents, because they made tempting targets for practicing marksmen.

A weathervane was an excellent target—distant, yet clearly visible against the sky; safe, up where a miss would not harm a farm animal; and obliging, spinning to tell the gunner he hit the mark and then settling to become an ideal target again. Young gunners often perfected their marksmanship aiming at vanes.

Marksmanship contests were among the first sport competitions in America. At the first Thanksgiving, the men of Plymouth "exercised" their "arms," a display of marksmanship which may have seemed to their Indian guests a sportsmanly show of skill and a word to the wise. On "training days" (the colonists regularly mustered to practice military skills), men displayed their shooting proficiency in marksmanship contests and competed in wrestling, running, and tumbling. In general, they disported themselves in diversions which on other than "training days" would have been condemned as a "mispense" of time.

Shooting matches were common at New England taverns in the early 1800s. As Basil Hall explained in *Travels in North America in the Years 1827 and 1828,* a gunner would pay to try, and

> If he kills the bird, he is allowed to carry it off; otherwise like a true sportsman, he had the amusement for his money.

So shooting practice, which had made the colonists good hunters and defenders of the settlements, made the new Americans true sportsmen. Shooting practice continued after "training days" and "tavern matches" were long gone, and generations of gunners have taken aim at barn weathervanes to develop the skill they would need to hit a flash of feathers in the woodlands.

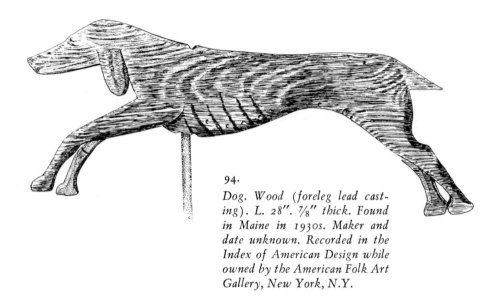

94.

Dog. Wood (foreleg lead casting). L. 28". ⅞" thick. Found in Maine in 1930s. Maker and date unknown. Recorded in the Index of American Design while owned by the American Folk Art Gallery, New York, N.Y.

The upland birds that dogs flushed from cover varied with the season and with the century. By mid-nineteenth century, the wild turkey of colonial times was gone from New England; the once numerous heath hen would soon be extinct; the quail's staccato "bob-white" was heard less each year. The grouse and woodcock grew scarce as excellent bird dogs and well-practiced marksmanship took their toll. Conservation was a necessity by the end of the nineteenth century. Government came to the rescue—not of the birds as much as of the hunters.

Because fowlers had little left at which to shoot, Chinese or ring-necked pheasants were acquired, bred, and introduced to American fields at the turn of the century. They flourished, and since 1914 pheasants have been hunted annually in New England. The imported fowl has become the principal game bird; Massachusetts alone breeds fifty-five thousand cock birds each year to meet hunting needs.

From the relatively recent introduction of the ring-necked pheasant to this country, we can deduce that the weathervane in Figure 95 is not very old. Although wood is often the medium of very old vanes, the wooden pheasant is newer than most mass-produced copper vanes. Probably because it was not aloft very long, it was not riddled with shot. Its fine condition is remarkable because it certainly presented a tempting target.

Waterfowl, as well as upland birds, were popular game birds. Hunters con-

95. *Pheasant. Wood, painted. L. about 34". Made in twentieth century. Maker unknown. Collection of Effie Thixton Arthur.*

cealed in low-lying, camouflaged duckboats or shrewdly hidden blinds on the shore, blazed away at migrating flocks so thick that at times they darkened the sky. As the nineteenth century progressed, increasing numbers of sportsmen took up this damp and merciless pastime and the migrating flocks grew steadily thinner. To lure the fowl within range, the hunters used decoys, carefully carved and cleverly arranged in the water or along the edge. Wooden plovers, curlew, and sandpipers stood on single legs in the sand; lifelike duck and geese "blocks" floated offshore. A sociable wild goose, seeing what seemed to be others of his kind, would glide down on motionless wings to feed—only to be met by gunshot.

Often the wildfowl hunters shaped their own decoys. Many grew skilled at carving and painting the deceptive wooden figures. Perhaps, after shaping some blocks of ducks and geese, some hunter made the flying goose shown in Figure 96 for a vane.

Hunting was a universal sport, popular with townsmen and farmers, in North, South and, as the nation went west, there too. Everywhere, deer were common game.

In New England's woods, wildlife was plentiful and varied. Wolves and moose roamed the colonial Northeast; squirrels and raccoons were regularly hunted; but a deer was most often down range of the gun barrel. Venison was commonplace on the colonial table, and during the early 1800s, it was eaten almost as often as beef.

The deer was a favorite subject for vanes. Many sheet-iron silhouettes were made of leaping or standing deer. In either pose, the animal's grace and decorative form make it an attractive silhouette for a weathervane like the iron one shown in Figure 97.

All weathervane manufacturers featured deer patterns; many companies made more than one design. Cushing showed two models (see Fig. 87), one leaping (his own design) and one standing (Jewell's pattern). Harris & Co.'s deer is depicted leaping over the very same log and greenery as served as a woodland prop for their Indian, Massasoit (Fig. 24). J. W. Fiske listed four deer vanes: a standing stag, two running designs, and a combination—a deer chased by a dog. The vane illustrated in Figure 98 is probably one of Fiske's running models.

Full-bodied weathervanes have an advantage over flat vanes—they can be effective when viewed lengthwise. From that angle too the antlered deer has a beautiful form. No wonder this attractive animal, a favorite quarry for hunters, was the commonest subject for hunting vanes.

The wily fox was not the kind of game New Englanders hunted. The fox hunt was an aristocratic sport in the elegant English manner—with horns and hounds, fine mounts and fashionable habits. It was occasionally enjoyed in colonial New York and Philadelphia and was quite popular in the colonial South where horse races and cockfights also entertained men who bet in pounds of tobacco and numbers of slaves. In New England, however, the sport of fox hunting was almost unknown.

New Englanders hunted singly with a dog and a gun, on foot. A fox hunt meant a group following the quarry on horseback, in a cross-country chase. Understandably, the sport was not popular where small independent farmers resented hounds and hunters upsetting their fences and trampling their fields. Besides, the fox hunt was traditionally associated with aristocratic leisure and thus resented by democratic-thinking Americans.

Even in the South, where plantation gentry, including George Washington, had enjoyed fox hunting, the sport waned in the early years of the new nation. If the sport

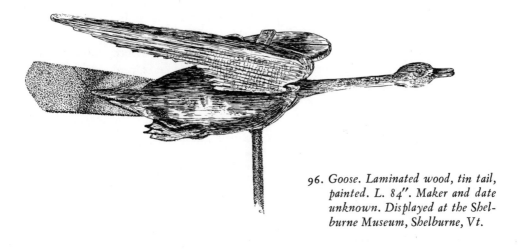

96. Goose. *Laminated wood, tin tail, painted. L. 84". Maker and date unknown. Displayed at the Shelburne Museum, Shelburne, Vt.*

97. *Deer. Sheet iron (strengthened on back with iron bands) L. 32½″. Mass produced in the late nineteenth century. Maker unknown. Abby Aldrich Rockefeller Folk Art Collection, Williamsburg, Va.*

was too aristocratic for Americans, where was the market for the mass-produced vane illustrated in Figure 99?

Late in the nineteenth century, a new aristocracy arose in industrialized America—a society which sought aristocratic European sports almost as much as its daughters sought aristocratic European husbands. The fox hunt was perfectly suited to that hunt-club society; the fox chase vane was perfect for their clubhouse.

Leonard Cushing designed a fox vane priced at fifteen dollars and a dog-chasing-fox combination (Fig. 100) priced at thirty-five dollars, probably with the hunt-club market in mind. Some of these vanes must have been bought by people who never hunted on horseback but chose the fleet-footed twosome simply for its appeal. The frightened fox and almost victorious hound convey a sense of delightful movement, sport, and action. The dog will never catch the fox, but the vane catches the eye.

The most popular weathervane subject in the last half of the nineteenth century was the trotting horse. Yet horse vanes which predate 1830 are rare. Quite suddenly in the 1830s Americans everywhere began breeding horses, racing horses, and talking about horses. Soon, they were hanging pictures of horses on parlor walls and placing weathervanes of horses on carriage houses.

A wood and copper vane (Fig. 101) made about 1840 probably depicts the trotter Lady Suffolk, the celebrated "old gray mare" whose career (1838–53) spanned the years when trotting was becoming America's first national sport. The vane, which has a short rein for a saddled rider, may commemorate Lady Suffolk's record mile (2:26½) trotted under saddle in 1843. At that time, trotters raced either saddled or harnessed to

98. *Deer. Copper, full-bodied. L. about 36″. Mass produced probably by J. W. Fiske, New York, N.Y., and Massachusetts, in the late nineteenth century. Privately owned.*

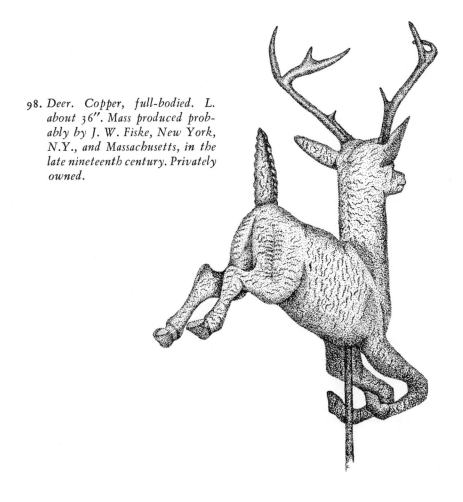

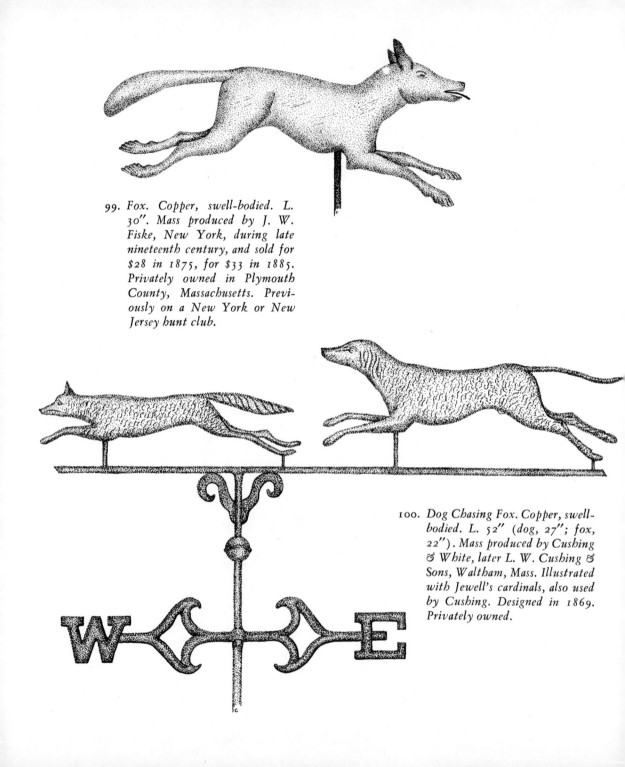

99. *Fox. Copper, swell-bodied. L. 30″. Mass produced by J. W. Fiske, New York, during late nineteenth century, and sold for $28 in 1875, for $33 in 1885. Privately owned in Plymouth County, Massachusetts. Previously on a New York or New Jersey hunt club.*

100. *Dog Chasing Fox. Copper, swell-bodied. L. 52″ (dog, 27″; fox, 22″). Mass produced by Cushing & White, later L. W. Cushing & Sons, Waltham, Mass. Illustrated with Jewell's cardinals, also used by Cushing. Designed in 1869. Privately owned.*

101. *Horse. Wood, copper mane and rein. L. 24". Made about 1840. Maker unknown. Found in Maine. Author's collection.*

vehicles. One quarter of the mare's 161 races were trotted under saddle, but after 1847 she trotted almost exclusively in harness. By then New Englanders, who had rejected horse racing, succeeded in shaping the national sport into their image of what an equine sport should be.

For two centuries, Puritans and their descendants had persisted in a feudal conviction that a horse was a "gentleman's mount." Unlike southerners, they did not consider themselves gentry, so they foreswore horseback riding. Although in the South a horse was for riding, in the North a horse was for pulling. North of the Mason-Dixon line there were "a hundred persons travelling in light wagons, sulkies, or chaises, . . . for *one* —on horseback."

New Englanders developed no interest in racing saddled, galloping horses because they seldom rode horseback. That, more than Puritan sentiment against wasting time and money in racing and betting, kept Yankees from racing "southern style." Also the northerners' horses weren't worthy of racing. They were small light-harness horses, far inferior to the southerners' fine mounts. In the early 1800s "it was rare . . . to hear any boasting of horses." Even wealthy Yankees had poor horses; those of stage companies were little better.

With the advent of the steam locomotive, Americans fell in love with speed.

Swift horses for fast road travel caught the imagination of all. Trotters were saddled up, or harnessed up, and raced to see which had the best speed and stamina. Each man boasted that his horse was best. In New England, the trotters raced while harnessed to light vehicles. Through the 1830s trotting under saddle and trotting in harness vied for popularity. By the late 1840s the Yankee style prevailed. Harness racing was supreme—a national sport that was distinctly American.

The heroes of the national sport, trotters, were commemorated in prints and weathervanes. The vane in Figure 101 has a copper mane and rein and an iron tube reinforcing the hole for a spire. Some vanes of wood and metal are probably of the late eighteenth century (see the cocks, Figs. 51, 52), but this vane is probably from the 1830s or early 1840s. Not until trotters were considered worth boasting about were they worthy subjects for weathervanes. The finely carved vane was originally gessoed and covered in gold leaf—not the work of an amateur but, rather, of some craftsman who often made vanes in the years preceding mass production and the copper weathervane industry.

One small corner of New England was far from puritanical—actually as aristocratic as any place in America. There, in Rhode Island, saddle horses known as Narragansett pacers were bred and raced and won renown by 1700.

The Narragansetts took naturally to the pacing gait. (A pacer lifts both feet of the same side at the same time.) The breed's easy gait and motion were desirable in a saddle horse ridden on primitive roads. The easy riding, surefooted Narragansetts were shipped in great numbers to the southern colonies and the West Indies. However, by the time harness racing became the nation's sport, the Narragansett breed had vanished.

Trotters were the harnessed heroes of the nineteenth century. (Whereas a pacer runs with his legs laterally paired, a trotter's legs are diagonally paired, although not exactly synchronized.) The trotting gait proved easy for a horse in harness and most agreeable to the driver. There was little competition for pacers, so many owners of natural pacers converted them to trotters by applying toe weights and correcting their balance.

Eventually, fine harness pacers were developed. Dan Patch, a swift pacer, won fame as an outstanding competitor in harness, but that was not until the early years of the twentieth century.

A pacer vane is exceedingly rare. One recorded in the Index of American Design (Fig. 102) is the only such piece of which I know. Perhaps some Rhode Islander with chauvinistic pride in the vanished Narragansetts, or some fan of Dan Patch (if this vane is of twentieth-century origin), wanted a weathervane of a pacer. He would not have

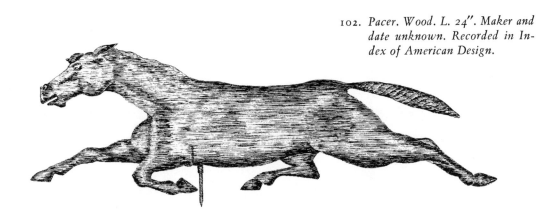

found a pacer listed in weathervane manufacturers' catalogues, so this vane was most likely especially carved. Its owner, like his favorite horse, was out of step with his times.

Most weathervanes were modeled after trotters, the most popular favorites of the turf. Although each weathervane manufacturer featured many horse vanes—some standing, most in action—almost every horse vane was named for, modeled after, and displayed the gait of a trotter. A few vanes were of thoroughbreds (i.e., gallopers) and depicted those horses standing or galloping. (Galloping is running by leaping: the front legs go forward together.) One rare vane (Fig. 82) featured a steeplechase horse jumping a gate. Few race tracks were equipped for steeplechasing, and in America it was a novelty. The sport was considered dangerous and was denounced by the Society for the Prevention of Cruelty to Animals in 1885. Few steeplechase vanes were made.

A copper vane manufacturer could have made a pacer vane, but it would have been a special order. By the time harness pacers like Dan Patch won fame (1902), copper weathervane manufacturers were no longer adding new designs to their lines. New weathervane catalogues rarely appeared after the turn of the century. Companies like L. W. Cushing & Sons continued to make vanes into the twentieth century but sold from old catalogues. (Cushing's 1883 catalogue, No. 9, was his last.)

The small horse depicted in Figure 103 was listed in Harris's catalogue as Black Hawk. Almost every weathervane manufacturer made a virtually identical Black Hawk model to commemorate an early harness-racing favorite.

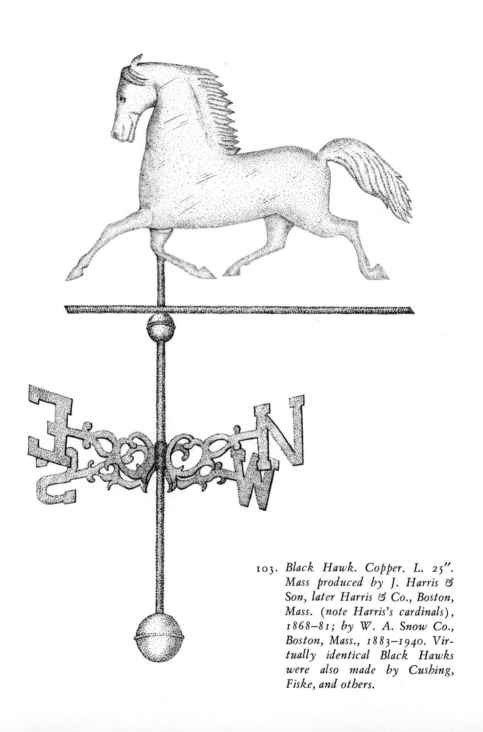

103. *Black Hawk. Copper. L. 25″.*
Mass produced by J. Harris &
Son, later Harris & Co., Boston,
Mass. (note Harris's cardinals),
1868–81; by W. A. Snow Co.,
Boston, Mass., 1883–1940. Vir-
tually identical Black Hawks
were also made by Cushing,
Fiske, and others.

Ethan Allen. Copper. L. 42".
Mass produced by A. L. Jewell &
Co., Waltham, Mass., from about
1853 to 1867. A 30" version
continued to be featured by
Jewell's successors, Cushing &
White, later L. W. Cushing &
Sons, into the twentieth century.
The 42" version was largely su-
perseded by the Cushing firm's
own 42" design.

Black Hawk, foaled in New Hampshire in 1833, strongly resembled several fast trotters from Vermont. All were strong but small and light in weight, with short legs, short tails, and mighty shoulders. Black Hawk made these physical characteristics the beau ideal by winning many trotting purses in the early 1840s. When he began a career at stud in Vermont (1844), farmers newly interested in selective breeding brought their mares great distances and paid one hundred dollars, the top price then paid for the service.

What were the "blood lines" for which they paid so handsomely? The ancestry of Black Hawk and the small Vermont horses was untraceable, so horse breeders substituted stories of a midget wonder horse. In 1842 a sixty-year-old Vermont storekeeper wrote to an agricultural journal claiming that the founding sire of the strong little horses was one his father, Justin Morgan, had owned a half century before. D. C. Linsley, a Vermonter, accepted the storekeeper's story and spent a decade listening to old men's tales and writing a horse "history." His saga, *Morgan Horses*, published in 1857 while Paul Bunyan and Pecos Bill were looming large in the West, told the story of a mighty midget horse of Vermont.

In 1795, Justin Morgan, musician and composer, went to West Springfield, Massachusetts, to collect on a debt and brought home to Randolph, Vermont, an under-sized two-year-old colt of unknown parentage. In Randolph, Morgan hired out the colt, named Figure, to Robert Evans for a year at fifteen dollars. Evans, the story goes, found that the pint-sized colt (about 14 hands, 900 pounds) could clear a wooded hillside of trees better than any other horse. Figure had power, stamina, and speed. He could out-race any horse on road or track with, Linsley wrote, "unvarying success."

Linsley repeated the tale of a log-hauling contest. Evans bet some loggers a gallon of rum that the undersized Figure alone could move a log which the loggers' teams could not move. Linsley recorded Evans's boast: "I am ashamed to hitch my horse to a little log like that, but if three of you will get on and ride, if I don't draw it, I will forfeit the rum." Evans won the rum and Justin Morgan's horse won a powerful reputation.

Soon, the story continues, mares were brought to Figure from everywhere. (Justin Morgan died in 1798, so he benefited little from Figure's two-dollar stud fees.) Figure then displayed his greatest quality—all his foals took after their sire whether their dams were large or small, sound or lame. Linsley decided that one horse, Figure, had sired all the fantastic little horses of Vermont; and that he was Black Hawk's grandsire. Linsley renamed the wonder horse Justin Morgan, in honor of its one-time owner, although Morgan had owned the horse for less than three of its thirty years. Linsley dubbed the breed Morgans.

By the time Linsley "documented" Black Hawk's ancestry, Black Hawk's sons were vying in harness races and Black Hawk probably had died, his death unrecorded, his grave unknown. "It is strange and sad that a horse so venerated should have no monument," laments Morgan-horse enthusiast Jeanne Mellin.

Actually, Black Hawk has more monuments than any other horse. New England's most popular horse weathervanes were small, barely three-dimensional Black Hawks. They were among the cheapest of horse vanes, costing about fifteen dollars. Every manufactured Black Hawk vane has the same pose as the Harris vane (Fig. 103). All, no doubt, were modeled after the same lithographic portrait.

While Figure had lived, no one thought of preserving his likeness. With no portrait to follow, no commercial vanes could be modeled after the breed's founding sire. Many owners of Morgan horses, wanting vanes clearly depicting the Morgan features—small stature, short legs, short tail, muscular neck, and heavy chest—bought Black Hawk vanes. They outsold all others.

Most famous of all the Morgan horses, however, was Black Hawk's son, Ethan Allen. In 1853 as a four-year-old he trotted the mile in 2:36, a record for four-year-olds, and became the darling of the racing public. For eighteen years he held the public's esteem, especially in his native New England. Many called him the "New England Champion," and throughout New England he was known as "Old Ethan."

That affectionate appellation appears on A. L. Jewell's 1867 brochure under the picture of the trotter and sulky vane (see Fig. 86). Jewell had modeled his No. 1 Ethan Allen, 29 inches long, and an identical No. 2 version, 42 inches long (Fig. 104) about 1853, when the famous Morgan was everyone's trotting idol.

Ethan Allen had a special appeal for Yankees because in New England a Morgan was often the family horse. This truly all-purpose breed was used as a light work horse, pulling the new lighter plows; as a riding horse—many Morgans went to war under Union Army saddles; but primarily as a driving horse, to pull the family "shay" or sleigh. During Ethan Allen's career, Morgans pulling family buggies, doctors' chaises, peddlers' wagons, and pleasure vehicles were common sights on the roads and turnpikes.

Pleasure driving was the great pastime for everyone who owned a horse, and almost everyone did. The United States had a higher horse-to-people ratio than any other country. City avenues were often clogged with drivers out for a fast ride. Rural roads were the scenes of friendly trotting matches, for trotting racing was not limited to the track—everyone enjoyed a trotting match with friends or acquaintances. Many challenged every stranger on the road lest another make better time.

In winter the "people's pastime" continued to clog the roads. Everyone found sleighing delightful. Enthusiasts sped over snow-packed roads, bundled in blankets against the frosty air, the quiet broken by the tinkling bells warning others of their approach and the crunch of snow under the trotters' hooves. Sleighing and sleighing matches were perhaps the greatest fun of all.

The nation had "fetlock fever," as one newspaperman called the obsession with fast trotters. While this fever raged, every young man dreamed of owning a fine roadster, as a horse for pleasure driving was called. Every fine roadster deserved a suitable stable; every stable sported a suitable vane.

Alvin Jewell wisely established his copper vane manufactory when the building of stables and carriage houses was booming. And at that time when many of these buildings housed Morgan horses, Jewell astutely designed his No. 1 and No. 2 models after the fastest Morgan of them all.

With the Morgan breed popular all through the North and the West (Ethan Allen helped carry the breed westward and died in Kansas in 1876), Ethan Allen vanes sold well and widely. All vane manufacturers made Ethan Allen models—usually one full-bodied vane and one cheaper, swell-bodied version. Harris's full-bodied Ethan Allen was his prime feature. Cushing, who continued to make Jewell's Old Ethan, listed four Ethan Allen models.

The Cushing & White Ethan Allen illustrated in Figure 105 is the most elaborate of the four. It came in two sizes and with several appurtenances.

No. 1.	29 inches long,			$ 25.00
" 2.	45 " "			65.00
" 1.	29 " "	to Wagon, full length, 40 inches,		50.00
" 2.	45 " "	" " " 50 inches,		100.00
" 1.	29 " "	to Sulky,		45.00
" 2.	45 " "	"		95.00
" 1.	29 " "	to Jockey,		35.00
" 2.	45 " "	"		85.00
" 1.	29 " "	to Bridle,		28.00

A sulky has two wheels, a wagon four. The one-hundred-dollar, 50-inch Ethan Allen harnessed to wagon was Cushing's most expensive trotter vane. (And these gilded copper trotters certainly were expensive. The 45-inch, No. 2. Ethan Allen without appurtenances cost, at sixty-five dollars, the price of a real horse.)

These Cushing & White full-bodied Ethans first went into production in 1868. On January 22 of that year, Leonard Cushing brought to Henry Leach, the carver, some illustrations of the fastest Morgan and a roughly shaped wooden horse—a jigsawed, glued together wooden form that could later be disassembled into its several pieces, each to be cast separately for the mold. Eight days later, Cushing picked up a 29-inch wood carving of Ethan Allen and praised it as "a splendid thing." By March, Hoopers Brass Foundry, Boston, had finished making the molds, and Cushing & White's 29-inch Ethans went into production. In May Leach carved the 45-inch Ethan.

The illustrations from which Leach worked probably included the excellent lithographic print of Ethan Allen made by C. H. Crosby, Boston, and dated 1868. Weathervanes of trotting horses were almost always modeled from lithographs. Jewell's Ethan Allen, the earliest known mass-produced copper weathervane, may have been an exception, having been modeled before weathervane manufacturers began their practice of copying lithographs.

Mass-producible lithographic prints, immensely popular in the mid- and late-nineteenth century, were excellent sources for craftsmen designing vanes of trotting horses. Lithographs were readily available. According to Peter C. Welsh (*Track & Road: The American Trotting Horse*):

105. *Ethan Allen. Copper. L. 29".*
Mass produced by Cushing &
White, later L. W. Cushing &
Sons, Waltham, Mass., beginning
1868.

Prints in infinite variety were sold by the thousands to a public eager to be reminded of the exploits of their heroes, political, military and sporting.

And people pictured their trotting favorites not as they remembered them speeding by on the track, but as they saw them day after day on parlor and office walls. Through lithographic prints, the faithful images of famous trotters lived on, long after the horses had retired from the track.

After Ethan Allen passed from the racing scene, the trotting favorites were no longer Morgans. Standardbreds, leaner, longer-legged trotters, became the top horses on the track and the most popular roadsters for pleasure driving. The standardbred won the appellation, the American Trotter. Morgans, however, continued to be popular as family horses and as business horses for the road. Ethan Allen vanes also continued in favor. Many people remembered that greatest of the Morgan racers. Many had Ethan Allen's name on their own horses' pedigrees (Ethan Allen spent years at stud), and many had Old Ethan's lithographic image hanging on the wall.

Smuggler (Fig. 106) was a natural pacer, but in 1874, the heyday of the trotting track, Smuggler came to Boston to race for the title of Fastest Trotting Stallion in the United States. Wearing two-pound toe weights to correct his gait, Smuggler trotted past more people than ever before had watched a race.

Urban America had found its sport—watching. Spectator sports grew as cities

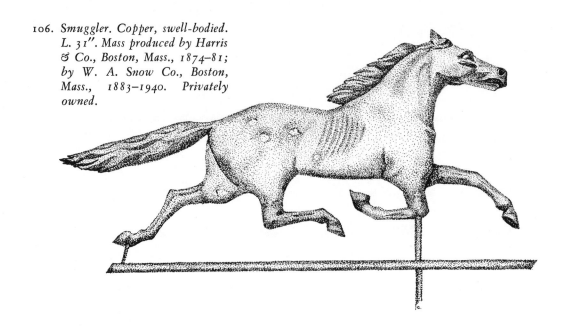

106. Smuggler. Copper, swell-bodied. L. 31″. Mass produced by Harris & Co., Boston, Mass., 1874–81; by W. A. Snow Co., Boston, Mass., 1883–1940. Privately owned.

brought together great numbers of people with little place to play. The first important spectator sport, America's first national sport, was trotting at the harness track. Virtually every town of five thousand had a track. Boston's big track was Mystic Park in suburban Medford.

The *Daily Advertiser* described the exodus from Boston the day of the race, Tuesday, September 15, 1874.

> Teams began to pour out from the city toward Medford as early as noon, and from that time until three o'clock a steady stream of conveyances of every description moved over the hill and along the dusty road—for it was dusty, although it had been watered —out to the track. Not a hack in the city, not a horse, not a conveyance, not a carriage of any kind could be hired in the afternoon, and even a funeral would have had to be postponed. It is estimated that something like 3000 carriages went over Winter Hill. The railroad trains were packed . . . three special trains were run and each of them carried nearly 2000 people. . . . The accommodations inside the park had been increased by the erection of a grand stand capable of seating 6000 people, and this was filled in every part. Every seat in the smaller stand was also taken, and the capacity was increased two or three thousand by putting in stools wherever any vacant spot could be found.

Carriages lined both sides of the track and in all, 40,000 spectators, one tenth the population of the greater Boston area, saw Smuggler win the $10,000 purse.

Lithographers quickly brought out Smuggler prints, and Harris and Cushing added Smuggler models to their weathervane lines. Smuggler vanes sold well.

An era of spectator sports is an era of champions. In the 1870s sports spectators (who exercised their emotions if not their bodies) idolized the standardbred Goldsmith Maid. The champion trotter was the subject of lithographs and weathervanes (Fig. 107), of memoirs, stories, sketches, and a full-length fictionalized biography. Forty-one years after Goldsmith Maid died on a New Jersey farm—forty-eight years after her retirement—Governor A. Harry Moore of New Jersey addressed a distinguished assemblage at the unveiling of a memorial at her grave.

During years when few people crossed the continent even once, Goldsmith Maid crossed from ocean to ocean and back three times in her own Pullman car accompanied by her pet dog. In thirteen seasons of competition, she trotted in 118 matches, won 95, was second in 16, third in 5, fourth in 1, and was unplaced but once. She ran another 26 races against the clock. In 1878 she retired at the age of twenty-one; her career winnings—$364,200—remained unequaled until 1931 when topped by a thoroughbred.

Alden Goldsmith, the mare's owner, had wanted to retire her to breeding when she was twelve years old. She had cost him $850 and had won ten times that amount. But instead he sold her to her trainer for $15,000. The next season (1870), Goldsmith Maid had eleven wins, one defeat, and earned $40,000. In 1871 the Maid, as she was affectionately known to the public, won all the fourteen races in which she ran and set a new world record, a mile in 2:17. Two years later, the sixteen-year-old mare crossed the country in a series of "farewell" appearances.

The Maid was back the next season, won all twenty-one races in which she ran, and repeatedly broke her own records: 2:16, 2:15½, 2:14¾, and on September 2, 1874, at Boston's Mystic Park, 2:14. A thrilled racing public thronged to every Goldsmith Maid performance and went wild. One woman, waving madly at the Maid, replied to the gentleman who pointed out that her child was crying, "Oh, I expect to have several babies, but I never expect to see another Goldsmith Maid."

The Maid's fame was nationwide. Her name and picture sold products. Children had Goldsmith Maid sleds and wagons. Nails from the Maid's shoes were preserved as watch charms. When she finished a race, admirers mobbed her, and her trainers had to cover her from head to toe to keep souvenir hunters from taking every hair from her mane and tail.

It was fortunate that her fans (the word evolved from the fanatical sports

107. *Goldsmith Maid. Copper, full-bodied. L. 28″. Mass produced by Cushing & White and L. W. Cushing & Sons, Waltham, Mass.*

spectators of the late nineteenth century) did not get at her tail or mane, for they were already pitifully thin, as was the rest of the Maid. This national institution, this Queen of Trotters, was a raw-boned bay mare with lean and wiry legs and a gaunt head and neck which admirers called "refined." She was noticeably undersized and had a ridiculously long tail.

Weathervane replicas of Goldsmith Maid were usually honest and therefore unattractive. They did not sell well. Had the Maid been a beauty, perhaps Goldsmith Maid vanes would have been more popular. Weathervanes of mares never sold as well as vanes of stallions or geldings. When Bent manufactured a copper vane of Flora Temple, a very famous trotting mare, Flora was placed face to face with a copper stallion and the vane was called Flora Temple and Mate.

Copper weathervane manufacturers offered a goodly selection, and although every manufacturer listed a Goldsmith Maid, a man choosing his carriage house vane could, and usually did, pick a handsomer horse. Instead of a skinny, gilded Queen of Trotters, many chose a handsome gilded King of the Turf—Dexter (Fig. 108).

That magnificent trotter became the national idol during the Civil War, while the war was making heroes of men and the sports world was making heroes of horses. The war suspended horse racing in the South. In the North, however, racing continued, although one racing enthusiast observed that "during the year 1863 the war caused a great diversion of public attention. . . ." In 1864 the war proved less of a "diversion": that year Dexter made his debut and won immediate admiration and much public attention.

A year later, in 1865, Dexter lowered the record and was dubbed King. The nation turned from warring to sporting competition with renewed vigor and thrilled as Dexter won twenty-four of twenty-five races in 1866. But in 1867, while all were cheering his triumphs, Dexter was suddenly retired.

Dexter posted his record 2:17¼ on August 14, 1867, at beautiful Buffalo Park, a year-old driving track in New York State. Among the excited spectators was the millionaire publisher Robert Bonner who had gone to Buffalo for the event, having stopped first to see Niagara Falls. Bonner reportedly wired a friend substantially as follows: "You know I like to own all the best things. I couldn't buy the falls, but I could buy Dexter, which I did within the hour."

Bonner acquired Dexter for $35,000 and retired the King from the turf. The public was dismayed. The national idol was now one man's private roadster. Racing fans could not even look forward to seeing Dexter's offspring on the turf, for the nervous horse had been so fractious he had been gelded. The fans were left with stories of Dexter's greatness, weathervanes of his glorious form in action, and colored lithographs of Dexter's easily recognizable likeness.

The handsome Dexter had a rich, seal-brown coat set off by a white nose and four white feet. Until Dexter's debut, horsemen had derided such markings:

> *One white foot, buy him;*
> *Two white feet, try him;*
> *Three white feet, sell him to your foes;*
> *Four white feet and a white nose,*
> *Skin him and give him to the crows.*

Dexter ended the crow-bait theory.

Dexter's blaze and spats, his hallmark, were clearly depicted in all lithographs. Oddly enough, they were even shown in weathervane catalogues, although the vanes were sold entirely gilded, with no natural coloration depicted.

Prints of Dexter in action usually show the trotter with his head down. The same pose is seen in most Dexter vanes. Cushing likely modeled his full-bodied Dexter from an 1865 lithograph entitled "The Celebrated Horse 'Dexter' The King of the Turf." Here the 42-inch Dexter (which alone cost fifty dollars) was mounted above a Buffalo Park scroll. Cushing & White made the vane in 1868, most likely for Buffalo Park, where Dexter had trotted his record performance and passed from the professional turf.

Dexter's admiring public kept an eye on its retired favorite. Print makers followed him from the track to the parks and lanes where Bonner enjoyed his renowned roadster. One day in 1869, while out for a fast ride in his road wagon, Bonner handed Dexter's reins to his friend and house guest, Ulysses S. Grant, then president-elect. A lithograph entitled "Taking the Reins" immortalized the scene and won widespread popularity, especially among Republicans.

The political-sporting print of the great war hero and the great racing idol depicted Dexter in his usual pose—head down, muscles straining, speeding along at his graceful gait. John Hervey wrote in *The American Trotter*:

> His gait was a revelation—nothing like it had ever been seen before. While long-striding, he had a magnificent roll of the knee and went with a dash, a fire, an impetuosity that . . . became the beau ideal of trotting action. With flashing eyes, ears pinned back, and an air of indescribable gallantry and gameness, . . .

All that was captured in copper in Cushing & White's full-bodied Dexter.

A full-bodied Dexter vane was the featured model in most weathervane manu-

108. *Dexter and Scroll. Copper. Dexter alone: L. 42". Mass produced Dexter, custom-lettered scroll by Cushing & White, Waltham, Mass., made in 1868, for Buffalo Park driving track, Buffalo, N.Y.*

facturers' catalogues. Dexter raced from 1864 to 1867 and held his title for four years after he retired; thus he was King in the era when weathervane manufacturing was growing. And Dexter vanes remained best sellers even after Goldsmith Maid dethroned him in 1871. Dexter, a year younger than the Maid, was still in Bonner's stable when he lost his title. He died in 1888. Many wondered how long the King could have retained his crown had he not become Bonner's roadster.

No horse had been Dexter's equal during his brief career. At times, he had raced in single harness against a competitor trotting in double harness (i.e., with a running mate to help pull the sulky). The versatile Dexter had raced in one-, two-, and three-mile heats; he had trotted under saddle and harnessed to wagon or sulky. Weathervanes of many trotters could be ordered with bridle (such vanes are extremely rare), or jockey (unusual), or harnessed to two-wheeled sulky (quite popular), or four-wheeled wagon (extremely rare). For a Dexter vane to have any of these appurtenances was not only enhancing to the vane but faithful to trotting history. The vane illustrated in Figure 109 is Dexter harnessed to a wagon.

With champions of the track national sensations and events at the track national news, trotting matches became big business. By the end of Dexter's career the experiments with saddled trotting and trotting to wagon ended; all trotted harnessed to sulky. Gradually the distances were standardized to three one-mile heats. Once agricultural fairs had been the principal arenas for matches designed, at least in part, for the improvement of the breed. Soon, huge driving parks (such as Buffalo Park, Mystic Park) were the scenes of what was unabashedly a sport.

By 1870 trotting was a sport of speed more than of competition. Horses often campaigned just against the clock. In 1878 Goldsmith Maid's mark was lowered one half second by Rarus, a bay gelding who soon joined Dexter in Bonner's stable. A year later, another gelding, St. Julien, set a new record—2:12¾—at the Oakland, California, track. Weathervane designers set to work on St. Julien models.

The glorifying of speed in trotting led to hippodroming—exhibition races where the public saw their favorite out-race all competition in a contest with prearranged results. How the spectators' sport had changed! The pastime which agricultural societies had organized for fun and agricultural science had been transformed into a mass-supported, immensely profitable business—the entertainment business. The stars of these commercial enterprises were superb animals. The agricultural interests and scientific breeders had done their job well. They had developed the magnificent standardbred horse.

The standardbreds, a family of trotters descended from Hambletonian 10, monopolized the track. Their accomplishments were compared to the locomotive; their virtues were proclaimed in race-park oratory. According to the *Daily Advertiser*, Boston, September 16, 1874, the Honorable George B. Loring, awarding medals at Mystic Park, extolled

> . . . the American horse, the Yankee horse, the horse of all horses (applause) . . . the American horse, the horse of all work combining many characteristics in one. How well he represented the nationality to which he belonged! How true to the character of the institutions where one was as good as another and was bound to beat every man he could catch on the road! (applause.)

St. Julien was an American trotter, a standardbred, as were Dexter, Goldsmith Maid, and Rarus before him. St. Julien's turfing feats were confirmation, if confirmation was still needed, of the excellence of the Hambletonian line.

By 1881 Fiske had copyrighted his vane design of St. Julien (always misspelled in Fiske's catalogues as St. Julian) and usually depicted him with sulky and driver, as in Figure 110. An oil painting by Scott Leighton, probably the source for Fiske's design,

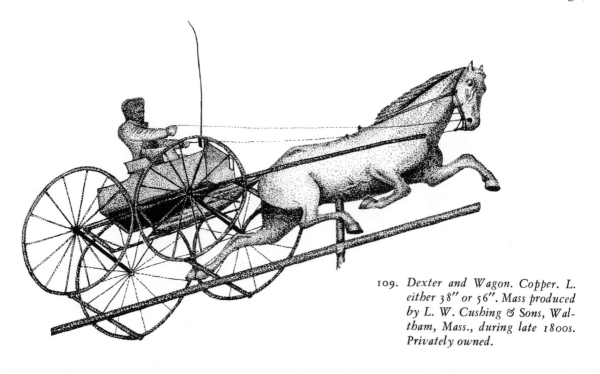

109. *Dexter and Wagon. Copper. L. either 38″ or 56″. Mass produced by L. W. Cushing & Sons, Waltham, Mass., during late 1800s. Privately owned.*

110.

St. Julien. Copper; horse's head cast in zinc or bronze. L. 38½". Mass produced by J. W. Fiske, New York, since 1880s. Illustrated with Fiske cardinals. Still available from J. W. Fiske Architectural Metals, Inc., Paterson, New Jersey.

shows St. Julien driven by Orrin Hickok. Hickok's brother, Wild Bill, was a hero of the West. St. Julien, too, was a western hero; he won his title in California. No doubt many St. Julien vanes were shipped westward.

In the South, where the draft animal was the mule, there was no call for the standardbred, "the horse of all work combining many characteristics in one." The horse a southern gentleman mounted was a thoroughbred. The thoroughbred turf, not the trotting turf, attracted southern sportsmen both before the Civil War and after the war when racing revived. For national popularity, however, thoroughbred racing could not rival the trotting track, not even at the end of the nineteenth century when the saddled sport prospered in southern and middle-Atlantic states.

Late-nineteenth-century copper weathervane manufacturers included only a few thoroughbred models amid their many trotter vanes. Thoroughbred vanes were no competition for trotters in the lucrative carriage-house trade. Not only were thorough-breds less widely renowned as sport horses, they were not particularly appropriate as carriage-house finials. They were riding horses, not carriage-pulling horses.

Thoroughbred vanes made in New England were primarily for shipment south, where they obtained positions on thoroughbred stables. And at the luxurious throughbred racing parks, galloper vanes—often with jockeys up—adorned grandstand, clubhouses, stables, and judges' stands.

A copper vane of a galloping or standing thoroughbred was more likely to carry a rider than was a trotter vane. Most horse vanes were trotters, but a trotter vane with jockey is unusual (as indeed saddled trotters had become unusual). Thoroughbred

111. *Kentucky with Jockey. Copper, full-bodied. L. 32". Mass produced in the late nineteenth century possibly by J. L. Mott & Co., New York, from a mold now owned by E. G. Washburne & Co., Danvers, Mass.*

vanes are far fewer in number, but it is not unusual for a thoroughbred vane to be mounted.

The copper vane illustrated in Figure 111 is of the thoroughbred horse Kentucky, probably made from a mold currently owned, and still used, by E. G. Washburne & Co. Among the weathervane molds and forms acquired by Washburne when the weathervane industry was collapsing after the turn of the century seems to have been those of J. L. Mott Iron Works. Mott's late-nineteenth-century catalogues listed this model (and many other designs which Washburne now makes). Whether Mott, Washburne, or even some other weathervane maker originated this design is unknown. (Fiske made an almost identical model.) What is known is that the vane illustrated is of old manufacture. It has the clean seams and the careful and detailed crafting of the bridle that indicate nineteenth-century workmanship.

Often a small, swell-bodied galloper was designated in a weathervane catalogue merely as "horse." The "horse" could be placed over a gate (Fig. 82) or a ball, or shown jumping through a hoop, or, as in the highly unusual vane in Figure 112, carrying a bareback rider.

The bareback rider, the horse and hoop, and an elephant vane of J. W. Fiske were symbols of the circus spectacle which began in ancient times with equestrian acts and culminated in America in the most spectacular of entertainments.

Wandering acts of jugglers, rope dancers, trained animals, and comics, each traveling on its own, had for centuries amused folk here and abroad. In nineteenth-century America, a unified show, joined by an equestrian ring, took to the road. When the traveling tent show added the menagerie and sideshow, the spectacle became distinctly American.

The sideshow had originated when menageries, freaks, and sharpers took advantage of the crowds attracted to agricultural fairs and set up just outside the fairgrounds. These "outside" shows did so well they were taken into the fairgrounds, becoming sideshows. Phineas T. Barnum ran a permanently located sideshow-type entertainment in New York City and called it a "museum." (Improving the mind was more acceptable than having fun.) Barnum's American Museum became an institution in the 1840s.

Twice, in 1865 and 1868, fire gutted Barnum's Museum. So in 1871 the sixty-one-year-old Barnum took his show on the road, combining it first with Coup's circus and then with Bailey's. This expanded show and others which followed brought glamor to the lives of rural Americans. For many it was the event of their lifetimes. They saw within the menagerie tent, the sideshow tent, and the immense main tent (three rings encircled by a hippodrome track and ten thousand spectators) what seemed to them all the sights of the world.

112. *Bareback Rider. Copper, partly filled and weighted with lead. L. 33½". Made in the late nineteenth century. Maker unknown. Shelburne Museum, Shelburne, Vt.*

The region of the southern Connecticut-New York border was called the "Cradle of the American Circus." Almost all the early circus men and circus money came from there. Much of the region's small industry serviced the circus. There, people might well have selected a circus vane. Among their native sons were P. T. Barnum, showman, legislator, and mayor of Bridgeport, Connecticut, and Barnum's greatest attraction—the talented midget, Tom Thumb.

The area which nurtured the minuscule entertainer and the giant of entertainment adjoined the Connecticut home of the Yankee tin peddlers. The circus men were itinerant peddlers too—vendors of entertainment. When the persuasive Barnum had finished peddling his wares, America no longer saw anything wrong in having fun.

With the acceptance of spectator sports came approval of participatory sports. All could play, but not at the same activities. The vane illustrated in Figure 113 possibly represents a circus equestrian, but more likely a gentleman engaged in the favorite pastime of the elite—horseback riding.

High society chose recreational activities which were too expensive to be anything but aristocratic pastimes: group hunts, yachting, and, most of all, horses. (Every man could watch the races but only the wealthy could support breeding farms and stables full of fine horses.) Polo, from its introduction in the United States in 1876, was a rich man's sport because the training and keeping of the necessary string of polo horses is exceedingly expensive. The horse show initially was open to all. (The first one, in 1883, featured an appearance by the twenty-six-year-old Goldsmith Maid.) But within a decade, the annual activities resembled a night at the opera more than a livestock exhibition, being an occasion for jewels even more than for judges.

The select few (four hundred when Mrs. Astor made up her famous guest list) had become alarmed by trends toward democratization, and in the late nineteenth century

113. *Man on Horseback. Galvanized iron, painted. L. 32½". Made in late nineteenth or early twentieth century. Maker unknown. Eleanor and Mabel Van Alstyne Collection, Smithsonian Institution, Washington, D.C.*

they embraced the aristocratic most ardently. Nothing was more aristocratic than a gentleman on his mount—the very idea of a gallant man was a man on horseback—so, in society, horsemanship was a requisite. One never mentioned a gentleman's attributes without noting his abilities as a horseman.

C. K. G. Billings's 1903 dinner invitations, therefore, although different were not out of keeping. This heir to a Chicago utility fortune invited a few gentleman friends to be his guests at Louis Sherry's in New York. His invitations included their horses. According to *The New York Times*, July 24, 1966, for the dinner, the ballroom

> was disguised as a woodland garden with sod on the floor, real birds singing from full-scale scenic backdrops lining the walls and a man-made harvest moon beaming down on the 36 guests and their mounts. A table was attached to each thoroughbred and as the diners ate an impressive number of courses they could sip champagne through rubber tubes leading to iced bottles in the saddlebags.

The Puritan notion that a horse was a gentleman's mount had not been dispelled but acknowledged. What had vanished was the Puritan determination not to behave like aristocrats.

The "four million," O. Henry's answer to the "four hundred," had their sports too, often games that high society shunned. A simple, inexpensive weathervane design (Fig. 114) depicts one such inexpensive pastime.

Bowling had been American since the Dutch settled Manhattan. The New England green, however, had never been a bowling green. In the years when Yankees frowned upon frivolity, ball sports had seemed especially frivolous. In 1816 Worcester, Massachusetts, passed a law "prohibiting the playing of ball in the public streets. . . ." In 1822 Yale College forbade playing "football" (a game played with a round ball) in the college building or yard.

But after the spectacular Goldsmith Maid and the spectacles of Barnum, in an era when some men dined on horseback, who could condemn playing ball? Between 1869 and 1875, the first professional baseball game was played, soccer and rugby were introduced to American campuses, modern football evolved, and ten-pin bowling began. The United States National Lawn Tennis Association was formed in 1881. Between 1888 and

1895, golf, basketball, ice hockey, and volleyball were invented or introduced, and ten-pin bowling was standardized.

Bowling at ten pins was not the game of the New York Dutch. They had bowled at nine pins (i.e., three rows of three pins each). Nine-pin bowling had spread to New England in the early nineteenth century but soon the sport was in trouble. Frank G. Menke, quoting Elmer H. Baumgarten in *The Encyclopedia of Sports*, asserts:

> Bowling alleys were frequented principally by hustlers, touts, hangers-on, cheap gamblers and disreputable individuals. The situation was such as to disgust business, professional and decent working-men who enjoyed bowling.
>
> Teams and individuals oftentimes permitted themselves to be beaten in match games rather than be beaten physically by rowdies upon leaving establishments where these matches were bowled. The entire situation was disgusting, deplorable, disorderly and chaotic.

So, several eastern states, including Connecticut, home of the "blue laws," passed laws prohibiting bowling at nine pins. Bowlers, disconsolate over the ban, used some Yankee ingenuity and developed the game of ten pins. The triangular arrangement of ten pins, four rows deep, skirted the ban on nine pins.

The vane's bowler is playing at ten pins, for looking broadside at the ten pins one sees four. Since the ten-pin game began after the Civil War era, the vane does not predate it and probably was produced about the turn of the century.

About 1900 a new style of vane came into vogue. The "modern style" vanes were silhouetted scenes usually cut from sheet iron, occasionally of sheet copper. Many mid-twentieth-century vanes in "modern" style are similarly scenes but are cast of aluminum. Scenic vanes depict not merely a symbol but some background as well: a ship with waves, a horse with grassy turf, a cow under a tree, a setter on grassy uplands, even an airplane with clouds. Few scenic vanes have the action and vitality of the ten-pin bowler at play.

9.
Fabulous, and Fancy Creatures

Imagination is not a talent of some men but is the health of every man.
RALPH WALDO EMERSON
Poetry and Imagination

Not all play is physical; minds play too, sporting with fantasy and fancy. Men pass the time conjuring myth and whimsy, and reinterpreting the fantasy of earlier times. The gods of ancient Greek and Roman narrative and sculpture reappear often in American fine and folk art, from paintings of Venus to fountains representing Bacchus. The sculptural art of American weathervanes was as susceptible as any art form to the charm of ancient mythological creatures.

Weathervanes of Greek gods were especially popular during America's classical revival. The citizens of the young nation saw their democracy as that of ancient Greece reborn, as Rome's republic made workable. They immortalized American dignitaries in paint and marble—wearing togas. They constructed buildings (from public edifices to backyard privies) to look like Greek temples, and painted them the white of Hellenic marble. They crowned many with gleaming weathervane-versions of Greek lyres (Figs. 43, 44) or Greek gods.

Of all the Greek deities none was so meaningful to New Englanders as Triton, a minor sea deity who was pictured as human from the waist up and fish from the waist down. The first Triton, according to myth, was the son of Poseidon, god of the sea. Triton symbolized the roaring sea; his chief attribute was the shell which he used as a horn, blowing loudly or softly as he chose, to arouse or calm the ocean. New Englanders, well versed in ancient myth, were as sea-minded as the seafaring ancient Greeks. Triton caught their fancy as a weathervane subject (Fig. 115).

The prime source of information on classical architecture for the architects and builders of America's "alabaster cities" was Vitruvius's treatise *De Architectura*, the only book on architecture to survive from antiquity. It contains a description of the earliest known weathervane.

The ancient Greek vane, a Triton, has been lost for centuries, but the building it turned above still stands and is now popularly known as the Tower of the Winds. The eight-sided marble tower, over forty feet high, is a horologium (hour recorder) built about 48 B.C. at the northwest foot of the Acropolis in Athens by Andronicus of Cyrrhus. It measured time by means of a clepsydra (water clock) housed within and a sundial incised on the outside walls. Its octagonal shape presented a wall to each of the eight principal wind directions. On each of the sides, above the sundial's lines, a figure was sculpted in relief representing one of the eight winds. These served as cardinals for the weathervane which once turned above the marble roof.

The weathervane was described by Vitruvius, a Roman architect who worked about 25 B.C.:

. . . and above it [the tower] he [Andronicus] placed a bronze Triton holding a rod in his right hand. He also contrived that it was driven round by the wind, and always faced the current of air, and held the rod as indicator above the representation of the wind blowing.

From Vitruvius's detailed explanation, it would seem that the wind-pointing device had not yet a name and certainly was not yet customary. When in 36 B.C., the Roman Marcus Terentius Varro described his aviary in *De Re Rustica*, he wrote that its domed ceiling was marked with eight compass winds around the axis "as in the horologium at Athens." Varro had a pointer under the roof turning to indicate to those within the aviary which wind was blowing. He made no reference to the shape of the wind catcher above the aviary roof.

115. *Triton. Copper, painted. L. 32¼″. Made probably early nineteenth century. Maker unknown. Eleanor and Mabel Van Alstyne Collection, Smithsonian Institution, Washington, D.C.*

Andronicus of Cyrrhus may have invented the weathervane when he made the Triton for the horologium. He fashioned it as a meteorological instrument (indeed his entire tower was a scientific instrument). Later, weathervanes became what they are in the American tradition—crowns for buildings. The American Triton depicted in Figure 116 even carries the classical crown, a laurel wreath.

Pegasus, the winged horse, was, according to Greek myth, the offspring of Poseidon's sea foam and the blood of the slaughtered Medusa. His name means "springs of water" or "vapors which rise from the sea." On a vane now in the Shelburne Museum (Fig. 117) the place where the wave ends and the winged horse begins is marked by paint alone. Pegasus, wave, and pointer are all of one piece of sheet iron. The vane is probably turn of the century or early twentieth century. That was the era of scenic vanes, the flat, silhouetted figures depicted with some scenery and usually cut out of sheet iron.

Many vanes have been made of sheet iron (early meetinghouse vanes, for ex-

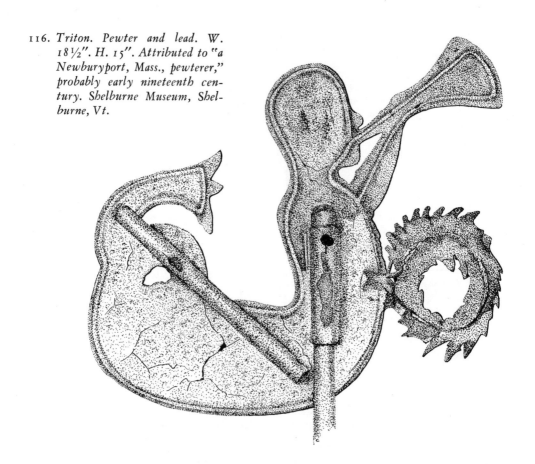

ample), and a few, such as the cock and the horse (Figs. 58, 59), were even cast of iron. But iron is not a durable weathervane material; it is severely corroded by the air and water to which weathervanes are continually exposed. When used outdoors, iron needs a protective film. On the old meetinghouse fanes gold leaf was used. The iron scenics of 1900, however, were usually protected with paint, at times in several colors. Over the years such vanes needed repeated and frequent repainting.

Wooden vanes were almost always painted. Paint is simply applied, effective, and decorative. Gilded wood is not particularly durable when exposed to weather and re-

117. *Pegasus. Iron, painted. L. 35".
H. 29½". Made early in the
twentieth century. Maker unknown. Shelburne Museum, Shelburne, Vt.*

quires an additional operation in the finishing—the wood must be given a coat of gesso (plaster) to provide the smooth surface needed for the application of the tissue-thin sheets of gold.

The Pegasus depicted in Figure 118 is one of few gilded wooden vanes. (For another which originally was gilded see Fig. 101.) Its finish, however, is not its most unusual feature. The carving is distinctive and successful. The simplified lines and slender grace impart an illusion of speed such as only a winged horse could attain.

The most common material for the construction of weathervanes—and the

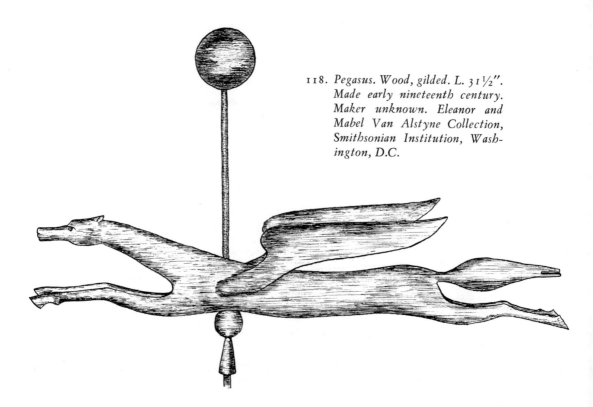

118. *Pegasus. Wood, gilded. L. 31½″. Made early nineteenth century. Maker unknown. Eleanor and Mabel Van Alstyne Collection, Smithsonian Institution, Washington, D.C.*

most durable—is copper. Copper resists fracture, is exceptionally malleable (thus easily wrought into complicated shapes) and extremely ductile (thus easily drawn into wire). Yet perhaps copper's most important property as a weathervane medium is its extraordinary ability to withstand atmospheric corrosion. When, after long exposure, it slowly oxidizes, it becomes coated with verdigris, a bluish-green patina. Unlike iron's rust, which is porous and brings on more rusting, verdigris becomes a protective coating. (It was for good reason that Andronicus's Triton was made of bronze, a copper alloy.)

Early American vanes had often been of iron simply because copper was then exceedingly scarce. Once rolled copper became readily available in the late eighteenth century, no other material could rival its popularity for weathervanes. As a result of the wide productivity of the late-nineteenth-century copper weathervane industry, copper vanes soon outnumbered vanes of other materials.

Nineteenth-century weathervane makers did not leave the copper of their vanes exposed. They did not want as a finish the soft sheen of copper or the bluish-green of verdigris. They wanted the gleam of gold, and copper's smooth surface takes easily to gold leaf and tenaciously retains it for about a half century. That is a decided asset for a vane, because regilding is an indoor job necessitating two lofty climbs by roofer or steeplejack.

Thus copper was a superior weathervane material to iron, which has to be laboriously worked to a smooth finish for gilding, and to wood, which has to be given a coat of gesso before gilding. Once exposed to weather, neither wood nor iron holds gold leaf nearly as long as copper. Neither can lead-alloy or zinc-alloy castings, which were often used for heads on vanes otherwise of sheet copper and was probably used for the torso of the centaur shown in Figure 119. Sometimes a trotter vane can be seen gleaming with gold over its sheet copper body but with a grayed head cast of lead.

One of the reasons for casting the forward part of a vane in solid metal was that the process allowed fine detail to be easily reproduced. But a more important reason was that the cast head gave weight to the part of the vane forward of the spindle. Because

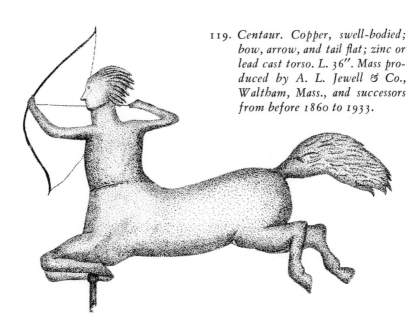

119. *Centaur. Copper, swell-bodied; bow, arrow, and tail flat; zinc or lead cast torso. L. 36". Mass produced by A. L. Jewell & Co., Waltham, Mass., and successors from before 1860 to 1933.*

120. *Mermaid. Wood, bronze mirror. L. 52½". Attributed to Warren Gould Roby, made in the mid-nineteenth century for his barn at Wayland, Mass. Shelburne Museum, Shelburne, Vt.*

most of the vane had to be behind the spindle to catch the wind, the cast head tended to balance the vane with the spire at the fulcrum. Vanes do not need to be balanced exactly, but when a vane is too unbalanced, it turns jerkily and its spindle wears badly. Vanes which are entirely of hollow sheet copper often carry weights within the hollow heads to achieve better balance.

The copper centaur (Fig. 119) with cast torso was among the early products of the copper weathervane industry and came from that early (if not first) weathervane manufactory of A. L. Jewell & Co. in Waltham, Massachusetts. Sometime before 1867 Jewell modeled the mythical creature—or astrological sign, because a centaur represents Sagittarius, the archer—and listed it in his brochure (Fig. 86) as No. 28. Other weathervane manufacturers also made centaur vanes, for the pattern is appealing, combining as it does two familiar weathervane themes—a running horse and an archer.

Wood has always been favored as weathervane material by men who wanted to make personal vanes as suggested by their imagination. Wood was readily available and easy to work with. A homemade wooden vane was usually painted, but not every painted wooden vane was homemade. The delightful wooden mermaid illustrated in Figure 120 was clearly the work of a craftsman. The carving is so elegant and sophisticated in design and detail that few would think it homemade.

One might assume the vane came from some coastal town, perhaps the home port of a vessel named *Mermaid*. Pauline A. Pinckney wrote in *American Figureheads and Their Carvers:*

> When the barque *Mermaid* was built, the carver, whose name was not given any publicity, ornamented the bow with a mermaid who held a comb in one hand and mirror in the other.

The arms of such a pine figurehead would be removable so they could be taken safely aboard while the vessel was on the high seas. The arms of this pine figure too are separable. The vane also has much of the forward and upward movement of a figurehead rising at the bow. Figurehead carvers occasionally worked on vanes. A Boston figurehead carver, E. Warren Hastings, made the wood model for Cushing's angel Gabriel (Fig. 40). Was this too the work of a figurehead carver, some companion-piece to a figurehead—a mermaid for the merchant's ship, a second for his cupola?

No. This mermaid was found, not on a boathouse, but on a barn; not in a seaport, but in Wayland, Massachusetts, sixteen miles inland. The barn had once belonged to Warren Gould Roby, a coppersmith and brazier. Town folklore says he carved the vane. Mr. Roby depicted the mythical sea nymph as she has been depicted since her origin in antiquity and throughout her widespread popularity in medieval Europe—combing her hair with one hand and holding a mirror in the other.

It was not strange that a man in Wayland would choose a sea motif; the New Englander's traditional love for the sea was possessed even by those landlocked in the Berkshires. Nor should anyone wonder why coppersmith Roby made his vane of wood. Coppersmiths and braziers were, of course, skilled in wood carving because the first step in making forms of copper or brass was usually making a model in wood. One can only guess, however, why Mr. Roby did not translate his carving into copper.

Perhaps he wanted his design, this female of his fancy, to be the only vane of its kind. Triton vanes, half man and half fish, were quite popular, but a mermaid vane, half woman and half fish, was most unusual. By putting his wooden carving on top of his barn, Mr. Roby kept his mermaid unreproducible. Had he translated his design into copper, the only way he could have ensured its uniqueness would have been to destroy the wooden model.

Who would blame him if he could not?

The fantastic creatures of amalgamation—the human-fish, Triton and mermaid; the human-animal, centaur; and the mammal-bird, Pegasus, originated in ancient

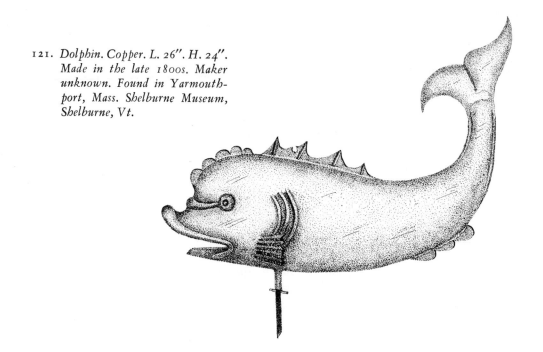

*121. Dolphin. Copper. L. 26″. H. 24″.
Made in the late 1800s. Maker
unknown. Found in Yarmouthport, Mass. Shelburne Museum,
Shelburne, Vt.*

times around the Mediterranean. The mammal-fish depicted in the weathervane shown in Figure 121 did not assume its improbable combination of characteristics until a later era.

This vane was intended to portray a dolphin, a favorite symbol of the ancient Greeks and a popular motif in American crafts during the period of the Greek revival. The Greeks put the dolphin on their coins much as we put the eagle on ours. The ancients knew the dolphin well and portrayed him accurately. Even in Greek mythology, the dolphin comes closer to nature's truth than this weathervane dolphin does.

The wine-god, Dionysus, the story goes, hired a ship to sail to Naxos. The sailors, really pirates, planned to sell Dionysus into slavery. The resourceful wine-god turned the masts and sails to snakes and filled the ship with ivy, driving the pirates to leap into the sea, where they at once became dolphins. Thus the Greeks explained the origin of the intelligent dolphin. Oppian (*Halieutica* I:649–52) wrote that "by the devising of

Dionysus they exchanged the land for the sea and put on the form of fishes." Not until Darwin did men again understand that dolphins were land-living mammals who returned to the sea and there evolved into "the form of fishes."

One "form of fishes" which the dolphin did not assume was gills. Among the nineteenth-century Americans who did not know that was the creator of this vane. He went beyond nature to make his dolphin appear seaworthy. He gave it gills and the fins of a fish instead of the dolphin's blowhole, flippers, and single dorsal fin. However, he shaped the dolphin's face and tail-flukes more realistically. He did make the flukes vertical although in nature they are horizontal, but that may be considered artistic license in vane making. The curve he gave the body is truly dolphinlike; a mammal arches his spine while a fish wiggles his backbone sideways.

Even if the vane has more of the "form of fishes" than a dolphin needs, it has every virtue that a weathervane needs. Its bottlenose serves as a pointer, whereas the sperm whale (Fig. 30) sorely lacks one. The bend of the back and the sweep of the tail make clear to the observer which end catches the wind. The grace of the creature's curving form and the bright-eyed look on its face say "dolphin" clearer than gills or fish fins can deny it.

The vane's creator probably got his concept of the dolphin from heraldry. Medieval Europeans portrayed the dolphin as exceedingly fishlike, even giving him scales. With far less knowledge of natural history than the observant ancient Greeks, they considered the dolphin the king of fishes. Like the king of animals, the lion, the dolphin was popular on coats of arms. Heraldic dolphins with fish fins, gills, and scales adorned the arms of the Fishmongers Company of London, of families with naval traditions or whose names were related to "dolphin," and of seaport towns. Whatever the name or occupation of this vane's owner, the dolphin certainly was fitting for his home town—Yarmouthport on Cape Cod.

The twelfth sign of the Zodiac—Pisces, the fishes—is usually depicted with the two fishes facing in opposite directions. The wind kept the two on the vane shown in Figure 122 facing the same way; nevertheless, they are easily recognizable as Pisces and make a fine vane for someone born under that sign. However, it was not customary for people to select vanes representing their astrological signs, and such vanes are exceedingly rare. (The only other one of which I know is the mass-produced centaur, probably made to represent the creature of myth rather than the Zodiac's Sagittarius.) Possibly this vane was

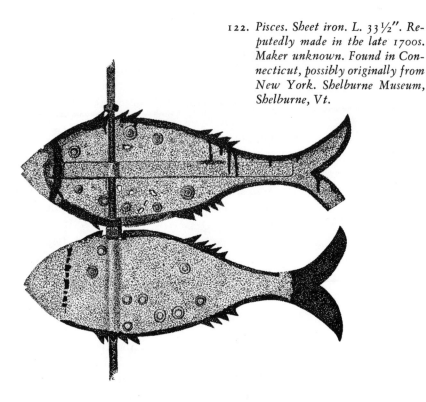

made for a practitioner of the ancient pseudo-science of predicting human events from celestial patterns.

Astrologers were not as commonplace in colonial America as they had been in Europe a few centuries before. Yet eighteenth-century slave traders in Newport, Rhode Island, customarily employed astrologers to cast horoscopes to determine the day and hour at which a vessel should weigh anchor. In a letter accompanying one such ship's horoscope, dated August 22, 1752, the astrologer boasted that his computations were much more rigorous than those in the almanac.

Astrological advice was, of course, readily available in most almanacs. No book other than the Bible played as intimate a part in the lives of New Englanders as the almanac. Often Bible and almanac were the family's entire library. Even on scholars' voluminous bookshelves, a place was assured for a farmer's almanac. The annual publication, designed to tell which days were best for which activities, was quite naturally astrological, as almanacs had been for centuries. In ancient Rome, farmers' calendars were carved on marble blocks with astrological data, earthly events, and agricultural advice concisely listed month by month, each marked with a sign of the Zodiac. Propitious days were commonly discerned through astrology until sixteenth- and seventeenth-century astronomers gave the world a new understanding of the relationships among sun, earth, other planets, and stars.

Astrology then lost much of its importance. Most seventeenth- and eighteenth-century Americans considered it a "false science." In 1690 the editor of *Poor Robin's Almanack*, acknowledging that horoscopes were as necessary to almanacs "as a Nose for a man's Face," included a spoof-horoscope entitled "The Ass-trological Scheme" so "a man may foretel things that never will be. . . ." Poor Robin's horoscopes were humorous and accurate, as, for example, this one published in 1697:

> This month [December] will be more Employment for Cooks and Fiddlers, than for Reapers and Haymakers; . . . very few poor Men this *Chrismas* will get Surfeits by over-eating 'emselves at rich Men's tables. . . .

By 1792 when Robert Thomas began publication of his highly successful *Farmer's Almanack*, it was possible to keep it free of astrology. Mr. Thomas, who adored "that devine science, Astronomy," filled his almanac with astronomical calculations while proudly eschewing astrology and horoscopes. Nevertheless, even Mr. Thomas's almanac used the signs of the Zodiac to illustrate each month's calendar just as the Romans had on their marble versions. (Pisces, February 19–March 20, was used as the sign for February in American almanacs, for March on Roman calendars.)

Other American almanacs did include astrology. Along with a horoscope, perhaps subtitled "Done for Fun," they included "the Anatomy" or "the Man of the Signs," a human figure surrounded by the twelve signs of the Zodiac, each with an arrow pointing to the part of the anatomy it "governed." Pisces, for example, "governed" the feet. The figure, of thirteenth-century or earlier origin, was widely consulted in the days when medicine was administered as much by the arrangements of the stars as by the nature of the ailment. This vane could have suited a podiatrist had there been such in the late eighteenth century.

The butterfly, unlike centaurs and mermaids, is a common creature of nature; but its grace and form make it uncommonly fancy.

Nineteenth-century Americans adored the fancy. Simplicity was beauty to

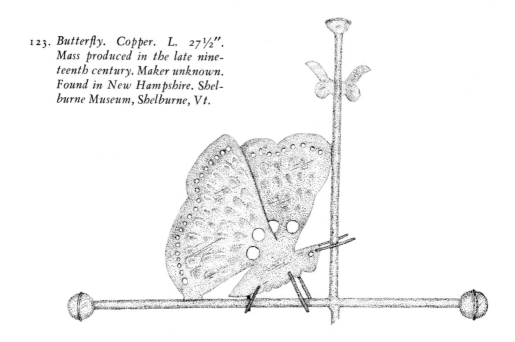

123. *Butterfly. Copper. L. 27½".
Mass produced in the late nineteenth century. Maker unknown.
Found in New Hampshire. Shelburne Museum, Shelburne, Vt.*

the Shakers only; to everyone else, fancy was beauty. Victorians mistook ornament for good design. Copiously carved animals, fabulous creatures, and flowers adorned their furniture and woodwork. Accumulations of innumerable objects cluttered every available space in their homes.

Later generations have been critical of the "dust collectors" in Victorian homes. But at the time, after generations of at best affording a few family treasures, the "art objects" and "fancy things" made available by the age of machines must have been irresistible. So knickknacks, "fancy goods," and "art-workmanship" crowded Victorian interiors, while similarly, ornaments crowded building exteriors. Among the latter were weathervanes.

The vanes were often of the same motifs as the fancy goods over the mantel. Butterflies, among nature's fanciest creatures, were prominent in late-nineteenth-century ornamental design. The butterfly motif in paint, porcelain, wood, and in gilded copper in the weathervane illustrated in Figure 123, lent its decorativeness to the restless anarchy that was Victorian decor.

On February 27, 1871, according to his business journal, Leonard Cushing made up a new price list to include the patterns which Cushing & White had added to the weathervane line they had acquired from Jewell. Between September 1867 and the start of 1871, they had added two Ethan Allens, two Dexters, new eagles, new roosters, the 60-inch Goddess of Liberty, the angel Gabriel, a locomotive, a clipper ship, a sloop, a yacht, a vane which Cushing called "carriages," a 42-inch cow, a new deer, the fox and hound, and the squirrel eating a nut depicted in Figure 124.

Squirrel vanes are unusual, but Cushing & White's was not the only squirrel design. For very "Victorian" reasons, this rodent seemed a suitable weathervane subject.

Several attributes of the fluffy-tailed tree climber seem most compatible with the wind-pointing job. The tree climber is often seen aloft as weathervanes are. However, being land-bound did not preclude a slithering snake at the elevated post. The broad surface of the squirrel's tail is ideal for weathervane wind catching. But, thin tails did not prevent the rat-tailed sheep from being weathervane subjects. The squirrel's plumelike tail is fancy, making him a decorative creature. The rabbit, with an equally fancy fluffy tail, became a popular motif in other nineteenth-century decorative crafts.

The rabbit, however, was too often a garden pest to be honored with weathervane eminence. (I know of only one wooden vane depicting the fabled hare and tortoise.) The squirrel was different. He was known as a frugal, hard-working creature, and Victorians esteemed thrift and industry. For them, the squirrel's fabled virtues (even more than his fancy tail) warranted the prestigious position of weathervane.

The fancy and frills of Victorian decor were not for the home alone. Women in hourglass corsets wore draped, fringed, and ruffled bustled dresses. Their hats were laden with ribbons, cloth flowers, and feathers. When hatless, women often wore feathers in their hair. The plume of the ostrich was a favorite costume accessory and came to be almost a symbol of the era. As Elizabeth K. Mitchel wrote in *The Ostrich and Ostrich Farming*:

> Something in . . . the spirit of the times during the latter half of the nineteenth century and the beginning of the twentieth, . . . harmonized well with the ostrich feather. Perhaps the generously curling plume with its grace and elegance and its soft fullness, expressed well something in the prevailing spirit; unhurried, but robust and fruitful.

Trade in ostrich feathers first threatened the bird with extinction, then led to

124. Squirrel Eating Nut. Copper, gilded. H. 18". Mass produced by Cushing & White, later L. W. Cushing & Sons, Waltham, Mass. Designed in 1870. Listed in 1882 catalogue at $30.

125. Ostrich. Copper. H. 40½". Mass produced by J. W. Fiske, New York, about 1890. Sold for $65.

the domestication of the ostrich, bringing prosperity to South Africa's cities of export. Feathers arrived in the United States by the ton.

Its fashionable plume made the African bird the subject of an American vane (Fig. 125). This Fiske vane, listed in his 1893 catalogue as No. 527, at sixty-five dollars, may have been used on a feather shop or a factory where plumes were cut, sewn, and wired together to make them even fluffier. Or the vane could have been placed on an ostrich farm in the American Southwest where, in the late nineteenth century, American farmers sought to cash in on the plume-prosperity.

While ostrich plumes decorated women, the splendid feathers of the peacock's train were used like flowers to decorate rooms. Pictures and figures of peacocks were featured in interior design; outdoors, the hardy birds decoratively roamed in the gardens of estates.

The shape of the bird and the design of its feathers made the peacock a favorite subject of art nouveau, a movement in crafts and decoration which flourished at the turn of the century. Art nouveau craftsmen, in reaction to an age of machines, tried to encourage crafts and return to natural subjects and nature's forms. They favored undulating lines and asymmetrical designs, and found both in the shape of the peacock.

The peacock motif was so much the rage in turn-of-the-century design that it overcame a long-standing superstition among theater people—a "horror of peacock feathers." In 1903 New York's New Amsterdam theater was decorated with "two peacocks in mosaic, in panels over two fountains . . . , and sixteen peacocks to decorate the proscenium." Not to be outdone, Florenz Ziegfeld presented his wife, Anna Held, in *Miss Innocence*, "a musical extravaganza in which a group of girls dressed as peacocks danced the 'peacock strut.' Miss Held made a spectacular entrance as a glorified white peacock." Even the ordinary woman with her bustled skirt trailing behind and ostrich plume topping her coiffure bore more than a casual resemblance to a strutting peacock.

Peacock vanes, typically with feathered crests—missing in the particular example illustrated in Figure 126—were part of the repertoire of most weathervane companies.

The sinuous swirls and flowing lines of art nouveau found another suitable subject in the swan. The decorative grace of its curving neck, the ease and beauty with which it swims, brought these decorative birds, also, to elegant estates and garden ponds. Though swans were more common than peacocks, a swan vane (Fig. 127) was much rarer than a peacock vane, for the peacock was the epitome of the age.

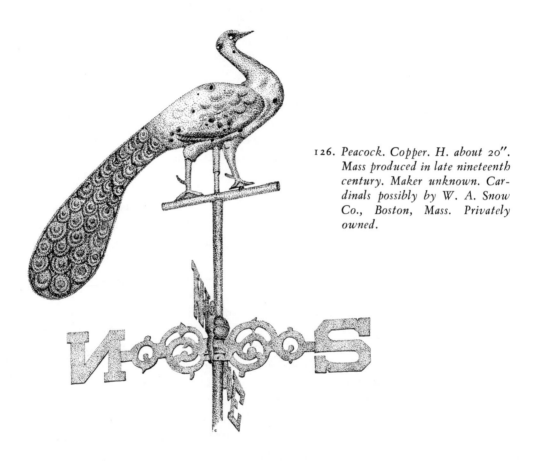

126. *Peacock. Copper. H. about 20".*
Mass produced in late nineteenth
century. Maker unknown. Car-
dinals possibly by W. A. Snow
Co., Boston, Mass. Privately
owned.

The white stork is an Old World bird well known in America for its fabled occupation. In myth, the stork brings good fortune and newborn babies. By repute, the stork is long-lived, monogamous, and returns to the same nest year after year. In actuality, storks commonly nest atop people's houses, and some Europeans build rooftop platforms hoping that the "lucky" birds will abide on their roofs.

The stork fable is so popular and widespread that the image of the bird is recognized by all, even in lands like the United States were the stork is not native. Everyone who saw the weathervane illustrated as No. 59 in Harris's 1879 catalogue knew the bird's identity and reputation. Few people, however, chose stork vanes. Although mass-produced, the one illustrated in Figure 128 is a rare bird.

Stork vanes are rare; the one (Fig. 129) made by a twentieth-century crafts-man for his nephew, an obstetrician, is unique.

In the 1950s Henry White, a sheet-metal worker who resides in Waltham, Massachusetts, began a new hobby. (Mr. White is no relation to Stillman White who, a century before, was Leonard Cushing's partner in the production of Waltham Weather-vanes.) White learned to model copper from a German-trained coppersmith whom White considered "an artist with a mallet," and looking forward to his retirement, began a hobby of making vanes. When a nephew moved to New Mexico and wanted a reminder of his native Boston, White made him a memento of Faneuil Hall's ancient insect—a grasshopper vane. To show no favoritism in the family, he then made this vane for his other nephew, the obstetrician.

White's technique is designed for making unique vanes. After studying photo-graphs and drawings of the creature he will depict, he decides on a pose. Most of his designs tell a story: a sailfish on harpoon, a kite with key and line. Then, White hollows out wood to make a concave form for each part of the vane. His carved molds are rough; they will be used only once. His anvil is an old tree trunk.

Like pre-twentieth-century artisans, White does not stint on labor. Each sec-tion is slowly and carefully wrought; the parts are neatly assembled with clean seams. But unlike the weathervane craftsmen of earlier centuries, White does not finish his

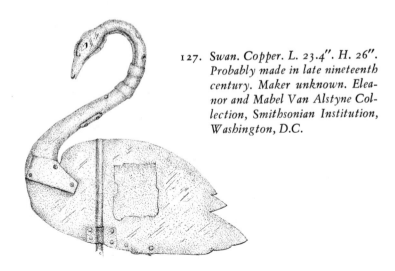

127. *Swan. Copper. L. 23.4". H. 26". Probably made in late nineteenth century. Maker unknown. Elea-nor and Mabel Van Alstyne Col-lection, Smithsonian Institution, Washington, D.C.*

128. Stork. Copper. H. 28.3". Mass produced by Harris & Co., Boston. Mass., in the 1870s. Sold for $25. Eleanor and Mabel Van Alstyne Collection, Smithsonian Institution, Washington, D.C.

copper vanes in gold; he allows the copper to age. The twentieth-century fashion in vanes does not demand golden emblems, but antiquelike ornaments or folk-art objects. Henry White is a twentieth-century folk artist.

In 1974, fate (and a weathervane-napper) brought Shem Drowne's grasshopper (Fig. 7) and Henry White's mallet together. The grasshopper was taken from its Faneuil Hall spire in the dark of a January night and secreted away in the Faneuil Hall attic. The ball and spike above the grasshopper's back were broken off and stashed in a bus depot locker.

The missing grasshopper made headlines across the country. Tips on stolen vanes and possible "hot-vane fences" poured in to police. As they searched for Drowne's missing vane, dozens of other stolen vanes were located. Several days after the theft, a steeplejack who had regilded the grasshopper eight years earlier turned himself in to the police, who wanted him on a drug charge. He said he knew the whereabouts of the grasshopper and wanted to make a deal. Two days later the vane was recovered.

Some restoration was needed, and coppersmith White was called in. A new ball was needed, and ball and spike had to be reattached to the vane. Two of the grasshopper's six legs had been replaced in the past with limbs of a thin-gauge copper, and they had become battered. After restoration, the vane was gilded. Today, Shem Drowne's grasshopper, with two legs by Henry White, and equipped with a special locking device, is again on Faneuil Hall. The symbol of trade has returned to the honored hall of liberty.

Because of its historic importance, Faneuil Hall survived the urban renewal which in the 1960s leveled the area surrounding it. But many old buildings in America do

129. *Stork with Baby. Copper. H. about 4½′. Made by Henry J. White, about 1955, for an obstetrician. Privately owned.*

fall to the wrecker's ball. Fortunately, their weathervanes are being salvaged. The day is past when the vane went down with the building. Some vanes go to adorn other buildings; even more go to private folk-art collections and public museums where they can be enjoyed as sculpture at close range.

Luckily, *in situ* weathervane viewing is still possible. Vanes atop buildings are the most enjoyable; they dignify the buildings they crown, lend charm to the entire landscape, and stand ready to surprise observant travelers just around the bend.

Appendix I.
American Weathervane Makers
and Vendors

A PARTIAL LISTING GLEANED FROM
SURVIVING CATALOGUES, ADVERTISEMENTS, ETC.

Of the forty-four firms in various regions of America, listed below, only three were shops of early craftsmen (Drowne, father and son, coppersmiths; Hamlin, pewterer; and Clark, brass founder). Numerous coppersmiths, workers in other metals, and wood carvers regularly or occasionally made weathervanes as part of their trade, but they remain anonymous. Because vane making was part of general coppersmithing, any list of colonial and federal period coppersmiths can also be considered a vane makers list. Hamlin and Clark are included here because Hamlin is known to have made the scroll vane shown in Figure 45, and Clark signed the swallow-tailed banner which he made in 1815 for the Waltham cotton mill, America's first complete factory.

The list is fuller in its coverage of companies of the late nineteenth century. But here too it is just a sampling of the many metalworking shops and retail stores of the era whose trade included in part, or on occasion, the making or selling of weathervanes. Most of the shops listed were merely retail outlets for vanes produced by others. The description "some vanes" signifies that the weathervane trade formed only a small part of the business. Although many of the firms were ironworks, the vanes sold by them were almost always of copper.

The list is more complete in its recording of the few late-nineteenth-century companies whose principal trade was in vanes.

Dates denote years when the shop was known to have been operating. An (e) or (t) after the date designates the year in which the company's weathervane trade was established or terminated.

AMES PLOW   Boston, Massachusetts   1868–70s
      agricultural supplies, some
      vanes, probably outlet for
      Cushing

BARBEE, W. T., WIRE & IRON WORKS   Lafayette, Indiana   *c.* 1890
      some vanes   Chicago, Illinois

BARNUM, E. T., IRON & WIRE WORKS   Detroit, Michigan   1870–1912
      some vanes

BENT, SAMUEL, & SONS   New York City   1875–88
      largely a weathervane
      business, also garden
      metalwork, a few designs
      copied from others,
      originally of Portchester,
      New York

BERGER MANUFACTURING CO.   Canton, Ohio   1889–95
      some vanes

BERGER, L. D., BROS. MFG.   Philadelphia, Pennsylvania   1895
      some vanes

BOLLES, J. E., & CO.   Detroit, Michigan   1884
      some vanes

BRECK, JOSEPH, & SONS   Boston, Massachusetts   1893–1916
      agricultural supplies, some
      vanes, outlet for Cushing

BROAD GAUGE IRON WORKS   Boston, Massachusetts   1892–1915
      some vanes

BUBIER & CO.   Boston, Massachusetts   1872–95
      ornamental ironwork,
      some vanes

CHELMSFORD FOUNDRY CO.   Chelmsford, Massachusetts   1859 (e)–1913 (t)

architectural metals, some vanes, removed to Medford 1910	Boston, Massachusetts Cambridge, Massachusetts Medford, Massachusetts	
CLARK, JOHN brass founder	Boston, Massachusetts	1815
CUSHING & WHITE, later CUSHING, L. W., & SONS primarily vanes, some emblems, acquired business from Jewell (1867), retail outlet in New York City (1870)	Waltham, Massachusetts	1867 (e)–1933 (t)
DORENDORF, D. some vanes	New York City	c. 1890
DROWNE, SHEM, later son THOMAS general coppersmithing and tinsmithing	Boston, Massachusetts	1715–71
FISKE, J. W. architectural metals, large weathervane trade at times	New York City	1858 (e)–present
tools, hardware, some vanes	Massachusetts	1858–64
large copper weathervane trade, general ironwork	New York City (retail) Massachusetts (factory)	1864–c. 1900
general ironwork, diminishing weathervane trade	New York City (retail) Brooklyn, New York (factory)	c. 1900–56
architectural metals, some vanes	Paterson, New Jersey	1956–present
FOSTER, C., & CO. outlet for Cushing vanes	Worcester, Massachusetts	1870
GOULD & HAZLETT coppersmiths	Charlestown, Massachusetts	1840–42
GOULD BROS. & DIBLEE some vanes	Chicago, Illinois	1875

HAMLIN, SAMUEL, later son SAMUEL E.
   primarily pewterer, also
   brazier and coppersmith
	Providence, Rhode Island	1771–1841 (t)

HARRIS, J., & SON, later
 A. J. HARRIS & CO., later
 HARRIS & CO.
   principally a weathervane
   trade, also railings, garden
   metalwork
	Boston, Massachusetts	1868 (e)–c. 1882 (t)

HAYES BROS. some vanes	Cincinnati, Ohio	1874

JEWELL, A. L., & CO.
   vanes, signs, lightning
   rods, cast iron, later years
   primarily vanes, acquired
   by Cushing & White
   (1867)
	Waltham, Massachusetts	1852 (e)–1867 (t)

JONES, M. D., & CO.
   ornamental ironwork,
   some vanes
	Boston, Massachusetts	1870–1902

MESKER, J. B. & G. L., & CO. some vanes	Evansville, Indiana St. Louis, Missouri	1877–91
METAL STAMPINGS & SPINNING CO. some vanes	Grand Rapids, Michigan	1894
MILLER IRON CO. some vanes	Providence, Rhode Island	1871–83

MOTT, J. L., IRON WORKS
   some vanes, a few designs
   not original, also retailed
   in Chicago and Boston
	New York City	1882–97

MULLINS, W. H., & CO. some vanes	Salem, Ohio	1896–1913
NATIONAL IRON & WIRE CO. some vanes	Detroit, Michigan	1884
OAKES MFG. CO. some vanes	Boston, Massachusetts	1881

PARKER & GANNETT	Boston, Massachusetts	1875
agricultural supplies, some vanes, outlet for Jewell and Cushing		
PHOENIX WIRE WORKS	Detroit, Michigan	1900
some vanes		
PURITAN IRON WORKS	Boston, Massachusetts	1903–31
some vanes		
SAVORY & CO.	Philadelphia, Pennsylvania	1850
some vanes		
SNOW, W. A., CO.	Boston, Massachusetts	c. 1885 (e)–c. 1940 (t)
in early years large weathervane trade, did not originate designs, acquired Harris's molds (c. 1883), sold molds to Washburne (c. 1940)		
SOUTHER, E. E., IRON CO.	St. Louis, Missouri	1900
some vanes		
SPOKANE ORNAMENTAL IRON & WIRE WORKS	Spokane, Washington	1890
some vanes		
UNION MALLEABLE IRON CO.	Moline, Illinois	1880
some vanes		
VAN DORN IRON WORKS	Cleveland, Ohio	n.d.
some vanes		
WALBRIDGE & CO.	Buffalo, New York	1895
some vanes		
WASHBURNE, E. G., & CO.	New York City Danvers, Massachusetts	1853 (e)–present
originally Isaiah Washburne, later son E. G., general coppersmithing, later large weathervane trade, many designs acquired from others,		

possibly agent for Cushing (*c.* 1870), acquired molds from others (1900s), removed to Danvers (1956)		
WESTERN GRILLE MFG. CO. some vanes	Chicago, Illinois	n.d.
WESTERVELT, A. B. & W. T., CO. considerable weathervane trade, other ornamental metalwork, most designs not original	New York City	1883–90
WINN, JOHN A. agent for Jewell and Cushing	Boston, Massaachusetts	1865–71 (t)

Appendix II.
Weathervane Cardinal Designs

In the past it was possible to identify the manufacturer of a weathervane from the design of the cardinals beneath. This is no longer true, because seldom are vanes and cardinals on their original posts. Nevertheless, some weathervane manufacturers' cardinal designs are illustrated and identified in the figures indicated below.

BENT: Upper cardinals in Figure 130, made with or without inset detail visible on E and N and omitted on S and W.

CUSHING: Figure 87; Cushing also used Jewell's cardinal design.

FISKE: Figure 110

HARRIS: Figure 103

JEWELL: Figure 100

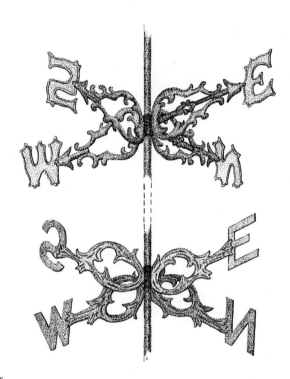

130. Cardinals
    Top: *cardinal design of Samuel Bent & Sons, New York, N.Y.*
    Bottom: *cardinal design of A. B. & W. T. Westervelt Co., New York, N.Y.*

MOTT: Figure 91. These are the same as Washburne's present cardinals.

SNOW: The cardinals shown in Figure 126 may be Snow's.

WASHBURNE: Figure 91; same cardinals as Mott's

WESTERVELT: Lower cardinals in Figure 130

Notes

1. HERITAGE FROM THE OLD WORLD

2 For a discussion of medieval fanes, see Albert Needham, *English Weathervanes* (Haywards Heath, Sussex, England, 1953), p. 12.

4 See D. Hamilton Hurd, *History of Essex County* (Philadelphia, 1888), pp. 1000–1001, for the history of the Middle Precinct, Salem, which became Danvers in 1752 and Peabody in 1868.

4 The "meeting howse" quotation is from *Wenham Town Records*, September 20, 1687, p. 60. (The *Records* are paged from the end of the book.)

5 Alonso Lewis's and James R. Newhall's *History of Lynn, Essex County, Massachusetts*, Vol. I (Lynn, 1865), p. 278, includes the story of the "Old Tunnel" and an illustration.

6 *Rededication of the Old State House, Boston, July 11, 1882* (Boston, 1882) includes a good history of Boston's Town House.

8, 10 Mary Kent Davey Babcock's book *Christ Church, Salem Street, Boston* (Boston, 1947), and Suzanne Foley's article, "Christ Church, Boston," *Old-Time New England*, LI, No. 3 (January–March 1961), p. 67–85, give full background information on the "Old North." A photograph of Drowne's bill for the vane appears opposite p. 183 in Babcock. See also Mrs. S. G. Babcock (Mary K. D.), "Weather-Vane on Christ Church, Boston," *Old-Time New England*, XXXII, No. 2 (October 1941), pp. 63–65.

10 Nathaniel Hawthorne's story, "Drowne's Wooden Image," in *Mosses from an Old Manse* (Boston, 1882), is literature but not history.

10   See Leroy L. Thwing, "Deacon Shem Drowne—Maker of Weather-vanes," *Early American Industries Association Chronicle,* II, No. 1 (September 1937), pp. 1–2, 7, for historical data on Drowne.

11–12   Abram English Brown, in *Faneuil Hall and Faneuil Hall Market, or, Peter Faneuil and His Gift* (Boston, 1900), gives the full history of Boston's market with "a place to sett" (p. 67), and an account of the grasshopper vane folktales (p. 138).

12   The original "Utter Ruin" note is in the Boston Public Library at Copley Square. J. Rayner Whipple quotes the note in "Old New England Weather Vanes," *Old-Time New England,* XXXI, No. 2 (October 1940), p. 2.

12–13   See also Daniel W. Baker, "The Grasshopper in Boston," *The New England Historical and Genealogical Register,* XLIX, January 1895, pp. 24–28. For the story of Gresham's grasshopper, see Richard W. Hale, "The Real Reason Why a Grasshopper Was Used for the Faneuil Hall Weather Vane," *Old-Time New England,* XXXI, No. 3 (January 1941), pp. 70–71.

13–15   The best historical discussions of early weathercocks will be found in Henri Leclercq's *Dictionnaire d'Archéologie Chrétienne et de Liturgie,* Vol. III (Paris, 1914), Part 2, col. 2901–2906 (concise and unbiased scholarship); Eugene Martin's "Le Coq du Clocher," *Mémoires de l'Academie de Stanislas,* I, ser. 6 (Nancy, 1904) (a thorough study); and Francesco Cancellieri's *De Secretariis Basilicae Vaticanae,* Vol. III (Rome, 1786), chap. XIV, sec. IV, pp. 1363–1389.

15   Needham, *English Weathervanes;* J. Starkie Gardner, *English Ironwork of the Seventeenth and Eighteenth Centuries* (London, 1911), pp. 300–320. These English researchers are not always accurate. Cancellieri, l'Abbé Martin, and Dom Leclercq are among the Catholic clerical researchers who explored the "whys" of weathercocks.

16   Frank Floyd records the weathercock's statistics in *Manchester-by-the-Sea* (Manchester, Mass., 1945), p. 60.

16–17   Ephraim Eliot tells the story of Peter Thacher and the crowing at the dedication ceremony in *Historical Notices of the New North Religious Society in the Town of Boston* (Boston, 1822), p. 15. The rather complete records of the cock among the papers of the First Church in Cambridge, Congregational, include "History of the Old Weathercock," William Newell's "The Cockerel of the New Brick on his Cambridge Perch" (1873), and Raymond Calkins' "First Church in Cambridge, Congregational" (1946).

19   Thomas Franklin Waters' town history, *Ipswich in the Massachusetts Bay Colony* (Ipswich, Mass., 1917), refers to the cock in Vol. II, pp. 440, 443, 449, 761.

21   John Updike, *Couples* (New York, 1968), p. 17.

21   The Waltham Historical Society has a letter from Charles Stone's son giving an account of the cock's career.

22   The records of the First Congregational Church, Waltham, Mass., include a clipping of the "jinx" letter, undated but probably from an October or November 1925 issue of the *Waltham News-Tribune.* (The fire occurred October 8, 1925.)

24, 25   *The Diary of William Bentley,* 4 vols. (Gloucester, Mass., 1962). The entry for June 26, 1814, tells of the cock's beginnings in June 1771. Other entries referring to the weathercock are dated September 10, 1789; July 16, 1791; August 19, 1795; August 20, 1795; August 25, 1795; June 23, 1814; and July 1, 1814.

2. FROM ENGLISHMEN TO AMERICANS

26   See Samuel Adams Drake, *Old Landmarks and Historic Personages of Boston* (Boston, 1900, 1873; Detroit, 1970), p. 235, for a view of the Indian atop the Province House.

26   See Nathaniel Bradstreet Shurtleff, *A Topographical and Historical Description of Boston* (Boston, 1872), for the history and description of the Province House.

Page

26 See Alden T. Vaughan, *New England Frontier: Puritans and Indians: 1620–1675* (Boston, 1965), for a history of seventeenth-century race relations.

29 The quotation about fishing is given on p. 223 of John Bakeless' book, *The Eyes of Discovery* (New York, 1961), which provides a fascinating view of a virgin land.

29 The "annoyances" are named in an early broadside quoted by Edward Weeks in *Boston, Cradle of Liberty* (New York, 1965).

30–31 On the snake symbol, see William Murrell, *A History of American Graphic Humor*, Vol. I (1747–1865) (New York, 1933), pp. 11–12; Ernst Lehner and Roger Butterfield, *American Symbols* (New York, 1957), pp. 7, 56; and George H. Preble, *The Flag of the United States and Other National Flags* (Boston, 1880), pp. 213–15. Preble gives the quoted rationale for the rattlesnake symbol on p. 215. *Antiques*, XIII, No. 1 (January 1928), p. 51, shows a rattlesnake cartoon with encircled armies.

31 See Clarence S. Brigham, *Paul Revere's Engravings* (Worcester, 1954), pp. 202, 209; plate 70 shows the masthead with snake and dragon.

33 *Antiques*, XLI, No. 2 (February 1942), p. 136, illustrates a rider-on-horse vane found in Chadds Ford, Pennsylvania; it is reputedly another weathervane portrait of "The American Fabius."

34 Douglas Southall Freeman quotes the "inn-cident" from *The Massachusetts Spy*, November 12, 1789, p. 3, in *George Washington: A Biography* (New York, 1954), p. 243n.

34 See George E. Shankle, *American Nicknames* (New York, 1955), for even more appellations for the "Sage of Mount Vernon."

34 When the "Sage" ordered a weathervane for Mount Vernon in 1787, he stipulated a dove with an olive branch in its mouth, the bird's bill to be black, the branch green ("Washington's Weather Vane," *Antiques*, XLVII, No. 2 [February 1945]).

34–35 See Gaillard Hunt, *The History of the Seal of the United States* (Washington, D.C., 1909).

36 Merle Curti, *Roots of American Loyalty* (New York, 1946), p. 131, has the quotation on the value of impressing the eagle on coins.

37 Franklin's often misunderstood opinions of the eagle and the turkey appear in his letter of January 26, 1784, to his daughter, Mrs. Sarah Bache. See Albert Henry Smyth, ed., *The Writings of Benjamin Franklin*, Vol. IX (New York, 1906), pp. 166–67. On the history of the eagle symbol, see also Clarence Hornung, "The American Eagle: Symbol of Freedom," *American Artist*, V, No. 9 (November 1941), pp. 10–13. Curti, in *Roots of American Loyalty*, p. 130, cites the strong qualities of the eagle as a symbol.

38, 40 George E. Shankle, in *State Names, Flags, Seals, Songs, Birds, Flowers and Other Symbols* (New York, 1938), explains the significance of the cap and its use on state seals.

42 The story of the lady of liberty and the *Boston Gazette* is found in Vol. I, p. 12, of Murrell, *A History of American Graphic Humor*.

42 The quotation about the Goddess of Liberty vane is from the personal journal of Leonard Cushing, May 9, 1868. The Waltham Historical Society. Leonard Cushing papers.

43 The excerpts from letters are from George M. Stephenson, ed., "Typical 'America Letters,'" *Yearbook of the Swedish Historical Society of America*, VII (St. Peter, Minn., 1921).

45 For Catlin's description of the Indians as he saw them, see Marjorie Catlin Roehm, ed., *The Letters of George Catlin and His Family* (Los Angeles, 1966), p. 30

47 Henry Clay's statement on the Indians is quoted from the *Congressional Memorial* on the transfer of the Cherokees westward.

3. CODFISH, SAILS, AND DARING MEN

49–50 Samuel Adams Drake gives interesting stories of the settlement of New England in *The Making of New England, 1580–1643* (New York, 1886). See also Charles Levi Woodbury, *The Relation of the Fisheries to the Settlement of North America* (Boston, 1880), p. 26.

50 For background on Paul Revere, see Esther Forbes's scholarly and readable study, *Paul Revere and the World He Lived In* (Boston, 1942).

52 For a detailed account of early Marblehead, see Samuel Roads, Jr., *The History and Traditions of Marblehead* (Boston, 1880). The Federal Writers Project guide, *Massachusetts: A Guide to Its Places and People* (Boston, 1937), p. 273, tells of Marblehead's reputation as "the greatest Towne for fishing."

53–54 For a fine account of the fishing industry of early New England, see Samuel Eliot Morison, *The Maritime History of Massachusetts, 1783–1860* (Boston, 1921), a classic in its field.

54, 55 G. Brown Goode, in *Materials for a History of the Sword-Fish*, a report of the United States fisheries (n.p., 1880), relates the adventures of the *Redhot* (p. 333) and the *Fortune* (p. 336).

55 Phil Francis, in *Salt Water Fishing, from Maine to Texas* (New York, 1963), p. 195, calls the swordfish "the ultimate game fish" and "the most challenging fish in the sea."

56–60 For the general history of whaling under sail, see Alexander Starbuck, *History of the American Whale Fishery* (Waltham, Mass., 1878); and Elmo Paul Holman, *The American Whaleman* (New York, 1928), an account of amazing inhumanity.

56 James Thacher, *History of the Town of Plymouth* (Boston, 1832), p. 21, has the quotation on "large whales of the best kind. . . ."

57 The "Landsmen Wanted" advertisement appears on p. 90 of Holman, *The American Whaleman.*

60 Lewis Holmes, in *The Arctic Whaleman* (Boston, 1857), p. 282, notes the "shoals" and "quicksands."

60 Holmes' *The Arctic Whaleman*, p. 20, contains the practical plea for humanitarianism made by Mr. J. Girdwood in New Bedford in 1857.

61 Morison, in *The Maritime History of Massachusetts*, p. 13, cites the Marbleheaders' opinion that "fish is the only great stapple. . . ."

61 Howard I. Chapelle lists shipbuilding sites in *The History of American Sailing Ships* (New York, 1935), p. 8.

62 See Robert Greenhalgh Albion, *Forests and Sea Power: The Timber Problem of the Royal Navy 1652–1862* (Cambridge, Mass., 1926), p. 246; and Harold Adams Innis, *The Cod Fisheries* (New Haven, 1940), p. 118, for the count of colonial vessels.

63–65 See Donald Barr Chidsey, *The American Privateers* (New Haven, 1962). On the privateer *Yankee*, see also Wilfred H. Munro, "The Most Successful American Privateer," *Proceedings of the American Antiquarian Society*, n.s., Vol. XXIII, pt. 1 (April 1913), pp. 12–62.

65–66 See Theron Brown and Hezekiah Butterworth, *The Story of the Hymns and Tunes* (St. Clair Shores, Mich., 1906), pp. 194–195, for the origins of the tune "China"; George R. Stewart, *American Place-Names* (New York, 1970), p. 94, for the naming of the town China; Morison, *The Maritime History of Massachusetts*, for the story of the trade with China.

4. FOR LOFTY STEEPLES

68   Homer Eaton Keyes, in his article, "And Joy a Vane that Veers," *Antiques*, XVIII, No. 6 (December 1930), p. 482, tells of the Whiting Gabriel and his church.

71   The headlines are from *The New York Times*, July 25, 1965 ("The Week in Review" section), and *The Pilot* (Boston), July 24, 1965, p. 1.

73–74 On the history of the meetinghouse, see Harris Thaddeus Mason, "The Meeting Houses of First Parish Church in Dorchester" (1817), reprinted in the church monthly, *The Up-Look* (October 1967). William Dana Orcutt, in *Good Old Dorchester* (Cambridge, Mass., 1893), p. 117, depicts the old church, from an early engraving.

79   See M. Ada Young, "A Weather Vane Made by Samuel Hamlin," *The Pewter Collectors Club of America Bulletin* No. 57, V, No. 8 (December 1967), p. 155.

5. ON THE FARM

83   For background on early cultivation methods, see Percy Wells Bidwell and John I. Falconer, *History of Agriculture in the Northern United States, 1620–1860* (Washington, 1925), pp. 11, 35, 123–125, 208–210.

83   Josiah Gilbert Holland, in *History of Western Massachusetts*, Vol. I (Springfield, Mass., 1855), p. 392, describes "the old plough."

85   On the Shakers, see Edward Deming Andrews, *The People Called Shakers: A Search for the Perfect Society* (New York, 1963).

85–86 See Bidwell and Falconer, *History of Agriculture in the Northern United States*, pp. 105–106, for the statistics on the self-sufficient farm.

85   Ralph Henry Gabriel's *Toilers of Land and Sea*, The Pageant of America, Vol. III (New Haven, 1926), is a concise, readable (and pictorial) history of evolving American agriculture.

89   Abram English Brown, in his *History of Bedford* (Bedford, Mass., 1890), p. 24, tells of breakfast at the Fitch Tavern.

91   Richardson Wright, in *Hawkers and Walkers in Early America* (Philadelphia, 1927), pp. 75–76, quotes the whole of "A Yankee Lyric" by Hugh Peters, while recounting the routes and practices of "strolling peddlers, preachers, lawyers, doctors, players, and others."

93   For Jean Lipman's discussion of Lombard's work, see *American Folk Art: In Wood, Metal and Stone* (New York, 1948), p. 51. See also *Antiques*, LVII, No. 5 (May 1950), p. 349.

93   For Picasso's comment, see Xavier Gonzales, "Notes from Picasso's Studio," *New Masses*, LIII, No. 12 (December 19, 1944), pp. 24–26.

97   The quotation is from Hilton Kramer's article, "Recovering the American Past," *The New York Times*, May 10, 1970, "Arts and Leisure" section, p. 21.

98   The improvements made in farming between 1846 and 1861 by using "judiciously chosen horsetools" were first noted in *Appleton's Cyclopedia* for 1861, and then in Edward B. Williams' article, "The Present Condition of the Farmer," *The New England Magazine*, III, No. 1 (1890–91), p. 12.

99–100 On swine in early America, see Bidwell and Falconer, *History of Agriculture in the Northern United States*, pp. 31, 111.

100   See Gabriel, *Toilers of Land and Sea*, p. 38, for a picture of razorbacks, and p. 109, for the quotation from *The New England Farmer* (1832) that the "raw-bones lank-sided" ones were gone.

100   For an account of American cattle husbandry see Bidwell and Falconer, *History of Agriculture in the Northern United States,* pp. 22–23, 106–109, 223–225.

101   On the Connecticut River Valley, see Holland, *History of Western Massachusetts.*

102, 103   For details on the farm buildings, see Byron H. Halsted, *Barn Plans and Outbuildings* (New York, 1881); the book gives all the farmer or builder would want to know about farm structures, including the barn belvedere (pp. 13–16), an icehouse (p. 155), and the "perfectly plain" wagon house (p. 127).

105   Bidwell and Falconer, *History of Agriculture in the Northern United States,* p. 404, tell of "noble teams."

107   Frederick Marryat, in *A Diary in America* (New York, 1962), a perceptive account of his 1837–38 journey to America, mentions whittling on p. 128.

108   Cuthbert W. Johnson's *American Farmer's Encyclopedia* (Philadelphia, 1844), p. 542, lists the useful qualities of goats.

109   On the sheep, see Bidwell and Falconer, *History of Agriculture in the Northern United States.* Gabriel, *Toilers of Land and Sea,* p. 103, notes the passing of the era of "inferior 'rat-tailed' " colonial sheep.

110   See Holland, *History of Western Massachusetts,* p. 393.

111   Elkanah Watson's words on the "first novel, and humble exhibition" are quoted from his *Rise, Progress and Existing State of Modern Agriculture Societies, on the Berkshire System* (Albany, 1820), p. 116.

6. INDUSTRIOUS YANKEES AND THEIR GLORIOUS MACHINES

112   Arthur H. Cole, *American Wool Manufacture* (Cambridge, Mass., 1926), gives the full story. Cole quotes a rhymed account of Merino-craze speculation:

> When first Merino's bless'd our land
> Thro' Humphrey's patriotic hand,
> Me thought I'd be a patriot too
> And buy a ram Merino true;
> One hundred eagles was the price,
> I paid the shiners in a trice; . . .
> Scarce did my hobby 'gin to thrive,
> 'Ere thousand Spanish ram arrive, . . .

115   Excerpt quoted from Jeremiah V. Murphy, "Lowell: Textile City on Painful Road Back," *Boston Globe,* March 12, 1967, p. 20.

116   See John Coolidge's *Mill and Mansion* (New York, 1942), a study of architecture and society in Lowell, Massachusetts, during the period from 1820 to 1865.

117   Henry J. Kauffman, in his fine work *Early American Ironware* (Rutland, Vt., 1966), p. 51, quotes Samuel Orcutt, *The History of the Old Town of Derby, Connecticut, 1642–1880* (Springfield, Mass., 1880), on blacksmith Smith. On p. 74 Kauffman quotes blacksmith Bryant's advertisement in the *Boston News-Letter,* July 6–13, 1732.

117–18   Carl Bridenbaugh discusses blacksmith specialties in *The Colonial Craftsman* (New York, 1950), pp. 84–86.

120   J. W. Fiske, *Illustrated Catalogue and Price List of Copper Weather Vanes* (1893), reprint by the Pyne Press (Princeton, 1971), p. 58 and historical introduction. See also J. W. Fiske, *Illustrated Catalogue* (1875).

121–22   For an illustrated account of colonial education, see Luther A. Weigle, *American Idealism,* The Pageant of America, Vol. X (New Haven, 1928), like Gabriel's *Toilers of Land and Sea,* one of the fifteen volumes in the excellent series published by Yale University Press. *The New England Primer* is pictured and quoted on p. 265.

124–27 See Arthur Wellington Brayley, *A Complete History of the Boston Fire Department . . . from 1630 to 1888* (Boston, 1889).

125 See A. J. Downing, *The Architecture of Country Houses* (New York, 1968), reprint of an 1850 volume, for 1850 prices for a workingman's cottage, pp. 78, 83; and for an elegant carriage house, p. 215.

126–27 See Brayley, *A Complete History of the Boston Fire Department*. See also *Report of the Commissioners Investigating the Great Fire in Boston* (Boston, 1922) and Harold Murdock, *1872, The Great Boston Fire* (Boston, 1909).

128–29 If there is any book wanting in American history, it is a history of American medicine.

129 *Collections of the Massachusetts Historical Society* revealed the prescriptions of "unicornes horn" and "lyons hair" among the letters of Wait Winthrop (1642/3–1717), dated 1682 and 1716/7, to his brother Fitz-John and his son John respectively; the former in 5th ser., VIII (Boston, 1882), p. 429; the latter in 6th ser., V (Boston, 1892), p. 336.

129 Oliver Wendell Holmes, *Currents and Counter-Currents in Medical Science* (Boston, 1861), p. 39, tells of the depths to which American medicines had fallen.

129 Richard Harrison Shryock, "Selections from the Letters of Richard D. Arnold: Medical Series, 1834–1875," *Bulletin of Johns Hopkins Hospital*, XLII (1928), p. 156. Richard Arnold was the physician who so busy in 1849.

130 Alvin F. Harlow, in *Steelways of New England* (New York, 1946), p. 67, cites Mr. Cogswell of Ipswich in debate; and on p. 43 quotes editor Buckingham (*Boston Courier*, June 27, 1827) on the uselessness of a railroad from Boston to Albany.

131 Seymour Dunbar, *A History of Travel in America* (New York, 1937). A basic work. Dunbar, p. 938, quotes the *Western Star* (Vincennes, Ind.), July 24, 1830, scoffing at the foes of the railroads.

132 Henry David Thoreau, *Walden, and Other Writings* (New York, 1950), pp. 105–106. The quotation is from chapter 4, "Sounds."

132 On early commuting, see George Rogers Taylor, "The Beginnings of Mass Transportation in Urban America, Part II," *The Smithsonian Journal of History*, I, No. 3, 1966, pp. 31–54. The impact of railroad commuter service, 1830s–1850s, was greater on Boston, a small city on the end of an isthmus, than on New York or Philadelphia (pp. 13–35).

133–34 On the Medford vane, see Frank W. Lovering, "Historic Weathervane Atop Depot Makes Home for Birds," *Medford Mercury*, August 16, 1956; "Search for B&M Vane on Estate Is Futile," *Medford Mercury*, December 4, 1957; "Search for West RR Depot Weathervane," *Medford Mercury*, November 17, 1966; and Frank Boches, "Here Is the Sad Tale of Final Days of Old Depot Weather Vane," *Medford Mercury*, March 11, 1957.

134–36 Dunbar, in *Travel in America*, gives a fine account of steamboat travel, including the steamboat rhyme on p. 410.

7. THE WEATHERVANE INDUSTRY

137 Quotation from the *Waltham Sentinel*, February 15, 1856, in which Jewell advertised his goods from hat trees to "Vanes of numerous patterns furnished and put up at the lowest prices."

Page

137-40 See Edmund L. Sanderson, *Waltham Industries* (Waltham, Mass. 1957), pp. 133–135, on A. L. Jewell, Cushing & White, and L. W. Cushing & Sons.

140 See Lawrence B. Romaine, *A Guide to American Trade Catalogs* (New York, 1960). The quoted title page of Tweedy's "Catalogue of Druggs" is on p. xi. This valuable work lists weathervane catalogues and the institutions which own them.

142, 143 See the list of nineteenth-century weathervane manufacturers' catalogues on p. 232.

143-44 *The New Yorker*, September 12, 1964, pp. 39–40, featured an interview with eighty-one-year-old Charles C. Kessler, who worked most of his life for E. G. Washburne & Co.

144 The Waltham Historical Society has the 1867–1871 journals of Leonard Cushing, in which Leach is mentioned repeatedly as doing specific carvings for the "Celebrated Waltham Vanes." Leach is listed in the *Boston Directory* from 1847/8 to 1872.

147 See "The Useful & Agreeable," *Time*, September 27, 1954, p. 80, a review of the show which recalls Mrs. Halpert's weathervane hunting. See also *Catalog of Weather Vanes*, Associated American Artists Galleries (New York, 1954).

149 The comment about the vanes not being gilded is from the personal correspondence of Winifred Cushing, September 27, 1954.

151 The quotation is from a six-page catalogue of cupolas, weathervanes, and other metalwork issued by J. W. Fiske Architectural Metals, Inc., Paterson, New Jersey, in the 1960s.

8. SPORTS AND LEISURE

155 Two basic books on American sports and leisure are Foster Rhea Dulles, *America Learns to Play* (New York, 1940), and Robert B. Weaver, *Amusements and Sports in American Life* (Chicago, 1939).

156 See John Allen Krout, *Annals of American Sport*, The Pageant of America, Vol. XV (New Haven, 1929), another fine volume. The "exercise" of arms and training days are discussed on p. 11.

156 Weaver, in *Amusements and Sports in American Life*, p. 49, discussing shooting matches for prizes, quotes Basil Hall, *Travels in North America in the Years 1827 and 1828* (London, 1830), p. 290.

157 See Bill Pollack and George Pushee, *The Pheasant in Massachusetts* (Westboro, Mass., 1963), pp. 1–2.

159 See Dulles, *America Learns to Play*, pp. 58, 241. See also Ralph H. Gabriel, "Sport in American Life," introduction to Krout, *Annals of American Sport*, p. 3.

160, 163-64 See Peter C. Welsh, *Track and Road: The American Trotting Horse* (Washington, D.C., 1967). Welsh's concise text and the "Visual Record, 1820 to 1900, from the Harry T. Peters *America on Stone* Lithographic Collections" combine to make a handsome, scholarly, and fascinating book. For the reference to Puritans and "mounts," see Robert West Howard, *The Horse in America* (Chicago, 1965), p. 44.

163 Henry Wm. Herbert [Frank Forester], *Horse and Horsemanship of the United States and the British Provinces of North America* (New York, 1871), p. 72, provided the quotation on a hundred traveling in vehicles as compared to one in the saddle.

163 See Bentley, *Diary*, Vol. III, p. 393, on the rarity of boasting in 1808.

166 John Henry Walsh, *Every Horse Owner's Cyclopedia* (Philadelphia, 1871), pp. 48–49, provides information on the Vermont horses.

166 *The Cultivator*, IX (Albany, 1842), p. 99, cites the letter by Justin Morgan's son Justin, which first linked his father's name (and his) with the Vermont horses.

166–67 D. C. Linsley, *Morgan Horses* (New York, 1857).

167 Jeanne Mellin's book, *The Morgan Horse* (Brattleboro, Vt., 1961), includes the quoted lament (p. 46).

170 Ethan Allan model numbers, sizes, and prices are listed in the Cushing *Catalogue,* No. 9, p. 8.

170–71 See Welsh, *Track and Road: The American Trotting Horse,* and compare Cushing's Ethan Allen (Fig. 105) with the print on p. 112; compare Dexter vane (Figs. 108, 109) with Dexter prints on pp. 19, 74, 86, 109. The quotation is found on p. 2.

172 *Daily Advertiser* (Boston), September 16, 1874, morning edition. The entire front page story is fun to read.

173–74 See William Cary Duncan, *Golden Hoofs* (New York, 1937); the Maid's 158-page biography. See also John Hervey, *The American Trotter* (New York, 1947), pp. 459–460. Peter C. Welsh, in *Track and Road: The American Trotting Horse,* p. 94, quotes the *Jackson Daily Citizen,* July 20, 1874, on the mother with Maid-madness.

175 John Elderkin, in "A History of the Turf and the Trotting Horse in America," *Atlantic Monthly* (1871), reprinted in Walsh's *Every Horse Owner's Cyclopedia,* p. 544, informs us that the war diverted public attention from trotting.

175–77 Hervey, *The American Trotter,* pp. 457–459, recounts Dexter's accomplishments.

176 Duncan, *Golden Hoofs,* p. 98, tells of Bonner's wire and the doggerel on white feet.

176 Hervey describes Dexter's gait in *The American Trotter,* p. 457.

178 *Daily Advertiser,* September 16, 1874, from the "short address" of the Hon. George B. Loring "preparatory to delivering up the medals."

180, 182 See Dulles, *America Learns to Play;* Marian Murray, *Circus! From Rome to Ringling* (New York, 1956).

184 Virginia Lee Warren describes the horseback-dinner scene at Sherry's in her article, "A New Day of Elegance for Sherry's," *The New York Times,* July 24, 1966, p. 56.

184 See Weaver, *Amusements and Sports in American Life,* p. 4, on prohibited ball games.

185 Frank G. Menke, *The Encyclopedia of Sports* (New York, 1963), p. 211, quotes Elmer Baumgarten on nineteenth-century bowling-alley adherents.

186 O. Maxwell Ayrton, "Some Modern Weathervanes," *The International Studio,* XIX, No. 73 (March 1903), p. 131, provides descriptions and illustrations of turn-of-the-century scenic vanes. See also Robert H. Van Court, "New Type of Weathervane," *American Magazine of Art,* VII, No. 12 (October 1916), pp. 489–493, which shows more scenic vanes.

9. FABULOUS AND FANCY CREATURES

188 Pollio Vitruvius, *On Architecture,* English trans. by Frank Granger, Loeb Classical Library (Cambridge, Mass., 1962), p. 57.

188 Marcus Terentius Varro, "On Agriculture," in *Cato and Varro on Agriculture,* English trans. by William D. Hooper, Loeb Classical Library (Cambridge, Mass., 1960), p. 457.

195 The *Mermaid* quotation is from Pauline Pinckney, *American Figureheads and Their Carvers* (New York, 1940), p. 133.

196–97 See Antony Alpers, *Dolphins: The Myth and the Mammal* (Cambridge, Mass., 1960).

196 Oppian: *Halieutica,* I: 649–652, in *Oppian, Calluthus, Tryphiodorus,* English trans. by A. W. Mair, Loeb Classical Library (Cambridge, Mass., 1958), pp. 269–271.

199 George Lyman Kittredge in *The Old Farmer and His Almanac* (Boston, 1904) gives a most interesting picture

of an American publishing phenomenon. For references to Poor Robin's attitude toward astronomy in 1690 and 1697, see pp. 40, 49.

201   The February 27, 1871, entry in Leonard Cushing's journal at The Waltham Historical Society states that he made up a new price list.

201   An illustration of a tortoise-and-hare vane of the 1930s appears in Lewis E. Stoyle's article, "Turtles, Hares, Dogs and Geese Tell Which Way the Wind Blows," *Boston Transcript*, July 8, 1931, "Travel Section," p. 1.

201   Elizabeth K. Mitchel, *The Ostrich and Ostrich Farming: A Bibliography* (Cape Town, South Africa, 1960).

203   Claudia de Lys in *A Treasury of American Superstitions* (New York, 1948), p. 30, mentions the traditional "horror of peacock feathers" among theatrical people, and the conquering of that superstition.

A Weathervane Bibliography

Over the years source material on weathervanes has been so limited that whatever had been written about vanes—fact or fancy, rumored or recorded—came to be repeated. Spurious information is iterated in many of the bibliographic sources listed below. Nevertheless, the sources in this rather inclusive list are worth investigation by collectors, enthusiasts, and scholars.

The bibliography includes the three books previously written on weathervanes (Needham, Fitzgerald, and Klamkin). A few, very valuable, foreign-language sources are cited, including Diderot, a notable exception to the lack of encyclopedic references to weathervanes. The chapters and articles included deal with weathervanes in general. Articles on individual vanes are listed in the Notes. Some articles on vanes outside the scope of this book can be found through the indexes of *Antiques* magazine. My own articles on individual vanes are in *Yankee* magazine, September, October, November, and December 1966, and January, February, July, and September 1967.

ALLEN, EDWARD B. "Old American Weathervanes." *International Studio*, LXXX, No. 33 (March 1925), pp. 450–53.

American Folk Art from the Shelburne Museum in Vermont. [Catalogue of the] Albright-Knox Art Gallery. Buffalo, N.Y., 1965, pp. 20, 23–28.

AYRTON, O. MAXWELL. "Some Modern Weathervanes." *International Studio,* XIX, No. 3 (March, 1903), p. 131. On turn-of-the-century scenic vanes.

CAHILL, HOLGER. *American Folk Sculpture.* [Catalogue of the] Newark Museum. Newark, N.J., 1931, pp. 40–45, 77–80.

Catalog of Weather Vanes. Associated American Artists Galleries. New York, 1954.

CHAMBERLAIN, S. "Le Coq Gaulois Comes Down from Its Perch." *American Architect,* CXLII (October 1932), pp. 14–16.

CHRISTENSEN, ERWIN O. *Early American Wood Carving.* Cleveland and New York, 1952.

———. *The Index of American Design.* New York, 1950, pp. 71–81.

———. "Weathervanes." *Antiques,* LIX, No. 3 (March 1951), pp. 198–200.

DIDEROT, DENIS (ed.). *Encyclopédie.* Facsimilé de la première édition de 1751–1780, Stuttgart, 1967. Diderot did not overlook the *girouette,* but American-published encyclopedias have been remarkably remiss in dealing with the weathervane.

EARNEST, ADELE. "Early American Folk Sculpture." [Catalogue] *California Palace of the Legion of Honor Bulletin,* XII, No. 5 (September 1954), pp. 61–67.

EBERLEIN, HAROLD DONALDSON. "Weather-Vanes." *American Homes and Gardens,* IX (November 1912), pp. 392–94, 403.

FITZGERALD, KEN. *Weathervanes and Whirligigs.* New York, 1967.

GARDNER, J. STARKIE. *English Ironwork of the Seventeenth and Eighteenth Centuries.* London, 1911, pp. 300–20.

HALPERT, EDITH G. "A Native American Art." *House and Garden,* LXXX (October 1941), pp. 51, 86–87.

HOLLAND, MURIEL. "Something in the Air." *Coming Events in Britain* (December 1965), pp. 24–26. On English vanes.

KELLY, J. F. "Three Early Connecticut Weather-Vanes." *Old-Time New England,* XXXI, No. 4 (April 1941), pp. 96–99.

KETTELL, RUSSELL HAWES. *Pine Furniture of Early New England.* New York, 1929. Plates 159–67 show vanes.

KLAMKIN, CHARLES. *Weathervanes: The History, Manufacture, and Design of an American Folk Art.* New York, 1973.

LECLERCQ, HENRI. "Coq des Clochers." *Dictionnaire D'Archéologie Chrétienne et de Liturgie.* Paris, 1914, III, Pt. 2. Col. 2901–6.

LIPMAN, JEAN. *American Folk Art in Wood, Metal and Stone.* New York, 1948, pp. 13–14, 49–72, 191. Well done, informative.

————, and WINCHESTER, ALICE. *The Flowering of American Folk Art 1776–1876.* New York, 1974, pp. 138–49.

LITTLE, NINA FLETCHER. *Abby Aldrich Rockefeller Folk Art Collection.* Boston, 1957, pp. 279–343, 379–80.

MACDONALD, W. A. "The Man Who Tells the World Which Way the Wind Blows." *Boston Transcript,* July 7, 1928, Magazine Section, Pt. 5, pp. 1–2. Charles Cushing is "The Man Who."

MARTIN, EUGÈNE. "Le Coq du Clocher." *Mémoires de L'Académie de Stanislas,* I, Series 6. Nancy, 1904, pp. 1–40.

NEEDHAM, ALBERT. *English Weathervanes.* Haywards Heath, Sussex, England, 1953.

ROMAINE, LAWRENCE B. *A Guide to American Trade Catalogs.* New York, 1960, pp. 385–86. A partial, sparse, but valuable list of weathervane catalogues and the institutions which own them.

————. "Weathervanes." *The Chronicle of the Early American Industries Association,* I, No. 21 (January 1937), p. 8.

SINNOTT, EDMUND W. *Meetinghouse and Church in Early New England.* New York, 1963, pp. 42, 65, 86, 108, 112, 118, 157, 162.

SONN, ALBERT H. *Early American Wrought Iron,* III. New York, 1928, pp. 82–105, plates 242–53.

STOYLE, LEWIS E. "Vane Fellows Always Found at Their Places of Business." *Boston Transcript,* March 25, 1931, Pt. 3, p. 1.

SWAN, MABEL M. "On Weather Vanes." *Antiques,* XXIII, No. 2 (February 1933), pp. 64–65.

THWING, LEROY L. "Deacon Shem Drowne—Maker of Weather-vanes." *Early American Industries Association Chronicle,* II, No. 1 (September 1937), pp. 1–2, 7.

VAN COURT, ROBERT H. "New Type of Weathervane." *American Magazine of Art,* VII, No. 12 (October 1916), pp. 489–93.

WELLMAN, RITA. "American Weathervanes." *House Beautiful,* LXXXI (January 1939), pp. 50–54, 69.

WELSH, PETER C. *American Folk Art: The Art and Spirit of a People.* Washington, D.C., 1965. Small but excellent.

WHIPPLE, J. RAYNER. "Old New England Weather Vanes." *Old-Time New England,* XXXI, No. 2 (October 1940), pp. 44–56. Good article, long a source of much weathervane information.

WINCHESTER, ALICE (ed.). *The Antiques Treasury.* New York, 1959.

NINETEENTH-CENTURY WEATHERVANE MANUFACTURERS' CATALOGUES

BENT, SAMUEL & SONS: *c.* 1875, *Portchester, N.Y.*
c. 1888, *New York City.*

CUSHING, L. W., & SONS: *c.* 1883 catalogue No. 9, *Waltham, Mass.*
A facsimile was privately printed in 1974 by Francis Andrews and Philip DeNormandie, Lincoln, Mass.

FISKE, J. W.: 1875, *New York.*
c. 1885, *New York.*
1893, *New York.*
A facsimile of Fiske's 1875 catalogue was published in 1964 by Gerald Kornblau Antiques, New York.
A reprint of Fiske's 1893 catalogue was published in 1971 by the Pyne Press, Princeton, N.J.

HARRIS & CO.: *c.* 1870, *Boston, Mass.*
1875, *Boston, Mass.*
1879, *Boston, Mass.*

JEWELL, A. L., & CO.: 1866, *Waltham, Mass.*
1867, *Waltham, Mass.*

MOTT, J. L., IRON WORKS: 1882, *New York.*
1890, *New York.*
1897, *New York.*

SNOW, W. A., CO.: *c.* 1883, *Boston, Mass.*
1889, *Boston, Mass.*
1894, *Boston, Mass.*

WESTERVELT, A. B. & W. T., CO.: 1883 catalogue No. 6, *New York.*
1884 catalogue No. 7, *New York.*
1890, *New York.*

Index

(See also Appendix I, an alphabetical listing
of American weathervane makers and vendors, pages 209–214.)